U.S. NAVY FUNDAMENTALS OF WAR GAMING

Francis J. McHugh

SkyhorsePublishing

All inquiries should be addressed to Skyhorse Publishing, 307 West 36th Street, 11th Floor, New York, NY 10018.

Skyhorse Publishing books may be purchased in bulk at special discounts for sales promotion, corporate gifts, fund-raising, or educational purposes. Special editions can also be created to specifications. For details, contact the Special Sales Department, Skyhorse Publishing, 307 West 36th Street, 11th Floor, New York, NY 10018 or info@skyhorsepublishing.com.

Skyhorse® and Skyhorse Publishing® are registered trademarks of Skyhorse Publishing, Inc.®, a Delaware corporation.

Visit our website at www.skyhorsepublishing.com.

10 9 8 7 6 5 4 3 2 1

Library of Congress Cataloging-in-Publication Data is available on file.
ISBN: 978-1-62087-641-1

Printed in the United States of America

"...war, itself has been declared to be a game,
and rightly so,
for it has the game characteristic of the
presence of an antagonist."

– Captain W. McCarty Little, USN

Fundamentals of War Gaming

Foreword

When I first arrived in the department over six years ago, I had a very good understanding of war gaming, especially how it was applied in the operational planning process. I must say that I also had a good understanding of the theory of war gaming and many of the people who were prominent in developing and writing about it. Yet, the more that I delved into the concept of war game design, the more I learned about the intricacies and considerations that have to go into a war game in order to make it successful. Then, with more research and study, I found that the person responsible for articulating many of these ideas was Frank McHugh, of our very own Naval War College War Gaming Department, in his manuscript *Fundamentals of War Gaming*, published in the 1960s. So, when we thought about what manuscript or book we would like to reissue in a hard cover edition, McHugh's work was the first choice for many reasons.

Frank McHugh's time in the War Gaming Department spanned over 40 years. Yet, it is not the longevity that is so important, it is the time period that he covered which is of such value. While many experts on the field, such as Peter Perla, have hailed the Naval War College as the birthplace of professional gaming in the United States, the College achieved its greatest recognition during the inter-war period following World War I. It was during this time that the War Gaming Department and the student body of the College continuously gamed the war plans against the potential enemies of what turned out to be World War II. Not only were 99% of the future admirals of World War II students during this period, but some of them, most notably Fleet Admiral Chester Nimitz returned for a tour on the faculty. It was during the mid-1930s that a young analyst named Frank McHugh joined the War Gaming Department where he cut his teeth alongside some of the Navy's greatest wartime leaders. McHugh learned a great deal in those days and carried those lessons forward as the Navy and the country entered into the Cold War period of the 1950s. Recognizing the value of war gaming, it was in the 1960s when McHugh penned his manuscript on the conduct of war gaming. His career carried on for another decade as VADM Stansfield Turner became President of the Naval War College in the 1970s.and established the model that has made and kept the college as the premier professional military institute in the world. It was at the end of this decade that the Naval War College War Gaming Department established another first when it started the annual "Global" War Game series. This eventually became known as the Navy's Title 10 War Game and was emulated by all the other Services to address their organize, train, and equip responsibilities. So Frank McHugh's career spanned from the interwar period to the establishment of the modern day Global War Games, making him not only an eye witness to history but an integral part of it.

The value of McHugh's *Fundamentals of War Gaming* is the intellectual underpinning that has given this work its enduring value. In just about every presentation today, the War Gaming Department faculty refers to one aspect or another of McHugh's fundamentals. Perhaps the one that is of most value is how McHugh described the importance of decision making in war games. It was McHugh who most clearly articulated that war games were interactions of humans and the critical function of that interaction was the necessity to make decisions and to be held accountable for those decisions. That human decision making aspect is what differentiates war gaming from other, purely quantitative styles of analysis. Yet, from a purely game design perspective, he provides one of the key aspects of developing the war game and that is understanding that every game is made of two parts, the decision making experience and the decision making information. For the war gamer, grasping how much of the game should be dedicated to decision making experience, such as education of the players, and how much should be dedicated to decision making information, for example determining what information is required to come from the game to provide further analysis, is of the highest importance.

Following a seven-year hiatus from the Global War Games, the Navy has resumed this important piece which helps link strategy to future force structure. Having just completed the most recent game in the series, I was again struck by the wisdom and insight of Frank McHugh. "Global" was primarily designed for gaining decision making information that can be further analyzed and presented to senior Navy leadership to help make more informed decisions. The game, which was conducted as a free play, two-sided game with, as William McCarty Little has stated, "a live vigorous enemy in the next room waiting feverishly to take advantage of any of our mistakes, ever ready to puncture any visionary scheme, to haul us down to earth," had the extra benefit of decision making experience. As declared by RADM Scott Swift, the Blue Cell Lead, "This was the best operational level leadership training on decision making that I have had in my entire career."

This not only attests to the power of the war game as ascribed by McCarty Little, but reaffirms the dual nature of the war game as laid down by McHugh.

The Latin author, Vegetius, has been quoted as stating, "Si vis pacem, para bellum." Translated it reads, if you wish for peace prepare for war. That is a quote that certainly applies to the art of war gaming. The concept of preparing for war has been around for generations. The formal approach to war gaming has been around for 200 years. Yet, it is through the words and efforts of people like Frank McHugh that the intellectual approach to war gaming has been advanced in recent decades. I take great pride as the Chairman of the War Gaming Department in carrying on this tradition. I take even greater pride in commending this book as one that will help better inform and educate on the value of war gaming.

DAVID A. DELLAVOLPE
Chairman
War Gaming Department
Naval War College

Table of Contents

Chapter IV

Chapter V

Chapter I
Introduction to War Games

Military officers, unlike other professional men, cannot practice their profession—war—except in time of war. Furthermore, when war does come, they may be promoted rapidly, and assigned to jobs that are far beyond their peacetime experience. Consequently, throughout a great deal of history the military has developed or has sponsored and supported the development of methods and techniques that will permit them to practice their profession in time of peace. One such technique is based on the simulation of war and is known as "war gaming."

Simulation. A simulation is an operating representation of selected features of real-world or hypothetical events and processes. It is conducted in accordance with known or assumed procedures and data, and with the aid of methods and equipment ranging from the simplest to the most sophisticated. John Clerk, a landsman with no actual experience in the ways of the sea, revolutionized British 18th century naval tactics by using a table-top for an ocean and wooden blocks to represent ships. In today's world Polaris missiles are test fired from machines that simulate the motion of a submarine. An accountant represents the past business of a firm by rows of figures; a high-speed digital computer simulates many things, a flow of traffic, a global air battle, and so on. Many aspects of naval and air warfare are simulated on the Navy Electronic Warfare Simulator, a large and complex system designed specifically for that purpose.

Simulation provides the means for gaining experience and for making and correcting errors without paying the real-world penalties. It offers opportunities to test proposed modifications in a system or process, to study organizations and structures not yet in being, to probe past, present, and future events, and to utilize forces that are difficult or impossible to mobilize. Simulation is of value as an educational device and as a heuristic device. One of its major forms, employed for both purposes, is the war game.

Conflict Situation. A situation in which two or more sets of interests represented by persons, sides, military forces, or nations are actively competing for the same goal, or have opposing desires and objectives, is known as a "conflict situation." A game of chess, a group of automobile manufacturers competing for consumers, a submarine attempting to penetrate a hostile barrier, a nation striving to gain control of a vital sea area while a second does everything within its means to deny that control are all examples of conflict situations.

War Games. Both in and out of the military services, training or testing exercises and maneuvers employing wholly, or in part, real forces and weapons and conducted under varying degrees of field conditions are often referred to as war games. Traditionally, however, the term is employed to describe conflict situations in which the operations are imaginary rather than real and when all of the forces, weapons, areas, and interactions are simulated.* It is in this latter sense that the term is employed in this text, and for current purposes the following definition is presented:

*A war game is a simulation, in accordance with predetermined rules, data, and procedures, of selected aspects of a conflict situation.*** It is an artificial—or more strictly, a theoretical—conflict "... to afford a practice field for the acquirement of skill and experience in the conduct or direction of war, and an experimental and trial ground for the testing of strategic and tactical plans."[3]

Following World War II the concepts and methodology of war gaming were applied successfully to non-military problems. This resulted in the development of "business," "political," and other specialized types of war games. Since many of these had nothing whatever to do with war, the term "operational gaming" has come into use to define the application of gaming techniques to non-military situations. It is also used to mean all war games, military and non-military. The definition of war games given above is also the definition of operational games.

War games evolved from military chess which in turn grew out of the ancient game of chess. The chief objective of both chess and military chess was to furnish amusement, although in some of the military chess games there seems to have been an intent to include some measure of military training. When the first war

---

* The first war game conducted in 1824 was a theoretical conflict between imaginary forces. An early Naval War College definition called war games, "exercises in the art of war, either land or sea, worked out upon maps or tables with apparatus designed and constructed to simulate, as nearly as possible, real conditions."[1] According to Young,[2] the *New International Encyclopedia* of 1916 (Vol. 28, Dodd, Mead and Co., New York) described a war game "as an imaginary military operation usually conducted on a map and employing various movable devices intended to represent the opposing forces, which are moved about according to rules reflecting conditions of actual warfare."

** *The Dictionary of United States Military Terms for Joint Usage*, 1 December, 1964, defines a war game as "A simulation, by whatever means, of a military operation involving two or more opposing forces, conducted, using rules, data and procedures designed to depict an actual or assumed real life situation."

game was devised in 1824 for the serious purpose of simulating actual military operations, it appeared obvious to the originator, Lieutenant von Reisswitz of the Prussian Guard Artillery, that the term "war game" was not an appropriate title for his invention. It had been applied to the military type chess games and implied a pleasant pastime rather than a serious endeavor. However, he did use the name war game "... only because he could not at that time find one more suitable.[4] Since then there have been other attempts to find what might be considered a more appropriate name for the simulation of military conflicts. Thus, as early as 1911, Captain W. McCarty Little, USN, who introduced the game to the Naval War College said: "... that the name, 'War Game,' has had much the same depreciating effect as the term 'Sham Fight' has had with regard to Field Maneuvers. To avoid this the Army had recourse to the expression 'Map Maneuver.' We, of the Navy, may in like manner say 'Chart Maneuver,' and we have lately decided so to do."[3] More recently the term "operational simulation" has appeared as a possible replacement for the traditional name, war game. Some writers retain the name but qualify their definition by a phrase such as "serious use of playing." Despite these proposals, the name war game (or, in its broader aspects, operational game) has never been uprooted, either by edict or suggestion. This may be because the title is too deeply embedded in the history and literature of the subject, or perhaps it is due to the more basic reason that was discovered by von Reisswitz, one cannot find a more suitable title.

Depending upon the available equipment and reason for play, a war game may employ any one or a combination of three basic methods of simulation: manual, computer, and machine. The manual method uses such tools as game boards, maps, measuring devices, tables and graphs. The computer method employs general purpose digital computers. Machine simulations are conducted on equipment such as the Navy Electronic Warfare Simulator which is designed especially for war gaming. However, regardless of the equipment and techniques, every game is conducted in accordance with a set of rules or procedures. These are known as the "Rules of the Game," or the "Model of the Game."

Models. A model is a representation of an object or structure, or an explanation or description of a system, a process, or a series of related events. Thus, a globe is a model of the earth; a flow chart is constructed to represent a communication system; a set of equations is formulated to serve as a model of a sector of an economy. Some models "look like" what they represent, others are analogue in nature, and a third type is symbolic.

Models are never intended to be anything more than useful approximations of reality. The globe merely duplicates the salient features of its massive counterpart.

A flow chart omits inessential currents and counter currents. A system of equations includes only the key variables. The details and variables incorporated into any model are those that are feasible and that are deemed necessary or desirable for the purpose for which the model is constructed.

Abstractions of broad overall processes might be considered to be "macro" models; representations that are somewhat detailed in nature, and that are focused on a segment of a process, "micro" models.

War Game Models. During the early days of war gaming, the word model, if employed at all, was used to designate those moveable pieces that to some extent resembled the forces or units they represented. The contour map, the chart of an ocean region, or the game board was a model of the battlefield or battle area. Later, and due, perhaps, in large measure to the introduction of digital computers and the entrance of mathematicians and other scientists into the field of war gaming, the term model, as applied to war gaming, began to be used in a less restricted fashion.

When a war game is conducted by means of a computer, it is necessary to analyze in advance the entire process, to select the features essential to the given problem, to specify every step to be taken, to determine and provide for alternative sequences of events, and to furnish in quantitative terms each item of data. Such a precise and complete description of the chosen aspects and processes of the conflict situation is in effect a model which serves as the basis or guide for the computer simulation. The conception and construction of the computer war game model are affected by the purpose of the simulation and by the capabilities of the computer.

War games that are not conducted on a computer, but are played by manual means with or without the assistance of a computer, or on the Navy Electronic Warfare Simulator, are also conducted in accordance with rules and procedures that reflect the nature and purpose of the game, and the simulation techniques that are employed. In recent years these rules and procedures, as in the case of computer games, have often been called the model, or in complex simulations, the models of the game.

The models or rules for non-computer games may be less precisely formulated than those constructed for computer simulation. More as well as a greater variety of inputs representing forces, operational and weapons characteristics, and the like are ordinarily possible. Many tactical decisions that must be considered and programmed on a computer are made by the players. The results of interactions are evaluated by a control group in accordance with rules and functions which they are frequently permitted to override, or these decisions may be based solely on their professional judgment. New forces may be injected during a game or old ones reactivated, if, in the opinion of the director, such actions will contribute to the purpose for which the game is being played.

In many war games a variety of situations and interactions are simulated: a landing operation, naval forces engaging air units, submarine versus antisubmarine forces, and so on. Each requires its own rules or specialized model. In addition to these representations of the various operational and battle processes, procedures or special models are usually required to control functions that are not features of the real-world events being simulated, but that are necessary to carry out the simulation. A communications flow diagram for a control group furnishes an example of such a model. The model of the complete war game, then, would constitute a macro model, a composite of the special or micro models plus an explanation or description of their interrelationships. That is, a war game model is the set of all the procedures and rules required for the control and conduct of a war game. When simulation methods are not altered, certain procedures might be changed or some specialized models or sub-models might be used in more than one type of game. Thus, an air-to-air model might replace a less sophisticated model without affecting the overall game model, or a surface action model might be utilized in several different kinds of games.

The model of a war game provides for the types of forces, the level or levels of command decision, and the modes of support, communication, and interactions which have been selected from the real-world, and includes a description or explanation of the processes needed to carry out the simulation. The model accepts inputs such as the number of forces, logistic factors, and so on, and produces outputs in the form of planes splashed, ships sunk, loss of effectiveness of units, residual capabilities, and objectives obtained.

Other Elements. The simulation equipment and the models or rules that are designed or chosen to guide the simulation represent but a portion of the overall gaming effort. A game needs a purpose, that is, a reason for its planning and conduct. Some sort of situation must be devised, and an area of operations, forces, and weapons selected so that together they will lead, naturally, into a simulated operation that will achieve the selected purpose. Consideration should be given to the form in which the results obtained during and from the game will be recorded, if a critique is to be conducted, and if so, what materials and equipment are necessary. Requirements for maps, forms, slides, and transparencies must be determined, and arrangements made for their preparation and reproduction. The coordination of the pregame planning for all of the elements necessary to play a game is usually the responsibility of the Director or Controller of the game.

War Game Director or Controller. The individual assigned the responsibility for the preparation, play, and postgame critique or evaluation of the simulation of a conflict situation is usually known as the Director or Controller of the Game. He may stop the play at any time, when, in his opinion, the game has served its purpose. In case of disputes and disagreements, he makes the final decision. During certain types of simulations the director has the authority to reverse or modify the assessments of umpires or the evaluations made by mechanical or electronic devices. He may add new units or materiel during a game, or increase or decrease the effectiveness of forces and weapons. It is also his duty to see that the results of the game are summarized and properly presented.

Control Group. This group comprises the director's staff. It exists in order to advise and assist him in the planning, conduct, and evaluation of the war game. The members of the control group should be cognizant of all aspects of the simulation, and should be furnished complete intelligence during the game of any areas over which they exercise control.

The size of the control group depends upon the type and scope of the game, and upon the simulation facilities that are available. It is usually composed of a well integrated team of military officers and professional war gaming personnel.

The military personnel aid the director in the military requirements of the pregame preparation. During the conduct of a game they monitor operations and logistics, and monitor or evaluate interactions. One or more may act as historians, or form an "analysis team" to observe, to deduce, and to present any lessons that might be learned from the game. In some simulations certain members of the control group may act as the "other side," or as lower echelon commanders in order to generate the kind and amount of opposition and intelligence that the director thinks is necessary for the purpose of the game. Members of the control group who monitor or evaluate are usually called umpires.

The war gaming personnel are concerned chiefly with gaming per se. They develop the models, prepare the programs for computer or simulation equipment, and coordinate the military requirements and the available facilities. During the play of a game they may be umpires, programming officers, etc. This group should function as part of the overall organization in such a way that its members provide the experience and continuity of gaming methodology that is essential to smoothness of operations and for the development and "phasing in" of new gaming concepts and techniques.

The control group may be assisted by war game or visual aids specialists, i.e., draftsmen, whose duty it is to prepare the maps and other graphic materials, and to maintain plots and situation maps. In addition, programmers, messengers, status board keepers, and clerical personnel are often required.

When mechanical or electronic simulation is employed, maintenance personnel are usually required; and in some instances an engineering group might be assigned to develop improvements or design new equipment in accordance with the operational requirements of the military and war gaming personnel.

Players. In most computer simulations the director and control group determine and program the limited number of decisions that the commanders of each simulated force could make, and provide methods so that the computer itself makes the choice. Once the game starts, there are no human commanders of the forces represented, no human reactions to affect the progress of the simulation. However, in many games a group of participants employ simulated forces according to their own plans and reactions and in pursuance of an assigned or deduced mission. This group is known as the "players."

Since most war games simulate an engagement or series of engagements between selected or the total military forces of two different nations or alliances, the players are usually divided into two opposing teams, each representing a range of command levels of one of the conflicting nations or alliances. Traditionally, opposing forces and players are designated by different colors; red and blue, green and white, etc. The players act out their assigned command roles, that is, they make the same decisions and take the same actions that they would if the imaginary forces and weapons under their command were real forces and real weapons. In order for a game to be successful, the players must enter, wholeheartedly, into the spirit of the play.

The players represent real-world commanders; the control group functions more as an all-seeing, all-knowing, strictly impartial deity.

Spectators. In addition to the control group and players, the progress of a game is often observed by spectators. There are two kinds: those that are interested, either from a military or gaming point of view, in watching all or specific portions of the game; and, those who are accidental spectators, that is, they should be in the game, but due to limited simulation facilities and personnel requirements could not be absorbed into either the control or player groups. The former need to be briefed on the purpose of the game, and given sufficient background to enable them to follow intelligently its play. The latter do not, as a general rule, derive as much benefit from the game as do the members of the control and player groups. Therefore, when possible, another game should be scheduled so that they may gain the benefit of active participation.

The Purpose. War games are not played for pleasure, although they may afford the designers and participants a great measure of satisfaction—or even frustration—much in the same manner as would the actual exercise of a professional function. They are conducted for a general purpose, and usually for one or more specific purposes that are considered to be commensurate with the efforts expended.

The ideal aim of every war game is to provide military commanders with both decision-making experience and decision-making information that will be useful in real-world situations. In practice, however, it has been found that it is better to point the game toward but one of these objectives, that is, to select as the primary objective or general purpose one of the following:

(a) Provide military commanders with decision-making experience, or
(b) Provide military commanders with decision-making information.

Thus, some games emphasize the first of these general purposes; others the second, although it is readily realized that by the very nature of gaming, all include both in one degree or another.

The relationship between the definition and the general purposes of war games is illustrated in Figure 1-1.

The general purpose of a war game is frequently stated by saying that the game is an "educational" (decision-making experience) or an "analytical" (decision-making information) type game.

Specific Purpose or Purposes. In order to achieve one of the general purposes to any practical extent, it is desirable to narrow the objective area. For example, a game may be conducted to provide decision-making experience at one or more specified levels and types of command; another to provide information and data concerning the employment of specific forces or weapons systems, test an organization or distribution system, or evaluate a type of operation or a tactical doctrine. These particular reasons, whatever they might be, are the specific purposes for conducting the game. They should be clearly defined.

The specific purpose of a game may be: To provide the players with experience in supervising a planned action of the operations of an attack carrier striking force

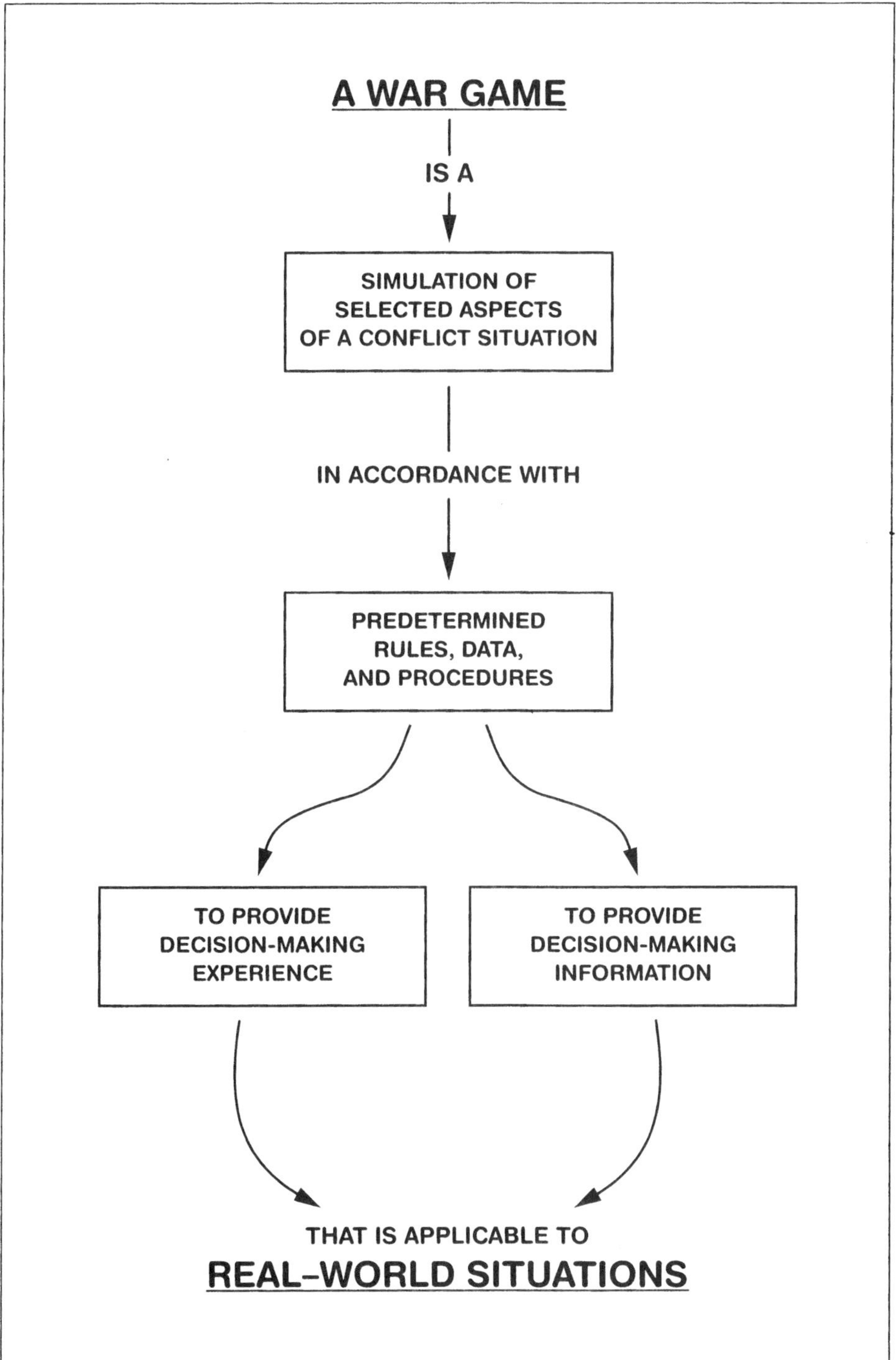
A WAR GAME
IS A
SIMULATION OF SELECTED ASPECTS OF A CONFLICT SITUATION
IN ACCORDANCE WITH
PREDETERMINED RULES, DATA, AND PROCEDURES
TO PROVIDE DECISION-MAKING EXPERIENCE
TO PROVIDE DECISION-MAKING INFORMATION
THAT IS APPLICABLE TO
REAL-WORLD SITUATIONS

Figure 1-1

when opposed by enemy surface, subsurface, and air forces. Or games may be played so that the participants can conduct a simulated amphibious assault based on their own plans, test a certain air defense formation, plan a future operation, or study an historical action. They may be used to develop tactics for the employment of a proposed missile system, or to teach decision-making under the pressure of real-time and when intelligence is contradictory and incomplete. Games may also be employed to give military commanders whose experience has been limited to a particular field of operations an opportunity to study and participate in activities of greater scope, or quoting the American Management Association's purpose for one of their business games, "To make generalists out of specialists."[5]

Types. As shown in Figure 1-2, war games may be classified according to six categories, some of which have a number of subdivisions. These categories are: purpose, scope and level, number of sides, amount of intelligence, method of evaluation, and simulation techniques.

General Purpose. When the primary purpose of a war game is to provide the players with decision-making experience, the game is known as an "educational" type game. When a simulation is conducted in an attempt to obtain information and data that will help the responsible commander to make decisions, the game is referred to as an "analytical" type game. As mentioned previously, educational games have analytical overtones; analytical games, educational connotations. The participants in any game designed and conducted to improve their decision-making ability obviously will receive and retain ideas and impressions concerning the relative merits of the plans, command structures, forces, and weapons systems that are employed, and gain some knowledge of the area of operations. This information should be of value in the planning and conduct of real-world operations. Those who organize and participate in analytical games will, of necessity, have to consider the factors that enter into the decision-making process.

Scope and Level. War games may range all the way from a contest between two units of a single service to a simulated global conflict involving coalitions of nations, the efforts of all services, and the impact of conventional and nuclear weapons on military forces and civilian economies. Games may be tactical, strategical, or a mixture of both. Some emphasize air operations; others, land or sea operations. Geographically, games may embrace a limited area, a single area of operations, or several areas of operations. Thus, a game could be played in a coastal area of, say, 2000 square miles, and involve a convoy and its escorts sailing from a harbor and opposed, possibly, by enemy submarines. Another might include divisions and missile battalions deployed along a portion of the German-Czechoslovakian border; a third, a global air battle involving thousands of aircraft and hundreds of bases.

General Purpose	Educational		Analytical
Scope and Level	Range of Command Levels		
	Military Services Involved		
	Type of Operations		
	Area of Operations		
Number of Sides	1	2	n
Amount of Intelligence	Open		Closed
Method of Evaluation	Free	Rigid	Semirigid
Basic Simulation Technique	Manual	Machine	Computer

CATEGORIES AND TYPES OF WAR GAMES

Figure 1-2

Related to the scope of a game is the range of command levels that are to be represented. In a game simulating a tank battle the levels might vary from the individual tank commanders up to and including the battalion commander. An imaginary carrier group operation may be played by participants representing command and staff levels from the task group commander right down to the commanders of individual ships. Or the lowest level of command represented could conceivably be at the division level. Moving up the ladder, a strategic war game may range from the national level to Army, Fleet, and equivalent levels.

The scope and range of command levels of a game determine, in part, the basic military units that will be represented. If the lowest level of ground command is that of army division commander and staff, the smallest unit represented may be the brigade; if the lowest command level of naval forces is the squadron, then the smallest unit might be the division, i.e., the smallest unit to which a naval squadron commander would normally issue orders.

When lower echelons of command are represented in a war game, the players may make the type of decisions that are sometimes referred to as "decisions of encounter" or a number of such decisions with varying probabilities of selection may be programmed in advance in a computer game. These are the types of decisions that must be made rather quickly; the sort that are constantly being made by small unit commanders in combat. The decisions to change course to avoid a torpedo or to open fire at an enemy tank are examples of encounter decisions. In planning a course or courses of action prior to a game, and during the play of games when the level of command represented is above the immediate tactical level, the need for near-instantaneous reaction is much less, and the commander usually has time to consider and to weigh possible alternatives. Such decisions have been called "decisions that are set pieces."*

The scope and command levels of a game stem directly from the specific purposes for which the game is conducted. Because of the limitless scope and the many possible ranges and numbers of command levels, classification according to scope and level is less well defined than classification under the other categories. It should include, however, the range of command levels represented, the military services involved, the types of operations contemplated and an indication of the size of the area of operations.

Number of Sides. A third category for the classification of games is based on the number of opposing sides or interests. Under this heading are one-sided, two-sided, and n- or multi-sided games.

The most common military war game is the two-sided. In this type of game two forces, two nations, or two coalitions oppose each other in a simulated battle, campaign, or war.

A one-sided game is conducted under two different sets of circumstances. In the first, a player or a team is attempting to reach a goal in a minimum period of time, or by employing the least number of forces, etc. An example of such a game might be the simulation of a replenishment operation when there is no enemy opposition. The objective is simply to complete the replenishment with the given forces in as short a time as possible.

This type of one-sided game is essentially a trial and error method for approximating an optimum course of action, or for testing existing procedures. It

* Professor William A. Reitzel, on page 37 of *Background to Decision Making*, (Naval War College, June 1958) refers to a Naval War College lecture by Professor Simon as a source of this method of classifying decision-making. Professor Reitzel then goes on to say: "... a warning should be given in connection with this observation: the two types are not unrelated — set-piece decisions often condition what can or cannot be done in an encounter situation, and encounter decisions are often called for in the course of developing set-piece decisions."

is analytical in nature and the problems it attempts to solve are often amenable to mathematical or graphical approaches.

The second type of one-sided game occurs when one side is opposed by forces employed by the control group. This sort of game permits the control group to confront the player team with situations specifically arranged to achieve the purpose of the game and to reveal to the players weaknesses and omissions in their plans and tactics.

One-sided games are not true games in the sense that there is no true opponent, no realistic conflict situation, no enemy to counter every move, to exploit fully every mistake. In the first type a single side is trying to do the best that it can against a completely impartial Nature; in the second, the side is playing against a control group that is not trying to win, but that is using the game as a teaching tool.

Games are multi-sided when more than two conflicting interests are represented. This is a rather common situation in business and political games, but does not occur too often in military gaming. As an example in the military field, the Japanese played such games prior to World War II. Teams of players represented such diverse nationalities and interests as Russia, the United States, England, China, Japan, etc.

Multi-sided games are also known as n-sided games, where n is an integer greater than two.

Amount of Intelligence. When a game is conducted in such a manner that all players have access to complete information on each other's plans and forces, the game is known as an "open" game. If the players receive the amount and kind of intelligence that they would probably receive under the real-world conditions being simulated, the game is classified as a "closed" game.

The closed game with its realistically simulated flow of incomplete information is, as may readily be realized, the usual type of military game. The open game simplifies procedures and reduces space and control group requirements. For example, a manual game may be played in a single room, and with one set of simulated forces and battle area. The players act, presumably, as if they possess only the amount of intelligence to which they are reasonably entitled. The open game balances the loss of real-world information patterns against a reduction in personnel, space, and time requirements.

Methods of Evaluation. In an actual conflict a patrol may sight an enemy tank, a ship pick up a plane on its radar, a submarine make a sonar contact, etc.; planes may be splashed, ships sunk or damaged, casualties inflicted, airfields attacked, and so on. Sooner or later true or distorted reports of many of these happenings reach the various command levels of the forces involved by messenger, radio, and other means of communication. In a simulated conflict such real-world effects are approximated and controlled by three different methods of evaluation or umpiring. These are known as the "free," "rigid," and "semirigid" methods.

Free umpiring is dependent upon the experience, the judgment, and the objectivity of those members of the control group whose duty it is to determine contacts, assess damage, and generate, monitor, and control the flow of intelligence. "At 1630 that Red aircraft gets an ECM contact bearing about 045." "Three Blue destroyers sunk, two lightly damaged; two Red submarines destroyed." "It will take that messenger 20 minutes to report back to his command post," etc.

When experienced control group personnel are available, free umpiring is a quick and simple method of evaluation that has worked well in many instances, particularly in educational games of great scope and large and varied forces. An umpire can select from among a broad range of realistic outcomes one that is not only probable, but that also furthers the purpose of the game. The free type of evaluation has also proven of value in games that are conducted to plan and to rehearse future operations.

Rigid umpiring is based on the models and data that reflect real-world interactions. Contacts, intelligence, time delays, number of hits, and amount of damage are determined by the use of functions and manual computation, by graphs, tables, and computing equipment. When manual techniques are employed, rigid umpiring is a slow and somewhat tedious process, and results in a low ratio of game to real time. For instance, three minutes of game time in a pre–World War II manual tactical naval game often required more than thirty minutes of evaluation time. In the NEWS, however, much of the intelligence is received automatically, simulated radio nets handle a great deal of the flow of information, and damage is computed and the results made known in about a second after a weapon is fired.

In some games both manual techniques and computers are employed. Certain types of evaluations are processed rapidly by the computer; others are handled by manual computations and graphical methods.

Rigid umpiring is most useful for educational games at the tactical level, and for analytical type games. The data employed are derived from past military engagements, and from tests, experiments, and exercises.

The semirigid method of evaluation combines both techniques.* It is employed when procedures have been developed to assess rapidly some but not all situations.

* Called free-rigid in earlier editions.

Qualified officers are then assigned to evaluate the latter. Thus, the results of conventional ground warfare might be assessed according to the professional judgment of the umpires; the effects of nuclear weapons by tables and curves.

In some games results are assessed according to rigid umpiring techniques, but the director or some members of the control group are permitted to vary the evaluations if, in their opinion, the outcome appears unrealistic, or if such a change will contribute to the purpose for which the game is played. Again, if some area of the game bogs down under rigid evaluation methods, the director may step in and render a decision in order to get things going. These games are included in the semirigid type.

A simple example of damage assessment will serve to illustrate the basic differences among the three methods of evaluation. During a game a commander skillfully maneuvers his submarine into position and fires a torpedo at a guided missile destroyer. Under the procedures of free evaluation the umpire, observing the excellence of the sub commander's tactics (and perhaps being a submarine officer from way back), rules a hit. The umpire operating under rigid procedures notes that the torpedo has an 80 per cent probability of a hit. He consults a chance device. Hit! Or, no hit! (In effect, a computer follows the same approach.) Assuming the latter result, if the game is conducted under the semirigid method, the director might accept the results, or he might say to himself: "That sub commander did a good job. Give him a hit!'" Or, "It will make a better game if that destroyer is sunk. Sink it!'"

In the application of the three basic methods, evaluation procedures are generally designed to conform roughly to the type or types of decision-making, i.e., encounter or set-piece, that will be employed during a game. Thus, if evaluations are made only in response to direct and specific command decisions and force actions, the assessment system is geared to the encounter type of decision-making, and might well be called "encounter-type evaluation." For example, intelligence gathering units such as patrols or aircraft are moved along specified routes. From time to time distances between these units or other units are measured or estimated, contacts determined, and information disseminated. Again, a decision is made to fire a salvo of two surface-to-air missiles at a specific enemy bomber. The range at the time of launching is noted, hit probabilities are considered, and an assessment given. If the decision to fire is not made, the bomber passes merrily on its way. In any of these instances, of course, each step could have been evaluated by rules, judgment, or by rules tempered with judgment.

The second type of evaluation procedure is associated more with the set-piece sort of decision-making, and for this reason may be termed "set-piece evaluation."

Under this procedure the evaluations are based on a sort of overall picture, and not on a step-by-step process. Thus, a Blue convoy transits a general route from Port A to Port B. Red has submarines in the area. Losses, if any, to both sides are determined from the detections and interactions that might logically occur during this phase rather than upon a detailed simulation and assessment.

Basic Simulation Techniques. There are three basic simulation techniques: manual, machine, and computer.

1. Manual Games. In this type of game the forces are represented by models, pieces, pins, or symbols, and the participants move them about by hand on a board, map, chart, or terrain model which depicts the area of operations. Contacts and interactions between forces are evaluated in accordance with the professional judgment of the umpires, or by or with the aid of rules, manual measuring devices, tables, graphs, and formulas. These games are also called "handplayed" games.

The manual game is the oldest type of war game. Because of its flexibility and low equipment cost, it is a useful technique, particularly for the simulation of ground warfare.

2. Machine Games. For the purpose of this text, a machine game is considered to be a game conducted on equipment or systems designed and constructed for the express purpose of gaming. These systems include such installations as the Navy Electronic Warfare Simulator (NEWS) at the Naval War College, Newport, R.I., the Trainer of the Joint Maritime Warfare School at Halifax, and the Submarine Tactics Analysis and Gaming Facility (SUBTAG) of the Electric Boat Division of General Dynamics.

In general, war gaming systems provide electromechanical or electronic aids for the movement and display of forces, the simulation of sensors and communications systems, and umpire bookkeeping and evaluation. These systems are, in essence, simply electromechanical or electronic versions of handplayed war games. Like their manual counterparts, games conducted on such systems require players and a control group.

3. Computer Games. These games are designed and programmed for general purpose digital computers. When the data and program are loaded into the computer and the start button is pressed, the computer itself simulates the conflict in accordance with the detailed instructions contained in the program, and then prints out or displays specified types of data.

Since all decisions in computer games are made by the computer in accordance with predetermined procedures and rules, they are sometimes called simulations rather than games. Because digital computers are occasionally referred to as machines, computer games are sometimes called machine games or machine simulation; however, it is usually clear from the context whether reference is being made to a machine game as defined above, or to a game conducted on a general purpose digital computer.

Due to speed of play and ease of replication, computer games are powerful analytical and research tools.

Mixed Simulation Methods. In order to achieve better the specific purpose (or purposes) for which a game is played, it may be desirable or necessary to use two or even three of the basic simulation techniques and equipment. For example, a digital computer may be employed to assess damage in a manual game. Or it might also be used to simulate detailed engagements, or record the logistics situation. The facilities of a machine gaming installation can be utilized to supplement a manual game, or manual techniques may be employed in conjunction with machine games in order to include details that the system is incapable of simulating, or to increase the scope of play. Additionally, it is possible to use a digital computer along with machine and manual methods for accounting, damage assessment, and so on.

The mixing of available simulation facilities to meet the requirements of a particular game enables the model designer to balance the advantages of one (or two) techniques against the disadvantages of another. If a manual game takes too long to play, a digital computer speeds the process. If a machine gaming system cannot simulate ground warfare in a theater play, or the search patterns of large numbers of reconnaissance aircraft, manual methods can. When manual techniques are needed for a high-level educational game, machine or computer support, alone or together, make it possible to include a greater number of selected aspects, and to increase the tempo of play. Hence the war gaming centers of the future will most likely feature integrated manual-machine-computer arrangements, any part of which will be able to be employed alone, or in conjunction with one or both of the other components.

The two simulation methods most commonly used in conjunction with each other are the manual and the computer. Games employing both these techniques are known as "computer-assisted" or "manual-computer" games.

Other Methods of Classification. In addition to the six categories previously described, games may be classified in three additional ways:

(1) According to the manner in which time is represented,
(2) The method used for treating chance events, and
(3) Free or rigid play.

When a game proceeds by constant and predetermined intervals, it is known as a "time-step" game. If the selected interval is three minutes, for instance, then all forces are moved every three minutes of game time and, at the end of each three-minute period, interactions are evaluated and the status of forces updated. The shorter the time-step, the longer the time required for play.

Games are also designed so that the play advances from event to event rather than by fixed intervals of time. For example, if there is no possibility of an interaction occurring for twenty-five minutes of game time, the forces are moved for that period of time and then the situation is evaluated. Games employing this technique are referred to as "critical event" or "event store" games.

The terms "time-step" and "critical event" are generally used when classifying computer games, although they can be used in connection with some manual games.

In machine games, game time is usually continuous. It may proceed faster, at the same rate, or slower than real time. Certain manual games also use continuous time. When this occurs, player decisions may usually be made at any time, but the forces are moved as the situation dictates and for discrete intervals of time.

Games, and the models upon which they are based, are sometimes classified according to the way in which chance events are handled. When the probabilities of the occurrence of chance events are used as average values, the game or model is known as an "expected-value" or "deterministic" game or model. If chance devices such as dice or tables of random numbers are employed to determine the outcomes of chance events, the game is called a "stochastic," "probabilistic" or "Monte-Carlo" game.

In the vast majority of pre–World War II games, the players, acting as military commanders and members of staffs, made decisions as they would in the real world. This freedom to make decisions holds true in many of today's games. However, in some analytical games, player-decisions in all situations are made in accordance with predetermined doctrines, procedures and decision-rules. To distinguish between the two types of play, the former are sometimes referred to as "free-play" games. Similarly, the latter might be called "rigid-play" games. Some writers prefer to call the first type a game and the latter, as in the case of a computer game, a simulation.*

The Value of War Games. War games reflecting in some measure the realities of combat have been conducted by the military forces of various nations since 1824, and in a more idealized form for many years prior to that date. In the United States before World War II, war gaming was limited to a very few service schools and the number of professional war gamers could probably be counted on the fingers of one hand. The Second Conference on War Games held at the University of Michigan in 1957 was attended by representatives of more than fifty military and civilian activities and groups. During the same year the American Management Association introduced its business game. Since that time such companies as General Electric and International Business Machines have employed games for training purposes. In addition, a number of colleges are using games in their business, operations research, and international relations courses. Today, more people and activities are gaming than ever before. This long and continuous use of war games, and the recent rapid growth in their popularity and scope of applications indicate clearly the value of gaming to both military and civilian activities.

War gaming possesses the inherent advantages of simulation, and provides a methodology for studying and examining almost any type of military operation from a patrol action to a major war. It "... offers the players the whole world as a theatre, and puts no limit to the forces either in numbers or kinds."[3] A 1914 article in the *Scientific American* observed: "Our army now numbers thousands—these gentlemen (officers at Army War College) play the map game with hundreds of thousands."[7]

Gaming provides a means of gaining useful experience and information in advance of an actual commitment, of experimenting with forces and situations that are too remote, too costly, or too complicated to mobilize and manipulate, and of exploring and shaping the organizations and systems of the future. When, as in atomic warfare, there are no precedents, no historical examples to furnish guidelines, war gaming creates its own history of artificial wars. The games may proceed at "fast time" or "compressed time," i.e., an hour in the simulated world of the game may take fifteen minutes of real time, or a month may take no more than

* "Simulations are to be distinguished from games. A *simulation* is a model in which decisions and choices are defined by explicit rules and procedures. A *game* is a model in which some decisions are made by players."[6]

a day. And when a critical situation develops, the game may be slowed, or even stopped, so that the situation may be examined in detail.

The preparation for and the conduct of a game illustrate vividly to all involved the complexity and ineffability of military operations, the difficulty of coordinating and utilizing the knowledge and conflicting opinions of experts in many fields, the need for employing balanced forces, and the desirability of gaining and maintaining an overall perspective. The participants are not taking part in a round table discussion where vague generalities will suffice, but are dealing with specific forces and weapons within a time-space frame. They learn to appreciate the "other fellow's" problems, to see that the Estimate of the Situation is a dynamic and not a static concept. Almost unknowingly, the personnel concerned with a game begin to think about variations in strategy and tactics, in organizations and support, and the effect of such changes on the overall scheme. In general, it might be said that they learn more than they realize at the time.

As an educational tool the war game gives a colonel his first opportunity to command a division, or an army, and to gain the insight and knowledge afforded by such an experience. It places a task force at the disposal of a navy commander and allows an air force major to employ more and better missiles and aircraft than the nation possesses. There are no peacetime budgetary limitations, no need for peacetime safety considerations and practices. There is an opportunity to make mistakes, and to profit by them; to have one's actions and decisions meet the acid test of competition. "... the great secret of its (the war game's) power lies in the existence of the enemy, a live, vigorous enemy in the next room waiting feverishly to take advantage of any of our mistakes, ever ready to puncture any visionary scheme, to haul us down to earth, ..."[3] The 1955 War Games Conference at the University of Michigan, attended by 43 representatives of the armed services, civilian research agencies, and universities, reached the following conclusion: "War gaming is an extremely important educational device for training senior officers—possibly the best available in time of peace—."

The war game is a valuable and proven method for developing and evaluating operational concepts and plans. It enables a commander and his staff to review assumptions, detect inadequate or untimely support, verify time and space factors, and reconcile divergent opinions. The game provides a means of testing ideas, of coordinating services and branches, and of exploring and considering all possible contingencies prior to the drafting of the final operational plan. During World War II the Germans frequently used both one and two-sided war games for testing and research purposes. Such simulations were employed to test the plans for the initial operations against France and against Russia; another aided in the evolution of Operation Seeloewe, the planned but never attempted invasion of England.[8] More recently, some elements of the Fleet "tried out" their plans on the Navy Electronic Warfare Simulator, and the War Games Division of the United States Continental Army Command has tested the feasibility of proposed operational and organizational concepts by using gaming techniques.

The simulation methods employed in war gaming have been utilized to fight the same engagement over and over in order to determine the effect of chance on the outcome, and then to run through additional series to measure, in turn, the results of variations in key parameters. Carmonette is an example of such a simulation.[9] It runs through, perhaps, 50 times, the same tank battle* between Red and Blue tanks, and comes up with a casualty distribution for both sides. Then the characteristics of, say, the Blue tanks, are changed and another series of engagements conducted. A comparison of the two casualty distributions provides one method of appraising the results of the changes in the Blue tank characteristics. In a similar manner, missile site locations may be evaluated against air raids at varying altitudes, speeds, and aircraft spacings; theoretical optimum attack characteristics determined for the penetration of assumed air and surface defense capabilities, etc. Interestingly enough, in what was probably the first war gaming of naval forces, this concept of many play-throughs was followed. "... as often as despatches with descriptions of these battles were brought home, it was my practice to make animadversions, and criticise them, by fighting them over and over again, by means of the aforesaid small models of ships, which I constantly carried in my pocket; every table furnishing sea-room sufficient on which to extend and maneuver the opponent fleets at pleasure; and where every naval question, both with respect to situation and movement, even of every individual ship, as well as the fleets themselves, could be animadverted on; ..."[10]

Because it can be played over and over again, the war game makes it possible to do what cannot be done in the field, that is, to vary characteristics, to extend the scope and value of limited peacetime experiments, to study the effects of atomic exchanges, to practice operations in any areas and with weapons of both the present and the future. Currently, war gaming appears to be one, if not the best, method available for visualizing and preparing for tomorrow's battles and for developing the organizations and tactics of the future. "Even if it is not possible to test plans conclusively with the techniques now available, it is at least possible to glimpse the elusive and manifold shape of future conflicts and to harden, by

* In addition to tanks, this game includes limited numbers of infantry, mortars, and self-propelled guns.

fictional exposure, the officers who may some day come face to face with the hideous visage of the real thing."[11]

The German general, Rudolf Hofmann, wrote in 1951: "Practical examples ... have proved the high value of these theoretical exercises and have saved the German soldiers much blood and labor. Perhaps modern warfare and new weapons will also indicate new ways of arranging war games. However, these games will always retain their high indisputable importance as one of the many theoretical aids."[8] This same officer also cautions: "... the value of war games should not be overestimated."[8] Like everything in this world, war gaming has its limitations.

Limitations. While war games are far less expensive than field maneuvers and fleet exercises, the preparation and conduct of even a game of limited scope and number of forces requires a great deal of time and work. (This expenditure of effort is offset somewhat when the model or procedures are used many times. For example, the war games rules formerly used at the Naval War College were employed for all the games then conducted at the college. They were revised from time to time to take into consideration changes in naval warfare.)

It is difficult, if not impossible, to include the impact of intangibles in a war game. "... missing are the impressions of combat, ..., the genuine tensions and the far-reaching responsibility."[8] Variables such as tradition, leadership, training, and esprit de corps are usually treated as constants. All pilots are equally skilled; all guns and missile systems of the same type, equally lethal. While such simplifications are necessary, and indeed are part of all models and simulations, the limiting effects of such restrictions must be considered in appraising a game.

In addition to the intangibles and the assumed homogeneity of similar forces, the use of simulation equipment and computers ordinarily limit the number of forces and weapons, and restrict in one manner or another some of their capabilities. Such constraints are overcome to some extent by aggregation, by omitting weapons that presumably will not be employed or that are considered to have a negligible effect on the outcome, and by various other subterfuges. For example, in the Navy Electronic Warfare Simulator, aircraft may fly at any one of five predetermined altitudes, hit probability curves are approximated by linear functions, and the rate of fire of a weapon is assumed to be constant for all ranges. Speed is correctly represented; rates of turn are approximated and are the same for all forces. Thus,—and this fact is not always realized—some characteristics may be simulated realistically; others may approach but not attain that goal. While these factors may have little effect on the outcome of a game, they should be appreciated and considered in every evaluation.

When damage assessments are according to the free or semirigid method, there is always the possibility of judgments being rendered by umpires who have had very limited or no experience in the particular type of situation being evaluated, or of national, service, or branch prejudice, either consciously or unconsciously, entering into the picture. A classical example of the latter instance occurred during the Japanese pre-battle gaming of Midway. The outcomes of rigid umpiring were sometimes set aside and new assessments injected—always in favor of the Japanese—with the result that they derived an overly optimistic appraisal of their chances of success.[12]

Educational games usually depict a conflict between the forces of two different nations. While in some cases there is a distinct tendency to assume that the "friendly" forces have a 1970 capability, and the "enemy" forces possess weapons of 1960 vintage, in most instances force and weapon characteristics are approximately correct, or when intelligence is lacking, the opponent is credited with the capability of the friendly side. However, both sides (in the game) usually employ the planning processes, the doctrines, tactics, the values of human life, and of military worth of the friendly side. Such a game, therefore, is not so much a contest between the military concepts and tenets of two nations as it is a competition between the plans of the military officers of one nation.

The permissible movement and endurance of forces, the reliability of weapons systems, detection capabilities, and the effects of interactions between weapons and targets are often based on fragmentary—and sometimes conflicting—data, on peacetime or controlled experiments, and upon the memory and experience of members of the control group. Interpolation, simplification, and subjective judgment, must, at least in some instances, decide the issue. Results and conclusions, therefore, need be tempered by the assumptions, the methodology, and the numbers which are injected into the simulation.

It sometimes happens in an educational type game that a player is in command of simulated forces that do not make any contact with the enemy. He may become bored, which is natural; or disillusioned with the whole idea of war gaming, which is scarcely fair. War itself, which is the subject of the simulation, provides many such instances. However, it is possible in a war game to keep these cases to a minimum.

In almost every educational game there is a tendency on the part of a few players to "fight the problem," to see the limitations of the simulation but not the advantages. Perhaps events do not always happen as they think they should, or interactions evaluated according to their liking. However, these things happen frequently in the world that is being represented, and do not necessarily indicate that the simulation is at fault.

Game Theory. The term "game theory" is heard frequently during discussions of war games, and at times the two names appear to be employed synonymously. Basically, they represent separate and distinct concepts. Game theory, or as it is sometimes called, "the theory of games of strategy," is a mathematical theory which, under certain conditions, can be employed to determine the optimum strategy or course of action to pursue in a conflict situation. War or operational gaming, on the other hand, is the simulation of a conflict situation. As pointed out by Andlinger, operational gaming " ... has no relation to 'game theory,' ..."*

Thomas and Deemer[13] showed that game theory may be used in lieu of the analytical game to solve generalized tactical problems of limited scope. But currently, at least, its chief value appears to be that of a potential decision-making aid. Both O. G. Haywood, a former Air Force colonel[14,15] and Captain R. P. Beebe, USN,[16] developed analogies between the doctrine of military decision (The Estimate of the Situation**) and the theory of games, and concluded that the terminology and concepts of game theory have possible military decision-making applications, and may, in some respects, be superior to the planning process now in use.*** In developing his analogy, Haywood employed two situations from World War II, the Rabaul–Lae convoy situation of 1943 and the Avranches-Gap situation of 1944; Captain Beebe used an example from a war game.

The first paper on game theory was presented in 1928 by the American mathematician, John von Neumann; the first extensive work on the subject was published in 1944 by Neumann and Oskar Morgenstern (*Theory of Games and Economic Behavior*, Princeton University Press, Princeton, N.J.). Since that time a number of books have appeared on the theory, among them an interesting and

---

* Gerhard P. Andlinger. "Business Games—Play One!" *Harvard Business Review*, March–April 1958, p. 115–125.

** The need for a formal military planning doctrine, at least as far as the Navy was concerned, was revealed by early naval war games. "This process which is thus briefly summarized is known as the *estimate of the situation*, and is the first grand step in the game; and let it be noted that it is the war game that has led us to adopt this systematic method described. It was the game that sought the method, and not the method that sought the game."[3]

*** "... there are certain conclusions which appear to be acceptable at the present time. The use of the matrix form for representing the interaction of strategies is superior to that recommended in the Naval Planning Manual. It should be used now as the Commanders summary and visual aid in place of the Manual recommendation. ... It is not recommended as *the* estimate."[16]

"Game theory provides the idea of a matrix to present the data required for a decision and a methodology for solution of the matrix. If a commander can not make a matrix of the opposing strategies for the situation, he is not prepared to make a decision. Unless he has made such a matrix, he may overlook the proper decision."[15]

readable introduction to the subject, *The Compleat Strategyst*, by J. D. Williams. (McGraw-Hill Book Company, New York, 1954).

In its very simplest form, game theory states that if a matrix is arranged as in Table 1–1, with Red Strategies, R_1, R_2, etc. along the top, Blue strategies, B_1, B_2, and so on along the side, and with quantitative payoffs from the point of view of Blue inside the boxes, then Blue can determine a course of action that will guarantee him a minimum payoff regardless of the strategy that Red chooses.* Thus, if Blue uses strategy B_2, he is assured of a gain of 5 if Red selects R_2, and more if Red chooses R_1.

Table 1-1

	R_1	R_2
B_1	-20	20
B_2	10	5
B_3	20	-10

Immediately, the question arises: Where do the numbers come from that appear in the strategy matrix? "In a real-world situation (aside from gambling and certain other fairly simple games), one does not know accurately the results of the strategies from which he may select."[17] However, "… in making a decision the Commander actually does express a preference for various outcomes."[16] His scale is qualitative rather than quantitative. For example, if a commander were using game theory to assist him in arriving at a decision, the matrix of Table 1–1 might look something like that shown in Table 1–2. The next question is: What happens if the commander's evaluations of the interactions of the various strategies are incorrect, or if he neglects to include all of Red's possible strategies, say R_3 and R_4? "If a commander's evaluation of the situation is incorrect, his decision may be in error regardless of how he arrives at this decision."[15]

Table 1-2

	R_1	R_2
B_1	Very Bad	Excellent
B_2	Good	Fair
B_3	Excellent	Bad

Exactly how, or by what means a commander reaches a decision—whether he employs the standard military process, game theory, or a crystal ball—is not the

* Red can arrange a matrix with payoffs from his point of view.

function of war gaming. In war games as in the real world that they simulate, it is the decisions and their implementation that count, not the method or methods by which those decisions were reached. Educational games are designed and conducted to provide the players with experience in the decision-making process, to give them an opportunity to attempt to carry out their plans in the face of enemy opposition, to test, if they wish, the relative merits of decision-making theories and methods, and to select for themselves the one that best suits their nature. Analytical games are played to provide some of the data and information that are needed in order to make decisions, regardless of the manner in which the decisions are reached. If game theory is used as an aid to decision-making, then the results of analytical games might furnish numbers or words that can be used in the boxes of the strategy matrix.[17]

Chapter II
History of War Games

From early times men have played games that featured the moving of pieces on a board in accordance with stated rules. In at least one of these, chess, the pieces were endowed with characteristics roughly representative of a few of the features of the military arms and forces common to the times. Hence, it is usually agreed that the war games of today had their origin in this ancient and still popular game.

Chess. Chess appears to have originated as a Hindu game known as "Chaturanga," although similar games were played in Iraq as early as 3000 B.C. The Hindu game required four players. The pieces represented elephants, horses, chariots, and foot soldiers—the arms then in existence. They were moved on a board according to fixed rules, but the effects of the various moves were determined by the throw of dice. Today's chess game, a later and somewhat simplified version of the older game, is sufficiently complicated for most players. It is a two-sided game in which the players employ forces with varying individual values but equal aggregated strength. Each player has complete knowledge of his opponent's disposition, but not his intentions. The players move alternately, not simultaneously, as in war games. Each plays to win, that is, to checkmate his foe. The results are determined by the actions of the players and are not subject to varying degrees of chance.

Military or War Chess. In Ulm in 1644 Christopher Weikhmann invented the so-called "King's Game," a game intended to train royalty in the art of war. It was in reality a modification of chess and was played on an enlarged board. Each player received thirty pieces: one king, one marshal, one colonel, one captain, two chancellors, two heralds, two chaplains, two knights, two couriers, two adjutants, three bodyguards, three halberdiers and eight private soldiers. There were fourteen different moves somewhat similar to those in chess. Because this game used pieces that were more closely identifiable with the military forces of the day than did the ordinary game of chess, it was called, as were many similar games that followed, "military," or "war chess." The inventor of the game stated "… it was not designed to serve merely as a pastime but that it would furnish anyone who studied it properly a compendium of the most useful military and political principles."[4]

Vogue of Military Mathematics. In Prussia in the latter part of the 18th century it became fashionable to consider war as an exact science, and particularly as a branch of applied mathematics resembling geometry.[4] Military formations were rigid; military tactics, highly formal. "The methods of exact science, and particularly mathematics, were applied to every phase of warfare. This gave rise to what was called the 'vogue of military mathematics.' It was axiomatic that above all a military leader must be a great calculator."[2] "... war itself tended to resemble a game played by gentlemanly contestants according to specific rules."[11] Of this period Von der Goltz, an outstanding general of the 19th century said "A true strategist of that epoch did not know how to lead a corporal's guard across a ditch without a table of logarithms."[4] "... Not only did military men open their arms to the new departure; savants did likewise. Learned men wrote of military science and the practical application of mathematics to war. The science of war was raised to a place in the curriculum of the most renowned seats of learning."[2] Military chess games devised during this era mirrored the prevailing theories of formal tactics and their relationship to mathematics.

Introduction of Additional Features. At someplace along the line in the development of war chess three important features were introduced. These were: first, the concept of aggregation, that is, having one piece represent a group rather than an individual or unit; second, depiction of terrain features; and, third, the assignment of a director to supervise the employment of the pieces. Just when these features first appeared is not clear, but they were all included in a game invented by Helwig in 1780.

Helwig was the Master of Pages at the court of the Duke of Brunswick. His game was designed to arouse the interest of young noblemen in the military problems of the day and at the same time to teach them something about military science. In this game the playing area was a chess-like board divided into 1666 small squares. These were tinted with various colors to indicate different types of terrain features. For example, red squares represented mountains; blue, water; light green, marshes; dark green, forests; black and white, level ground; and half-red, buildings. A dotted line across the middle of the board divided the sides at the beginning of the game. Each side was given a fortification at opposite corners of the board. The object of the game was to capture the enemy's fortification, just as in chess the object is to capture the opponent's king.

The pieces were similar to the pawns of chess but represented battalions of infantry or squadrons of cavalry. A number of players were permitted on each side and an additional person acted as the director of the game. The pieces were moved according to rules that were similar to chess. Thus, infantry traveled a stated number of squares in a straight line; light cavalry behaved somewhat similar to the knight in a chess game.

Helwig's game was rather successful and spread to France, Austria, and Italy. As could be expected, a number of imitations and variations soon appeared. One that attracted a great deal of attention was devised at Schleswig in 1797 by Georg Vinturinus (Venturini), a writer on the science of war. In that year he published the "Rules of a New War Game for the Use of Military Schools." The British *Military and Naval Magazine* of December 1827 referred to Helwig's game as the "War Game of the Continent," and to Vinturinus' as the "New Kriegsspiel."

In Vinturinus' game the board represented an actual area of operations, the Franco-Belgian Border. It was divided into 3600 squares which were marked to indicate terrain characteristics. As in Helwig's game, this resulted in square or rectangular mountains, plains, and water areas. Some pieces represented brigades, infantry or cavalry; others of various shapes and sizes depicted footbridges, parapets, magazines, etc. Artillery, convoys, provision wagons, and bakeries were included. The moves of the pieces approximated the real world. Troop movements were restricted in winter, and the rules attempted to consider their feeding and support.

Vinturinus' game was intended chiefly for use in the military schools. It related the play to a geographical area and included attempts to introduce the restraints imposed by weather and logistics. "In keeping with the prevalent technical theories of warfare, complex rules governed the movement and the fighting of the troops. These transformed the game into an extremely tedious operation, which was welcomed with enthusiasm by members of the military profession."[2]

Military writers of the 19th century criticized the game although it is sometimes difficult to know whether it was the game or the military concepts of the age which were being censured. Von der Goltz wrote: "This war game is a bad product of the refined military education of the period, which had piled up so many difficulties that it was incapable of taking a step in advance."[4] *The Journal of the Military Institution of the United States*, IV: (1883), as quoted by Young,[2] says of Vinturinus' game: "His work is a masterpiece of military acuteness, combined with technical and tactical absurdities. However, that age loved whatever appeared difficult and abstruse. The (New) Kriegsspiel, in reality, was merely a play, a series of tricks, the utmost benefit of which could only be an acquaintance with the conditions and principles which were regarded as essential to the management and maintenance of armies. A knowledge of the rules and principles required a long and attentive study. They evidently failed in their object, the intelligent development of the ideas of a student of the art of war."

In the military chess types of war games, of which there were many versions, the game features seem to have predominated. Apparently these games were, in general, designed first as a pleasant pastime for officers and members of the nobility and secondly, as a means of "sugar coating" their contacts with the largely prevailing idea that the operations of war could be reduced to rigid rules. War chess resembled rather than simulated warfare. In some ways it might be considered as having the same relationship to later war games as the game of Monopoly bears to current business games. The games required a great deal of time to learn and their successful play depended more on a knowledge of the rules than on a knowledge of war. What, if any, transfer of learning from the game to real-life situations took place is not apparent. Sayre, however, makes this comment: "They (war chess games) probably illustrated the science of war, as taught at that time, better than it could have been represented on a map or on the ground."[4]

About 1730 a Dutch engineer conceived the idea of using contour lines to delineate river bottoms. Toward the end of the century contour lines began to be used to represent relief on land maps.* Somewhat later Napoleon's tactics changed the character and concepts of European warfare. Together they furnished the means and the motive for supplanting military chess with more realistic representations of warfare.

Early War Games. The first game to break away from the chessboard pattern was invented in 1811 by von Reisswitz. The terrain was modeled in sand. Troop units were represented by wooden blocks and their movements were no longer restricted to chessboard squares. The following year an improved form of the game was presented to the king, Frederick William III. In this game the terrain was modeled in plaster at a scale of about 27 inches to the mile. Woods, buildings, roads and streams were painted in color. Troop units were depicted by porcelain blocks. "Later, in 1816, when the Grand Duke Nicholas came to Potsdam, the King spoke to him enthusiastically of the new invention, matches were got up in honor of the Grand Duke, who gave himself up to it with extraordinary ardor; and the following year, when Prince William visited the Court of Russia, a war game was

---

* "... the tactical game for land forces ... did not attain real value until maps were produced which showed the configuration of the ground."[4]

improvised at Moscow by joining several card games together and tracing the terrain thereon in chalk."*

It is not known whether the "tracing the terrain" on the card tables, the reports that Napoleon planned his campaigns in advance by maneuvering colored pins on maps, or just what inspired von Reisswitz's son, but in 1824 the younger von Reisswitz, a lieutenant in the Prussian Guard Artillery, transferred his father's game to a map and developed it into a practical tool for the simulation of military conflict situations. This game is generally conceded to be the first true war game,[2,4] although some writers give that credit to the older man.[18,19]

Young von Reisswitz's game was an immediate success and received a warm welcome from many high ranking Prussian officers. "It is told that in 1824, Von Mueffling, then Chief of the General Staff, consented to witness an exhibition of the game. He received the players somewhat coldly, but as the operations expanded on the map, the old general's face lit up, and at last he broke out with enthusiasm: 'It's not a *game* at all, it's a training for war; I shall recommend it most emphatically to the whole army.'" The general kept his word and issued a letter which "... may be said to be the formal introduction of the war game to the Prussian army." In this he said: "Whoever understands the art of war can, in this game, perform the functions of a commander of troops ... even if he ... has never seen the game played."[4] What better recommendation could any war game have?

The scale of the maps used was about eight inches to the mile. Forces were represented by properly proportioned and labeled lead pieces, red for one side, blue for the other. Dividers and scales were employed to measure distances and ranges. The game was supervised by a director. Prior to the game he issued to both sides in writing the information that they would possess in a similar real-world environment, that is, the general situation known to both contestant teams and a special situation for each side. The teams then prepared written orders. During the game the moves represented two minutes of real time, but at the discretion of the director several moves could be made at one time. The play continued until a predetermined result was achieved, or until the director considered that the game had attained its objective. In this regard von Reisswitz remarked: "It is not a question of winning or losing as in cards or chess, ... the approbation of one's comrades is the best possible reward. Whoever follows out his plan best, adopts the simplest and most natural means to the end, and departs least from the general idea of the operation, will have won the match, even though he may have lost more pieces than

---

* Quoted by Young[2] from H.O.S. Heistand (transl), Maj., Office of Asst Adjutant General, U.S. Army, "Foreign War Games," from the *Revue Militaire de L'Estranger*, 1897.

his adversary .... The advantages they will derive from it will be to acquire skill in reading maps, in the selection of movements best suited to the different arms of the service, in the choice of positions, etc. The interesting discussions which are sure to follow a match will be of incontestable value in the study of the military art."[4]

The game was conducted according to the "Instructions for the Representation of Tactical Maneuvers under the Guise of a War Game." These rules had been prepared by von Reisswitz with the assistance of other officers. They were based upon realistic troop movement rates, time delays between the sending and receipt of messages, and upon the concept of realistically limited intelligence. Only those forces that could be seen by the enemy were placed on the map. Thus, the players gained only the intelligence that they would presumably gain under similar field conditions. Interactions between forces were assessed with the aid of dice. The remaining strength of forces sustaining losses was indicated by substituting pieces of corresponding value. Casualty rates appear to have been based on theory and not upon experience factors.

The classification of this war game according to the categories shown in Figure 1-2, Chapter I, might look something like this:

1. General Purpose . . . . Educational
2. Scope and Level
   (a) Range of Command Levels . . . . Battalion to Brigade
   (b) Military Service Involved . . . . Army
   (c) Type of Operations . . . . Tactical, Ground
   (d) Area of Operations . . . . 4 square miles
3. Number of Sides . . . . Two
4. Amount of Intelligence . . . . Open
5. Method of Evaluation . . . . Rigid
6. Basic Simulation Technique . . . . Manual

While initially, at least, von Reisswitz's game was somewhat limited in scope, it brought together for the first time most of the features and underlying concepts of modern war games. The chief criticism of the game stemmed from the idea that young officers commanding, even on a map, forces larger than they normally commanded would lose interest in their lesser real-world assignments.[4] Today, on the contrary, the opportunity afforded by war games for officers to gain experience at higher command levels is considered to be one of the most valued facets of the games.

"The War Game of Prussia," published in *The United Service Journal*, Part I, London, 1831, compares Helwig's game with that of von Reisswitz's. Concerning the latter game, the following observation was made: "There can be no doubt that much advantage to the officers of the army would follow the introduction of this game, as it would tend to preserve a knowledge which now exists only among those who had attained rank during the last war, whose numbers are fast diminishing, and whose dearly bought experience must soon be lost to the service."

The enthusiastic acceptance of the game by high ranking officers caused a certain amount of envy among von Reisswitz's fellow officers and immediate superiors and he was transferred to a border fortress at Torgau. There, apparently becoming disheartened by what he considered to be an injustice, the young officer committed suicide three years after the appearance of his war game.[4]

Von Reisswitz's game, as were some of the military chess games that preceded it, was often referred to as "Kriegsspiel." It was played in the Prussian Army and at several Kriegsspiel clubs such as the Magdeburg and Berlin Clubs. Count von Moltke who became Chief of the German General Staff in 1857 was, throughout his entire career, a strong believer in the war game and supported and encouraged it in every possible manner. The original limited tactical scope of the game was extended to encompass increasingly larger military situations until in 1848 a game was conducted in Berlin that represented a war between Prussia and Austria. This appears to have been the first strategic war game.

Changes in the art of war and greater experience with the game led to modifications of the rules of play. The extension of the area of operations and the increase in the number of forces engaged resulted in the adoption of more rules to cover the larger number of possible contingencies. These actions caused further reexaminations of the procedures with the idea of reducing the number of rules and of simplifying their application. (This process has been repeated many times throughout the history of war gaming.) The Berlin War Game Club and such authors as Decker, Witzleben, and von Trotha contributed to these modifications and changes in the rules of the game. "The work of von Tschischwitz which appeared in 1862 made some improvements in the way of less complicated rules and more practical methods of computing losses."[4]

The Seven Weeks' War of 1866 (Prussia vs. Austria) and the Franco-Prussian War of 1870–71 provided procedures and data based upon experience rather than theory. This resulted not only in revisions of the rules of the game, but in the introduction of new evaluation techniques. In addition, the surprising success of the Prussian Army in both wars led to the adoption of the war game by other military powers. According to Sayre,[4] Captain Baring of the British Army stated in his version of the war game published in 1872 for the British service: "The increasing importance which is now attached to the game may be, in some measure, due to the feeling that the great tactical skill displayed by the Prussian officers in the late war (Franco-Prussian) had been, at least partially, acquired by means of the instruction which the game affords." Captain Little of the Naval War College said: "... it was generally admitted that the War Game was a notable factor in the result."[3] Colonel Middleton of the British Army commented: "The game of war, like the breech-loader, is by no means a new idea, and it doubtless owes its present fame to the late wonderful successes of its inventors, the Prussians. Now, without going so far as some of its greatest admirers do, who attribute those successes principally to its use by the Prussians, I have no doubt that the lessons taught by tolerably frequent and careful playing of the so-called 'War Game' must be of great value to the thinking soldier anxious to master his profession."[20]

New Methods of Evaluation. Up to the time of the Franco-Prussian War, the results of interactions occurring during war games seem to have been determined entirely by the rules of the game. After the war, according to Lieutenant Meckel, an instructor in the war school at Hanover, "... military ideas ran into more practical channels, when a general desire for practice and training in troop leading existed, and the war game was encouraged by imperial decree, it received a new, extraordinary, and universal enthusiasm—which, however, is not to be attributed to the old systems with their complicated rules, but which rather existed in spite of them. It is a question whether in the German Army there was a war game played in strict conformity with the rules. The exercises, under the leadership of officers of high rank who had no liking for the old systems, cut loose more or less from the cast iron rules and assumed, under a free leading, the form of serious exercises in the leading of troops."[4]

The directors used the rules that were helpful and replaced those that in their opinion were unrealistic or that hindered the progress of the game with decisions based on experience and judgment. In other words, the director conducted the game according to the semirigid method. Meckel, in his *Instructions for the War Game* published in 1875 acknowledged the trend and proposed that the director be freed from some of the rules, but that he follow them in assessing the effects of fire.

The following year General von Verdy du Vernois published *A Contribution to the War Game* in which he described a method of war gaming "... without rules, tables of losses, or dice."[21] In this game all evaluations of contacts and assessment of damage were left to the judgment of the umpire. It was the first example of the free method of umpiring.

Von Verdy's game was a two-sided game between Red and Blue. Prior to the play of the game, a general situation was issued to both sides, and a special situation to each opponent. The contestants then prepared their initial plans and orders. Two rooms were required. In one was the umpire and his assistant (control group) and a general map of the area of operations drawn to a scale of 2 to 3 inches to the mile. The second room was for the alternate use of the Red and Blue teams and contained a larger scale map of the area. Blocks represented the forces. Each commander was given a sufficient number of these blocks to depict all possible deployments of his command. For example, a battalion commander might be issued two half-battalion blocks, four company blocks, as well as additional blocks representing platoons and patrols.

During the game one side explained their intended movements and actions to the umpires while the other made plans and studied the situation on the large scale map in the adjoining room. The teams then reversed rooms. The director correlated their intentions in time and space, evaluated intelligence and assessed damage, and explained the prevailing situation to one team at a time. The assistant director kept an account of the movements and interactions for post game discussions. When one side was viewing the map only those enemy forces that were visible were displayed. Other enemy forces were either covered or removed.

The only data supplied to the director in this game were the assumed distances occupied by troop formations and the rates of march per minute under ideal conditions. For instance, a battalion took up 200 yards; a troop, 100. Fresh infantry on good roads marched 80 yards in a minute; cavalry trotted at 235.[21] The director was at liberty to degrade these figures to account for fatigue, terrain, and poor roads. Distances traveled by bodies of troops were computed and transferred to the map by means of scales and dividers.

While von Verdy left almost everything in the hands of the director, and Meckel chose a middle course, other adherents of the war game endeavored to devise procedures that would facilitate the conduct of games based on the rigid method. One of the most successful of these attempts was Captain Naumann's *Das Regiments-Kriegsspiel* which appeared in 1877. Naumann proposed that a "standard" value based on experience be used to assess losses, and that variations be evaluated by use of a "multiplier" applied to the standard.

German War Games, 1880 to World War II. The war game originated in Germany and practically all of its early development took place in that country. After the Franco-Prussian War other nations began to experiment with and use war games, but Germany still maintained the greatest interest, published the largest amount of literature on the subject, and found the most applications.

In the German Army two-sided games were called war games proper; one-sided were referred to as map exercises. Situations and forces were selected so as to provide a series of games at varying command levels. Games simulating the tactical employment of units ranging from patrols to regiments were conducted at each regimental headquarters one evening per month during the winter season. These were called "regimental war games" due to the places in which they were conducted and not because the forces involved were always of regimental size. What were known as the "Great War Games" were used chiefly for the manipulation of divisions and the study of their transportation and supply problems. These games were for the senior regimental, division and corps staff officers. General staff officers played the "Strategic War Game" which embraced the operations and employment of armies. Methods of evaluation tended to shift from the rigid to the free or semirigid methods, although the rigid method was continued to some extent in games involving small forces such as companies and battalions. Such games provided information that aided in rendering evaluations based on judgment and experience.

Some of the early games, for example von Reisswitz's and Meckel's, were played on the so-called "ideal" maps.* These were terrain maps of imaginary rather than actual areas. They were used because suitable maps of actual areas and of varied terrain were difficult or impossible to obtain. As maps of actual areas improved and became more plentiful, the use of ideal maps was no longer necessary. About the beginning of the 20th century the following scales were in general use for war gaming purposes: 1:5000 to 1:8000 (12 to 18 inches to the mile) for the regimental war games; 1:10,000 (6 inches to the mile) for the great war games; and 1:100,000 (2/3 inches to the mile) for the strategic war games.

According to Sayre,[4] Lieutenant General v. Litzmann, Director of the German War College, made the following observations in a work published in 1905, *Introduction to the War Game*: "It is essential to success that the director should not assume that he or other participants in the exercise have knowledge or skill which they do not really possess .... Beginners at the war game must be taught by means of preliminary exercises how to find their way about easily on a war game map, and how to use the blocks, scales and other apparatus. When they have learned this they are prepared to act as commanders, at first in simple exercises

* "Three plans, on a scale of about eight inches to one mile have been lithographed in Berlin, expressly for this (von Reisswitz's) game, ... One of these plans contains Ligny and Quatre Bras; another Austerlitz; and the third the neighbor of Leipsick, ... " *The United Service Journal*, Part I, London, 1831.

and afterwards in maneuvers presenting greater difficulties .... The difficulties must be mastered step by step ... Dissatisfaction with the war game is generally a consequence of not having thoroughly mastered its technicalities."

In Germany war games began to be used as heuristic devices to assist in solving military problems. During World War I, for example, the spring offensive for 1918 was tested and rehearsed by means of strategic war games. The game revealed that there was very little chance of this offensive producing decisive results.[8]

The restrictions imposed by the Allies upon the German military establishment following World War I stimulated the use of war games at all levels of command. During the period between wars, and during World War II, war games were employed extensively both for educational and analytical purposes. While no new methods were introduced, a great deal of experience in the use of gaming techniques was obtained. There appears to have been no official publications issued on war gaming, presumably because it was felt that such instructions might hinder the free development and application of gaming methods. However, many unofficial manuals and articles were written. "On the whole, the Officer Corps was firmly convinced of the great importance of theoretical exercises and did not cease until years after the beginning of World War II to employ them as a training device—even out in the field during the preparation of new operations."[8]

Tactical war games were conducted to provide lower level commanders with decision-making experience and to train them to issue the orders that were needed to implement the decisions. Some of these games were one-sided and the control group directed the movements of the opposing forces. Large scale tactical and strategical games were conducted by higher echelons, particularly at the War College and in the general staff. Military-political games were also played. The participants included politicians and businessmen as well as representatives of the armament industry, the Propaganda Ministry, and all branches of the armed forces.

Games were employed to test combat principles. In these games one side employed the tactics and strategy of the nation that was assumed to be the enemy. The "friendly" commanders were changed several times in order to "... bring the decisions of several persons to bear on the principle to be tested."[8]

Plans for future operations were tested and plans for impending operations tested and rehearsed by a series of war games. In a somewhat similar manner games were employed to assist in briefing the various command levels. The army group commander used them to describe the situation and to explain his intentions to the army commanders. The army commander in turn employed a game of lesser magnitude to instruct the division commanders, and so on down the line to the company commanders. In this way each became thoroughly familiar with the situation, "... and with the difficulties he would have to overcome with respect to both the enemy and the terrain."[8]

During the study of military history past campaigns were refought by means of war games. These games were also used to test or improve certain doctrines that had been developed and employed in the past. The actions and situations that occurred on the flanks of the German Army in World War I served as the basis for some of these historical games.

War games were conducted in order to study or test logistical feasibility and transportation problems. In such games the tactical and strategical aspects were handled by the control group. The participants were concerned with deciding where food, ammunition, medical supplies, etc., were needed, how much, and how to get them to those places.

After the establishment of the Reichswehr Ministry, Field Marshal von Blomberg conducted a series of high level war games in an attempt to "... solve the problems which the military and political situation had created for German national defense and, especially, to establish a theoretical basis for the joint action of the Supreme Armed Forces Command and the high commands of the Army, the Navy, and the Luftwaffe in all the important sectors of warfare."[8] Von Blomberg was later dismissed, and perhaps for this reason the results of the games were never recorded.

About 1933 war games were employed to assist in the planning of the west wall. When a special commission headed by Generaloberst Beck worked out the new operations manual for the German Army, the principles contained therein were tested by numerous war games. In 1938 the Chief of Staff of the German Army used the results of a war game to support his contention "... that no matter how successful the campaign against Czechoslovakia might prove, it would be only a 'pyrrhic' victory with all the catastrophic results of such an event for Germany and all Europe."[8]

In planning the western campaign of early World War II the German Army high command was faced with the problem of "...where the main force of the first offensive thrust was to be directed and how the obstacle of the Ardennes was to be overcome by large motorized units." To help solve this problem both two-sided and one-sided war games were employed. In the two-sided game the opposition "... did not have to act according to German principles, but was supposed to adopt decisions and measures which in our opinion the allied commander presumably would follow."[8] The one-sided game was used to determine the feasibility of moving through the Ardennes with large armored units. For this game data based on peacetime experience and the Polish campaign were used. The information gained from these games was employed in the preparation of the final operations plan.

After the collapse of France, plans for the invasion of Russia were prepared and rehearsed with the aid of war games.

During lulls in the fighting, games based on the actual situation were conducted to explore the effectiveness of alternative courses of action and to rehearse impending or probable events. Thus, in November of 1944 the staff of the Fifth Panzer Army under the direction of Army Group Model played a war game with the purpose of rehearsing defensive measures against a possible American attack. During the game such an attack did occur. All of the participants whose commands were not directly affected by the attack were ordered to continue the game and to base their decisions on reports from the fighting front. When the situation became so critical that it was necessary to commit the division that comprised the army reserve "... the division commander, General von Waldenburg, who was present in the room and engaged in the game, received his orders one after another from the army group, the army, and the commanding general in question. After only a few minutes General von Waldenburg, instead of issuing purely theoretical orders at the map table, was able to issue actual operational orders to his operations officer and his couriers. The alerted division was thereby set in movement in the shortest conceivable time. Chance had transformed a simple map exercise into stern reality."[8]

Japanese Use of War Games. Translations of the works of Meckel and von Verdy appear to have introduced the technique of war gaming to the Japanese. Educational games became a part of the curriculum of the Japanese War College, and the successes of the Japanese Army in the Russo-Japanese War of 1904 were attributed in part to the "lessons learned" by Japanese officers in war games.

In 1940 the Total War Research Institute was established for the purpose of determining Japan's future courses of action with the aid of analytical gaming. Players represented not only different nations such as the U.S., Britain, Russia, China, Germany, etc., but also the conflicting interests within Japan: Army, Navy, and civilian. "These games resulted in detailed military and economic plans that were actually put into effect on December 8, 1941."[2]

War games conducted in the fall of 1941 at the War College in Tokyo were employed to analyze the effectiveness of a surprise attack of Pearl Harbor, and to rehearse such an operation. Other games "resulted in a carefully worked out schedule for occupying Malaya, Burma, the Dutch East Indies, the Philippines, the Solomons, and the Central Pacific Islands. These games were essentially three-sided exercises with teams of players representing Japan, England, and the U.S."[2]

In early 1942 tentative naval plans including the capture of Ceylon, the destruction of the British fleet, and the gaining of air control over the Indian Ocean were tested by means of war games. These plans, which had as their ultimate goal the joining of German and Japanese forces in the Near East, called for the use of army troops in amphibious operations against Ceylon. However, the army refused to cooperate on the grounds that it had to be—"on guard against the Soviet Union and therefore could not afford to extend itself any further in Southeast Asia."[12] Naval planners then turned their thoughts to the east and prepared ambitious plans for the capture of Midway and the western Aleutians in early June, the seizure of strategic points in New Caledonia and the Fiji Islands in July, air strikes on southeast Australia, and operations against Johnston Island and Hawaii in August. These proposed operations were tested in a series of war games in the spring of 1942. During the play the Nagumo Force was attacked by land-based air while its own planes were attacking Midway. Following the rules of the game, an umpire determined that the carriers received nine hits and that two of them, the Akagi and Kaga, were sunk. Rear Admiral Ugaki, the director of the game, arbitrarily reduced the number of hits to three, and the number of sinkings to one, and then permitted the sunken carrier to participate in the next part of the play dealing with the New Caledonia and Fiji Island invasions. These and other arbitrary rulings, always in favor of the Japanese, caused the authors of *Midway: the Battle That Doomed Japan*[12] to write: "No more vivid example of thoughtless and stupid arrogance can be conceived than the attitude which pervaded the war games in preparation for the Midway operation."

Allies, World War II. While the Americans and British conducted war games for educational purposes during World War II, they did not use them to the same extent as did the Germans and Japanese for planning, testing, and rehearsing operations. However, the Allied Forces employed war gaming techniques "... in the detailed planning for the D day invasion of Normandy."[2] An interesting example of a somewhat informal use of war gaming by General Montgomery in planning a battle in the desert is described by Moorehead.* The intelligence officer arranged the forces of the Axis Army on a map, and then played move for move against Montgomery.

* Alan Moorehead, *Montgomery, a Biography* (New York: Coward-McCann, Inc., 1946), p. 132.

War Games in the United States. Little seems to be known about the first war games in the United States beyond the fact that they were introduced into the army in 1867.[4,19] However, it may be assumed that they were copies or adaptations of German games. Thus, Major Livermore, one of the early American authorities on war games, first learned about them in 1865 from a civil engineer who had been an officer in the Bavarian Army.

In 1872 Captain Baring of the Royal Artillery adapted the works of a German writer (von Tschischwitz) to British use, and this book formed the basis for the conduct of voluntary war games at a number of U.S. garrisons.

During 1873 the *Explanation and Application of the English Rules for Playing the War Game*[20] was published in London. This book was based on lectures on war gaming that were delivered by Lieutenant Colonel Middleton of the English Army to the Brigade of Guard and the Aldershot Division. It also contained some of the rules of the Aldershot War Game Society, a group formed for the purpose of playing and improving war games. This book became available in the United States, and it is interesting to note that there is a well marked copy of the book in the Naval War College Library stamped, "Received, March 27, 1887."

Middleton wrote: "The war game is intended to be a representation of some operation of war, on a map drawn to a large scale, … the troops being represented by metal blocks of two different colors, red and blue, which are moved according to certain fixed rules as they would be moved in the field." He noted that the games "… may be arranged as to be suitable for all ranks, by representing the minor operations of war as well as the greater," and believed that the war game was of particular value to general officers. The author cautioned: "The only thing to be guarded against is putting too high a value on the game which, after all, can only be considered as an attempt to carry out theoretically in the closet what is done practically in the field."

The first major American work on war gaming was *American Kriegsspiel*[19] by Major (later Colonel) Livermore. It was published in 1879 and a second edition printed in 1898. In the preface to the first edition Livermore wrote: "The American Kriegsspiel, or War Game, has been developed from that of the Germans, its purpose being to represent military operations upon a geographical or topographical map, by small colored blocks, and auxiliary apparatus to which a conventional meaning is assigned." He further stated that he had consulted the works of von Verdy, Meckel, von Trotha, and von Tschischwitz of the German Army, Captain Baring of the British Army, and several Austrian authors, but that his work was closer to the *Regiments Kriegsspiel* of Naumann than to any of the others.

The following appears in the preface to the second edition: "… an effort has been made to bring … the tables up to date; but now we have no recent war like the Franco-Prussian or the Turko-Russian to test the value of our estimates, …." However, a postscript notes that "The war with Spain … has solved several of the problems depending upon the new weapons." Comments were also made about the use of partially smokeless powder and black powder by United States troops as opposed to the smokeless powder of the Spanish.

Livermore classified war games as follows:

1. The Tactical Game, representing an engagement in all its details.
2. The Grand Tactical Game, representing an extensive battle in a more general manner.
3. The Strategical Game, involving the movements of armies over an extended area and for a period of several days or months.
4. The Fortifications Game, representing siege operations; and
5. The Naval Game.

The author considered the first two of the greatest importance to the army and the militia and consequently described them in great detail. He did not describe the naval game.

The rules were designed to cover every conceivable situation, and the games were conducted under the supervision of a director. In this regard, Livermore commented: "Although usually conducted under the direction of an umpire this is by no means essential for the rules are specific enough in their present form to enable the players to agree very well about their applications." Whether or not such umpire-less games were ever played does not seem to have been recorded; that they could have been successfully conducted is somewhat unlikely.

Livermore observed that in Germany where there were many officers with wide experience both in the field and in war gaming, the free method of evaluation "… answered well …. But such men are not always available for umpires in the small garrisons into which the American army is divided: …." Therefore, he based his original game on rigid methods of evaluation, but attempted to devise and employ improved equipment and procedures that would make "The American Game proceed almost as rapidly …" as those German games that used free methods of evaluation.

Major C.W. Raymond in a book* published in 1881 supported Livermore's contentions concerning free and rigid methods of evaluation. As quoted by Young,[2] Raymond wrote: "However possible such an exercise may be in Germany, it will certainly be found generally impractical in our own country (USA). In Berlin, where there are officers of the general staff who devote their undivided attention to the study of war it may be possible to obtain competent directors, ... but in this country ... only in a few exceptional cases would it be possible to obtain a director, the superiority of whose experience and attainments would be so undoubted that his decisions would receive unhesitating acceptance .... My own experience as a director has convinced me that ... the director, after he has conducted a few exercises, finds inevitably that he is acting in accordance with rules which he has consciously or unconsciously formed. Thus the choice we have to make is not between rules and no rules but between rules based upon the careful study of all available data, which have stood the test of practice and the fire of criticism, and rules extemporized by a single authority to be accepted without demonstration and to be varied by every new director."

Experience with Livermore's game, however, did not bear out the author's optimistic appraisal of the speed at which it could be conducted. And the second edition which was prepared with the assistance of Major Hugh G. Brown stated: "The tables in the American Kriegsspiel have been prepared with a view to expressing all that could be learned of the influences that affect a battle or campaign, and umpires are cautioned that they are only to be used as required: ... Although the methods ... described will enable the umpire to determine with the utmost rapidity any doubtful point that may arise in the course of the game, it cannot be too strongly stated that all these computations not only need not, but must not, be made in every case. They are intended to facilitate and hasten the game, and should not be so perverted as to retard it."

The maps used in Livermore's tactical games were drawn to a scale of approximately 12 inches to the mile with a contour interval of ten feet. They were ideal maps probably because suitable maps of actual areas were not available.** The maps were gridded as an aid in the taking of measurements and determining the locations of forces and events.

Troop units were represented by small blocks of wood, metal, or porcelain. The opposing sides were red and blue, but other colors and tints were used in

* C.W. Raymond, *Kriegsspiel*, U.S. Artillery School, Ft. Monroe, Va., 1881.

** According to Sayre,[4] the earliest American map made especially for war games depicted a four by six mile area around Fort Leavenworth. It was drawn in 1906 from surveys made by student officers of the Army Staff College. The scale was 12 inches to the mile; the contour interval, 10 ft.

combination with these colors to distinguish the different types of troops and formations. If a unit suffered a loss of two tenths of its fighting power, the block representing the unit was turned so that its face showed a single mark called a "score." A four-tenths reduction in combat effectiveness resulted in the face with two marks being turned up, and so on. Somewhat similar means were employed to indicate ammunition levels, states of fatigue, times of completion of fortifications, bridges, etc. The idea was to eliminate the keeping of records, a major problem in any war game.

Troop movements and firing were indicated by pointers. Damage was assessed and recorded by means of a firing board. This was an ingenious arrangement of scales and three matrices of holes which represented respectively a computing table, a record of losses, and the time. It took the players some little time to learn the meaning and manipulation of the blocks and pointers, and the control group even longer to master the specialized computation technique. Sayre[4] noted that Livermore's game was the best in its class but went on to emphasize, perhaps a little too strongly, that "... it cannot be readily and intelligently used by any one who is not a mathematician, and it requires, in order to be able to use it readily, an amount of special instruction, study and practice about equivalent to that necessary to acquire a speaking knowledge of a foreign language."

About the same time that Livermore's game appeared, Lieutenant Totten, in an article in the *Journal of the Military Service Institution*, Volume 1, 1880[18] observed that at that time some twenty-three independent sets of rules existed for the conduct of war games. He thought that these rules and the games that they governed were useful in the European nations with large professional armies, but felt that these foreign games were too advanced for the citizen soldiers of our nation and too complicated and too time consuming to be played "in the thinly soldiered and widely scattered outposts ..." of the "... little American (professional) army ...." He, therefore, described a series of games which he had devised and named "Strategos." These were intended to "... blend and fade one into another so gradually and so naturally that the student will be almost unwittingly entrapped into continually higher and higher forms of study until at length the mere tyro ... will find himself actually venturing to command an army, and essay with growing confidence those deeper, and more absorbing problems which alone test generalship and seal the fate of nations."

Totten's game was divided into a "Battle Game," and an "Advanced Game." The former was subdivided into a "Minor Tactical Game" and a "Grand Tactical Game." Concerning the Battle Game Totten said it is "... a compromise between a game and a study, between chess and 'war upon the map.' ... The rules of the game conspire toward concentration and arrangement, as a means of securing victory, rather than toward captures and losses, and the aim has been to make these rules suggestive of military ideas." Of the Advanced Game he remarked that it "... affords to the professional military man every opportunity that could be desired for pursuing studies, commenced in more elementary fields, to their legitimate termination. In this, the last branch of the subject, therefore, all arbitrary assignments of values and moves are of course entirely out of the question and improper. The whole game is required to base itself upon actualities, upon the results of careful investigations, and upon the tabulated statistics of experience, of actual practice, and of former battles and campaigns ... the constant endeavor will be seen to represent the mimic battle or campaign in all its features, save the dreadful wastes of blood and iron."[18]

The Battle Game was similar to the older war-chess type of games. Both versions were played on a 48 by 40 inch board which was ruled into inch squares. The surface of the board was covered with slate so that notations could readily be made and erased. The board was divided into four folding sections for ease in carrying. Pieces representing military units were also covered with slate. They were colored red for one side, blue for the other. Increased versatility was provided for by additional blocks which had topographical symbols printed on one side and a slate surface on the other. These could be used to depict either topographical features or troop units.

Pieces were moved according to fixed rules. An infantry unit could move one square forward, backward, or sideways. Cavalry pieces, in one move, shifted two squares diagonally in any direction and then one forward, backward, or sideways.[22] Arbitrary numerical values were assigned to the various pieces and fixed rules governed the capture and displacement of opposing forces. In the Grand Tactical Game the players sometimes made their initial dispositions while separated by a screen. The screen was then lifted for a short interval of time so that the opponents might see but not study each other's dispositions. Subject to the approval of an umpire, the players then adjusted their dispositions, the screen was lifted, and play began.

Totten's Advanced Game was played on maps, although in some instances contours were sketched on the game board and the topographical blocks used to indicate towns, woods, lakes, etc. Forces moved according to tabulated values compiled from real-world activities. These values were modified by one or more multipliers when conditions varied from those given in the tables.

The control group followed a series of steps, each of which referred to the tables that were needed for implementation. Whether or not a unit could advance, maintain its position, etc., was determined by the use of ratios expressing chances of success and reference to a throw of dice. For example, when veteran troops engaged new troops the ratio was 4 to 1 for the veterans. (Totten noted that Caesar's estimate was 2 to 1.) The author believed that the use of "chances of success" was not only a sound and realistic method for evaluating interactions but that "... 'chances of success' have deep meaning for the battlefield itself."[18]

The slated surface of the blocks was used for bookkeeping purposes and was, according to Totten, "... universally admitted by devoted players of the war game as perhaps the solution to one of the most perplexing and apparently insurmountable drawbacks to rapid and satisfactory study."[18]

The tables in Totten's work were based in great part on War Department records of the Civil War. Appendix E of Part II[22] contains data of interest to students of that war, and Appendix G provides information about the military establishment of the United States up to 1880.

The first naval war game appears to have been invented and patented about 1878 by Captain Philip H. Colomb of the British Navy. It was called "The Duel," and was designed to simulate an interaction between two opposing ships. In 1886 Captain Hammill of the British Navy said: "I know that some years ago Captain Colomb brought out a very capital war game, which, I believe, has been widely taken up abroad, by Russia especially. I have read occasionally of naval war-game battles having been fought in that country. For my own part, although I have seen a great deal of what has been going on in the Service the last six or seven years, or since the war game was invented, I have seen one naval war game fought, and one only, and that on board the 'Vernon,' I think, in 1879. No doubt many others have been fought, perhaps even in my own ship, without my knowing it ...." Rear Admiral the Hon. Edmund R. Fremantle commented: "... As regards the naval war game, I quite agree with Captain Hammill. I think I have fought two games, but that is about all. I bought the blocks, and intended to go at it. In one ship we had, as I say, two or three games. I am very sorry that it has not been adopted in the Navy. It certainly was extremely useful. It gave you certain rules which were of great service, and it also afforded some general information as to the tactics of a gun and torpedo action between a couple of ships."*

Some of the earliest references on naval war gaming to appear in this country were contained in the Bibliographic Notices of the *U.S. Naval Institute Proceedings.* The following two are listed on pages 201 and 116, respectively, of the 1881 volume: "The Duel, or the naval war game," *Revue Maritime Et Coloniale*, February, 1881; and "Game of Naval Warfare (translation)," *Revista General De Marina*, March, 1881.

* *The Journal of the Royal United Service Institution*, v. XXX, no. CXXXIII, 1886.

In 1886 William McCarty Little, a retired naval lieutenant who was living in Newport, delivered a lecture on "Colomb's War Game" at the Naval War College, Newport, R.I. This lecture appears to have had little impact, and was apparently soon forgotten. It is not mentioned in Knight and Puleston's *History of the Naval War College*. The following year Little became a member of the staff of the College, and delivered a series of six lectures on war gaming. It was this series of lectures that seems to have first aroused the interest of the College in war gaming, and "... led to their adoption as part of the College work, where the games soon took a large place in the College course."[23]

The free method of evaluation for war games became more widely known in the United States in 1897 with the translation by Captain Swift, U.S.A. of von Verdy's book, *A Simplified War Game*.[21] In the preface to the translation, Swift wrote: "Some years ago the distinguished General I. von Verdy du Vernois, whose ideas upon the education of officers and the peace training of troops rule the military world today, prepared this little manual for the purpose of aiding those who were discouraged by more difficult methods. After hard struggles with many systems, my experience led me to believe that this was the only system that could be successfully applied by American students, ..."

In 1908 *Map Maneuvers and Tactical Rides*[4] by Captain Farrand Sayre, U.S. Army, was published by the Army Service Schools Press, Fort Leavenworth, Kansas, and later editions appeared in 1910 and 1911.[2] This book was based on a series of lectures presented at the Army Staff College. The author discussed military chess and the history and value of war gaming. He described the maps then available both in this country and abroad that were suitable for war games, and the scales, blocks, and other accessories that were necessary or useful for conducting such games. Sayre noted that up to the time of the publication of his book no systematic division of map maneuvers (war games) had been made in our army. He stated that the "... character of the maneuver is controlled by its (the map's) scale," and recommended the following: "1. Maneuvers in Minor Tactics—embracing tactical exercises from patrolling to the operations of small detachments of all arms, for use at army posts and the Army School of the Line—maps on a scale of twelve inches to a mile, with contours at a vertical interval of five feet. 2. Maneuvers in Grand Tactics—embracing the employment of large detachments of all arms and of divisions, for the older officers at the larger posts and for the Army Staff College—maps on a scale of six inches to a mile, with contours at a vertical interval of ten feet. 3. Strategic maneuvers—embracing the operations of armies, for the Army War College—maps of the U.S. Geological Survey, scale 1:62,500 (about one inch to 1 mile)." Sayre also commented on a fact that is familiar to all war gamers, namely, "… the more minutely we wish to consider the details of military operations the larger should be the scale of the map."

Sayre observed that the situations upon which war games are based should be plausible and suggested the use of problems based upon actual situations or on events that occurred in military history. He believed that the forces assigned to opposing commanders need not be equal in strength or similar in composition, and when they were there was a tendency for the game to become a long drawn out affair. To add interest and realism, the author suggested that, when possible, problems be so formulated that "… one or both commanders may be forced or induced to abandon their original missions and adopt new ones on their own initiative."

One-sided games were explained and the author expressed the opinion that they had never received the attention that they merited. He believed that they were valuable types of games, especially for beginners, and that they gave the director an opportunity to bring out the tactical lessons that he wished to teach. "In a two-sided maneuver, it may happen that many of the mistakes which are made are not pointed out; this would, perhaps, be the case in actual war; but the lesson is none-the-less bad; the repetition of the same mistakes or uncorrected carelessness tends to establish bad habits. It may be objected that the part of the director, commanding one of the forces and knowing the movements of the other, is too easy from a tactical point of view. This would be true if it were a contest or a game; but there is no contest and no game; the director does not compete with the student officers, he teaches them." (Quoted by Sayre from "Jeu de Guerre et Manoeuvre sur la Carte," *Revue Militaire Generale*, Jan. 1907.)

The two-sided games were considered to be a higher form of war gaming, and the type most frequently conducted because they more closely approximated the real world. In these games the director's chief job was to furnish each side with realistic intelligence, to monitor rates of march, to determine contacts, and to assess damage. Sayre stressed the fact that a two-sided game provided a commander with "… an opportunity to gauge his opponents, to make use of his knowledge of their personal characteristics, and to shape his own course accordingly." To illustrate this point, he noted that "Such decisions as that of General Lee in halting behind Antietam Creek and accepting battle with the Potomac at his back—or in dividing his forces at Chancellorsville in the presence of a superior enemy—would, in a one-sided maneuver or in a map problem, be regarded as mistakes; but when the personality of the opposing commander is taken into account they may be very far from being mistakes."*

Four methods of starting the game were explained. In the first, the opposing commanders were assigned the problem some time in advance of the game and were required to prepare a written estimate of the situation. The second method gave the players about a half hour in which to familiarize themselves with the situation and to get ready to select their courses of action. The third way was to bring one side and then the other to the map, to brief orally each in turn on the situation and forces, and then start the game. "This method, no doubt, offers less opportunity for reflection than would ordinarily be the case in war. But one of the greatest benefits to be obtained from map maneuvers is practice in estimating situations rapidly and in forming decisions promptly...."

The fourth method, Sayre noted, was frequently employed in the German Army, and had been used to some extent at the Army Staff College. It is very familiar to officers who have attended the Naval War College and is frequently used in today's educational type war games. In this method the players are divided into two sides. Each player then prepares an estimate of the situation for his own side, and the courses of action that he would take were he in command of his side. The director examines all of the solutions and selects the two that he thinks would lead to an interesting and instructive game. The players whose solutions are selected act as commanders of their respective sides, and the other players are assigned subordinate commands.

In games that started with the opposing forces a considerable distance apart, Sayre proposed that they be conducted on a small scale map until such time as the forces came into contact. At that time they would be transferred to the large scale map and the game would proceed in a more detailed fashion.

The difficulties of simulating the engagements of large forces, which usually stem from an attempt to include too great a range of command levels, were recognized by Sayre. He recommended that the number of participants in such games be limited, that they be assigned to high level command jobs, and that they only make the decisions and issue the orders normal to those billets. "For instance, in mixed brigades the officers assigned to commands would be the brigade commander, the regimental commanders and the commander of the cavalry: ... By assigning no officers to command battalions or smaller units and by permitting the participants to decide only such questions as properly fall to the province of the

* For some interesting speculations on how computer gaming might have affected the outcome of Chancellorsville, see F. X. Kane, "Security Is Too Important to Be Left to Computers," *Fortune*, April 1964, page 146.

brigade, regimental, ... and cavalry commanders, the director may keep the control of the execution of all details in his own hands and greatly simplify the conduct of the exercise."

Sayre defined the strategic war game as one intended to give practice in such work as, in war, would fall to general staff officers. "The organization and concentration of armies, the establishment of lines of communications, the service in rear of an army and on the lines of communications, the use of railway and telegraph lines, the service of information, ... and the preparation of reports, etc., are taken up."

Meckel (*Anleitung zum Kriegsspiel*) was quoted by Sayre on the duties of the director in a strategic war game. "The most important and most delicate duty of the director is the communication of information of the enemy. It is the most important because operations depend upon this information, and it is the most delicate because it is very difficult to give just the right measure of information and no more .... The more experience the director has had in high staff positions in war, the more familiar he will be with the peculiarities of messages and other sources of information, and the better will he be able to hit on the right amount and kind of information to be given, and to mix correct, inaccurate, incomplete, and false information together in proper proportions." It was observed that there were few officers in our army with this sort of experience but "... the experience of our Staff College shows that well instructed officers—such as the students of the Staff College—are able to conduct strategic map maneuvers well enough to make them interesting and profitable."

Sayre based his game on the free method of evaluation. "Losses are estimated by the director in accordance with his judgment, based on his experience and study of modern wars." However, in an appendix which was a reprint of a pamphlet that had been used at the Army Staff College for about a year prior to the publication of *Map Maneuvers and Tactical Rides*, it was noted that while losses were no longer calculated in war games, many officers, based on their observations of target practice, had formed exaggerated ideas on the effectiveness of firearms. It was, therefore, recommended that fire effect tables be used in hypothetical situations to train the directors and umpires in estimating losses and to gain familiarity with the important factors which influence the effect of fire. Such a table and examples of its use were included in the appendix.

As noted by Sayre, Captain E. Dubois of the French Army recommended that plates of ground glass be placed over each commander's map and the movements of his forces drawn on it in colored pencil. The control group could then lay the plates over each other in their map and evaluate the situation. Sayre observed that "A modification of this method has been in use for several years at our Naval War

College and has recently been tried in our Army War College with satisfactory results. Sheets of transparent celluloid are used instead of the ground glass recommended by Captain Dubois." This method facilitated the mechanics of the game by eliminating the need for various size blocks to represent different troop formations, and the covering or removal of blocks on the control group's map. Since much intelligence could be indicated on the plates before they were returned to the players, this technique simplified and speeded the flow of intelligence.

With the introduction of overlays for transmitting information, most of the basic procedures now in use for conducting manual games had been tried at one time or another. Since, however, these techniques have been refined and extended by the use of projection, communications, and reproduction equipment, and by the production and availability of more and better maps.

A Coast Artillery War Game described by Major William Chamberlaine in a book of the same name[24] was developed in the Department of Artillery and Land Defense during the winter of 1912. The purpose of the game was "... to train Artillery Officers for their duties in time of war." It was used daily as part of the course of the Coast Artillery School. In the preface to the first edition the following appears: "It is considered unfortunate that some name more descriptive of its purpose could not be found but the present one has been adopted after considering several others."*

The Coast Artillery Game was a two-sided land vs. naval game. It was played on a game board which consisted of 36 four-foot square sections mounted on trestles. The coastal region was a model of some specific area such as Guantanamo Bay, Fort Monroe, etc., with a contour interval of 25 feet. Shore batteries, buildings, ships, etc. were constructed to scale; the ocean area painted blue. Searchlights for use in simulated night engagements were cleverly contrived with the aid of mirrors and lights.

Prior to a game, training in the identification of ship types was given with the aid of a baloptican (slide projector), and the usual general and special situations prepared and distributed to the players.

At the commencement of play a curtain concealed the board from the land players. The naval players placed their ships and retired from the room. The curtain was pulled open and the land players looked over the situation and issued their orders. The curtain was closed, the director rang a bell, and the naval players entered and made their moves and decisions concerning the selection of targets, opening fire, etc. Moves represented one minute of real-world time.

---

* As noted in Chapter I, von Reisswitz used the name war game "... only because he could not at that time find one more suitable."

Coast Artillery War Game Board

Figure 2-1

If a battery was firing, a metal flag was raised. Similar flags were employed to indicate to a target that it was under fire and the nature of the fire. This assisted in keeping to a minimum the flow of information between players and umpires.

Hits on ships from land batteries were determined by drawing one cube for each round fired from the proper bag of 100 cubes. For each cube drawn with a number on it equal to or greater than the range, a hit was scored. Just where the hit landed on the target was determined by spinning a random device (called a "localizer") numbered from one to twenty, and locating the corresponding number on an outline drawing of the ship. Whether or not the hit penetrated the armor of the ship was determined by the use of graphs known as "armor attack sheets." The number of hits required to destroy a particular type ship was compiled from data adapted from Naval War College games.*

The effectiveness of naval gunfire against shore targets was determined by dividing the land area into subdivisions, and then following somewhat the same procedures as outlined above.

A 1914 article in the *Scientific American*[7] described war gaming as then conducted at the Army War College. Redheaded pins represented artillery, strings

* Appendix II contains a table showing the numbers and types of hits and damage suffered by naval vessels in the Russian-Japanese, Chinese-Japanese, and Spanish-American Wars.

of beads indicated lines of skirmishers, and so on. The control group used a large scale map, the players the smaller scale maps they would use in the field. The article noted that "Kriegsspiel ... is used now in the instruction of every army of the world," and emphasized that a war game was "... not played as a game to see who will win, but to get results and experience, to profit by the mistakes made."

In *The Solution of Map Problems*[25] published during 1925 the student was cautioned not to "... waste time in criticizing the problem. The problem may not be perfect, but it must be solved." It was also noted that "It is not the aim of the General Service Schools to graduate officers highly proficient in the art of solving map problems alone, but through this medium (the solution of map problems) to bring about that state of mind wherein the individual, when confronted with a situation in the field, goes about its solution with full confidence in his ability to see things in their proper relations, to weigh conditions one against the other, and to reach a sound decision without undue loss of time." Colored markers, pins, colored pencils, and charcoal were used to indicate locations and movements.

While there is some indication that U.S. mobilization plans were war gamed by the War Plans Division in the late thirties, for the most part war games in the United States were conducted at such service schools as the Command and General Staff College, the Army War College, the Naval War College, etc. "Such games appear to have been played primarily for training purposes in conjunction with course work ...."[2] In some of these the student teams prepared plans and, prior to the play of the game, switched sides and during the game executed the plans prepared by their opponent.

In March of 1941, a translation and condensation of the German General von Cochenhausen's booklet on war gaming appeared in the *Military Review*.[26] The editors of the review stated: "It is believed that no better means than the 'Kriegsspiel,' or war game, has been devised for training commanders and general staff officers, approaching as it does the semblance of actual battle.* It demands definite decisions and orders for the commitment of troops, also being conducted within the realm of time and space thereby leading to exactitude in troop leading."

The article describes the then current German gaming techniques and concepts, and indicates the type of gaming literature then available. It describes the conduct of a one-sided game (called a map exercise by the Germans) and a two-sided game (referred to as a war game by the Germans). For the latter three rooms were required "... one for the actual game, another for the party not playing at the

* Compare with conclusion reached by the 1955 War Games Conference at the University of Michigan: "War gaming is an extremely important educational device for training senior officers—probably the best available in time of peace ...."

moment and a third into which officers of the playing party may retire for brief intervals." Sides were called to the map in turn, and enemy symbols were covered except when the locations of such forces were known. It was noted that the commanders should have one or more assistants to relieve them of the details of setting up the symbols, etc.

In one-sided games it was pointed out that the director should "... lead the enemy so as continually to introduce a new situation demanding prompt decision and action of commanders."

Of the game leader (director) in a two-sided game it was said: "He studiously determines which methods will keep play on the right course and avoids everything which might tend to have a semblance of force or influence on his part. He strives to give the war game charm and reality, a natural development of accomplishments out of the thinking and desires of the commanders."

During World War II, scientists conducting military operational research studies began to employ war gaming techniques to assist them in formulating and solving operational problems. In an article published in 1954, for example, Dr. Philip M. Morse told how war gaming was employed to develop some wartime antisubmarine air-search tactics,* and another article in the same book mentions the use of war gaming in mine warfare.**

Since World War II, and particularly during the past decade, tremendous advances have been made in war gaming, its techniques and its applications, and many new war gaming organizations—military and civilian—have been established.*** A few of these developments are outlined in succeeding paragraphs.

During the postwar years operations research personnel continued and expanded their wartime gaming and simulation experiments, and a number of hand-played games were devised by such organizations as the RAND Corporation, the Operations Evaluation Group, and the Operations Research Office (ORO) of Johns Hopkins University.**** As digital computing equipment became available, schemes were advanced for devising computer equivalents of board and map games. One of the first such games was Carmonette, a computer simulation of a tank battle.[9]

---

* Philip M. Morse, "Progress in Operations Research," Joseph F. McCloskey and Florence N. Trefethen, eds., *Operations Research for Management*, (Baltimore: Johns Hopkins Press, 1954), p. 115.

** Florence N. Trefethen, "A History of Operations Research," Joseph F. McCloskey and Florence N. Trefethen, eds., *Operations Research for Management*, (Baltimore: Johns Hopkins Press, 1954), p. 15.

*** A directory of war gaming activities has been compiled by the U.S. Army Strategy and Tactics Analysis Group, Bethesda, Maryland.[27]

**** ORO was dissolved as a research organization on August 31, 1961. Its work is being continued by Research Analysis Corporation (RAC), a nonprofit research organization under contract to the United States Army. *Operations Research*, September–October 1961, p. 770.

Another early computer game was devised by the RAND Corporation for the simulation of air warfare.[28]

Monopologs, a military inventory management game was devised by RAND in 1955. Two years later the American Management Association introduced the first practical business "war game," Top Management Decision Simulation. During this same general period, political factors were introduced into war games, and a number of political and political-military games were devised and conducted.[29]

The Air Force established a service-headquarters-level gaming activity, the Air Battle Analysis Center (ABAC), in mid 1957. The Navy set up Op-06C, the Office of the Assistant to the Chief of Naval Operations for War Gaming Matters, in early 1958. About two years later the Army established the Strategy and Tactics Analysis Group (STAG); the Marine Corps, the Landing Force War Game Group (LFWGG) at the Marine Corps Landing Force Development Center. In early 1961 the Joint War Games Control Group (JWGCG) was activated to plan, control, and supervise joint war games for the Joint Chiefs of Staff. Two years later this group was expanded and redesignated the Joint War Games Agency (JWGA). Its mission remained unchanged.[30]

Service war gaming organizations receive technical support from military groups and civilian research organizations such as Technical Operations, Incorporated. For example, the Navy's Office of the Assistant for War Gaming Matters receives technical support from two naval activities (The Strategic Analysis Support Group, and the Computation and Analysis Laboratory of the Naval Weapons Laboratory) and one civilian organization (The Planning Analysis Group of the Applied Physics Laboratory, Johns Hopkins University).

The Joint War Games Agency is staffed by personnel from all of the Services, and the position of the Chief of the Agency is filled on a rotational basis from among the Services. Except for certain political-military games, this agency does not conduct its own games, but utilizes service-gaming facilities and personnel and the technical support of contract organizations. The Joint War Games Agency coordinates the joint-gaming activities of the various service-gaming groups, and provides supervision and overall control, guidance, and advice.[30]

A game (or set of games) was played in 1964 that required the personnel and facilities of three Navy activities, and utilized all three of the basic simulation techniques. The given problem was to examine, by means of war gaming, an Atlantic Fleet contingency plan for the employment of amphibious forces. The game used three of Op-06's amphibious warfare models to play the load-out of the amphibious forces, the ship-to-shore movement, and the naval gunfire and air support. These plays were conducted on digital computers at the Naval Weapons

Laboratory. The movement of the amphibious task force to the objective area was played on the NEWS at the Naval War College. This portion of the game employed remote-play techniques. The commander and his staff operated from the flagship which was tied up at its pier; the control group in the NEWS simulated the units of the task force and the opposition. Troop operations ashore were played by means of a manual game conducted by the War Games Division at the Marine Corps Landing Force Development Center.*

Gaming at the Naval War College. The simulation of naval engagements between forces in which individual naval units are represented does not present some of the difficulties encountered in the gaming of land forces. Unlike a company of infantry, for example, a ship cannot vary the area that it occupies, nor can it be hidden by an intervening ridge, or seek concealment in a wooded area. Naval games are less dependent upon the production of good maps, and of course, can be conducted in areas representing open water without any maps at all. Consequently, it is not surprising to find that the use of gaming techniques was applied to the realistic appraisal of naval actions prior to its similar employment for land battles.

During the latter part of the 18th century, John Clerk studied naval tactics and evolved a highly successful theory with the aid of gaming methods. In the preface to *An Essay on Naval Tactics*[10] Clerk wrote: "As I never was at sea myself, it has been asked, how I should have been able to acquire any knowledge in naval tactics, or should have presumed to suggest my opinion and ideas upon that subject." In the explanation that followed he said: "... I had recourse not only to every species of demonstration, by plans and drawings, but also to the use of a number of small models of ships which, when disposed in proper arrangement, gave most correct representations of hostile fleets, extended each in line of battle; and being easily moved and put into any relative position required, and thus permanently seen and well considered, every possible idea of naval system could be discussed without the possibility of any dispute." Captain F. E. Chadwick, USN, while President of the Naval War College, had this to say of Clerk's efforts: "It may not be generally known that for a hundred years previous to the appearance of Clerk's work on Tactics ... all actions between the French and the English were of a very indecisive nature. Rodney made a first application of Clerk's principles in his action with de Grasse. The final and successful tactics under sail were thus worked out in the

* Thomas Bush, "War Gaming in the Navy," A lecture delivered at the School of Naval Command and Staff, Naval War College, Newport, R.I.: September 29, 1965.

solitude of a student's study ...."* Little observed in 1911 that Clerk, in order to analyze the tactics of opposing forces "... used little blocks representing ships which he moved about on a table representing the sea: practically the naval tactical or fleet war game of today!"[3] In a manner somewhat similar to that used by Clerk, Captain Mahan employed "... cardboard vessels of different colors for the contending navies ..." in developing his early lectures at the Naval War College.** However, despite the proven value of Clerk's techniques, the war game as used by naval officers "... was suggested by the German Army Kriegsspiel, brought prominently to view in 1870 ...."[3]

As noted earlier, war gaming was introduced to the Naval War College and, no doubt, to the Navy, in a series of six lectures delivered in 1887 by Lieutenant William McCarty Little, USN, retired.*** These lectures were continued during 1888 and 1889 and the staff conducted occasional games during the period from 1887 to 1893. In 1889 Major Livermore, author of *The American Kriegsspiel*, visited the College, and it can be assumed that the two authorities on war gaming, Livermore and Little, had a great deal to talk about.

Classes were not held at the College in 1890 and 1891. In 1892 a war game in which students participated on a voluntary basis was started but not completed. No classes were held in 1893. During the following year war games became a part of the regular course of the College, and have continued in that role to the present day. Throughout this early period, Little continued his studies of war gaming, and in 1892 translated into English a description of a naval war game proposed by Lieutenant A. Colombo of the Italian Navy.**** In the introduction to this game, Lieutenant Colombo wrote: "The practice of simulated war is also wanting to us, because the resources of our country do not permit organizing every year large manoeuvers with this scope, and even if they permitted it, it would be necessary to neglect other manoeuvers no less important. There is, however, a medium path, in my opinion, sufficiently sure and not expensive, and it is that of making these manoeuvers methodically by all the officers, marking them on the chart, according to such fixed rules as will cause the exercise to approach actual practice. With a little good will, a little patience and a little perserverance, I believe it possible to

---

* F.E. Chadwick, "Explanation of Course at the Naval War College," *U.S. Naval Institute Proceedings*, June 1901, p. 304.

** Alfred T. Mahan, *From Sail to Steam*, (New York: Harper and Brothers, 1907), p. 294.

*** The lectures on war gaming, "... mark(ed) the beginning of the official activities of Lieutenant Little at the College. With but one relatively short interruption these activities continued for 28 years until his death in 1915."[23] Lieutenant Little was appointed Captain in 1903 by a Special Act of Congress.

**** A. Colombo, "A Naval War Game," *Rivista Marittima*, December 1891.

succeed and to succeed well, I believe even more; that we will see a day in which this exercise, which I would call a Naval War Game, will succeed in interesting, and will form a useful and voluntary occupation of many officers in the weary hours passed ashore, or on board in an unamusing town, and will be the source of long discussions, perhaps at times a little bitter, but very often of very useful exchange of ideas, ... I will assemble a certain number of rules, in the hope that someone may be tempted to examine them, to test them and then complete them, and I am certain that something useful will come from it."

Concerning Little's efforts in behalf of the College and of war gaming, Rear Admiral Luce wrote: "... the College owes a deep debt of gratitude (to) Captain William McCarty Little, U.S.N., who vigorously fought its battles when the great body of the Service was either actively opposed to it, or wholly indifferent. The Naval War Game is his special contribution to the work. It was he who demonstrated all the possibilities of that method of investigation—now known as the laboratory method.

"It was through the ingenuity of devising and working out details, and the indefatigable labors of Lieutenant Little that the Naval War Game became a recognized part of the College curriculum. His work has contributed very largely to whatever success the College has achieved."*

In 1894, when the first curriculum games were conducted at the Naval War College, the President was Commander, later Captain, Harry C. Taylor. The staff consisted of four officers; the class, 18. In addition, officers of the R.I. Naval Militia and some foreign officers attended some of the classes. The course started June 12 and ended September 30. It consisted of lectures, war problems, war charts and defense plans, war games, steam launch exercises, torpedo instruction, and reading. The main problem of the course was based on assumed hostilities between Red (Great Britain) and Blue (U.S.). Due to Red's great naval superiority, most of Blue's actions were defensive in nature and led to a study of tactical defense plans for the waters of Narragansett, Gardiner's, and Buzzard's Bays. During the autumn and winter the staff completed these studies and forwarded them to the Secretary of the Navy.

The rules for the first games at the College in which students participated were compiled by Little under the title of "Introduction as to Conduct of War Games." Three types of games were recognized: "The Duel, or Single-Ship Game; the Fleet Tactical Game, which includes the Melee, and is the tactical maneuvering of hostile squadrons in the presence of each other upon the open sea or in restricted waters;

* Stephen B. Luce, "The U.S. Naval War College," *U.S. Naval Institute Proceedings*, September 1910, p. 684.

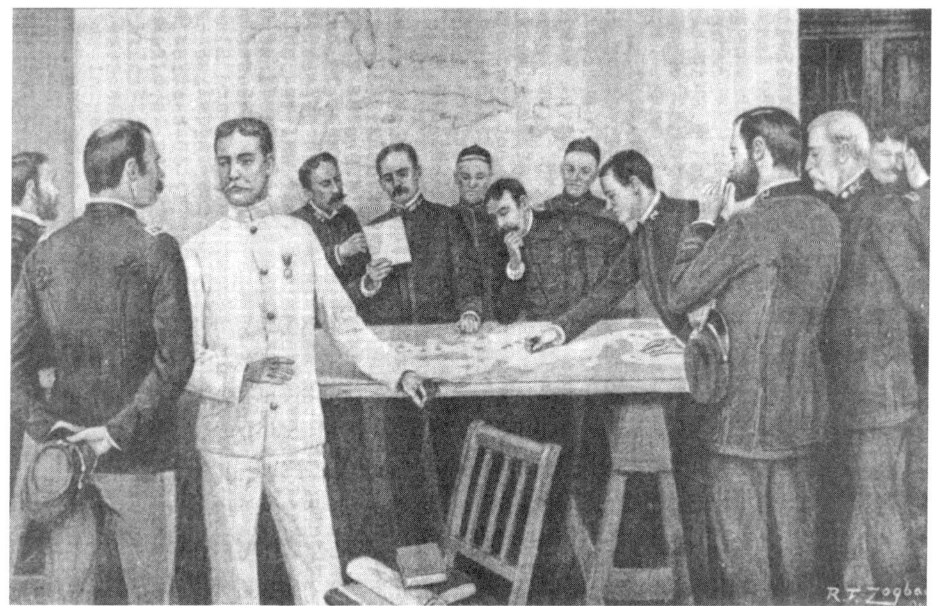

A Problem in Naval Tactics-at the Naval War College, Newport, Rhode Island

Figure 2–2

and lastly, the Strategic Game. The Strategic Game, as its name implies, governs the strategic disposition of the various units of the fleet and their subsequent mobility in a specific operation of war in some imaginary campaign."[1] Captain Chadwick, the President of the Naval War College in 1901 observed: "The principles of strategy and tactics may be gleaned from history, but the games afford the only practicable means known whereby these principles may be applied. The strategic game teaches the Admiral how to dispose his forces in a maritime campaign, the tactical game how to handle his fleet in action, while the duel game shows the commander how to best fight his ship."[23]

The 1894 games were described in an article that appeared in *Harper's Weekly* in February of the following year: "... the War College has taken a new and successful departure, and the year's work just closed has been peculiarly practical and progressive. It consisted, first and foremost in working out a problem in strategy—an application to American naval tactics of the 'Kriegsspiel' to which the German Army, and particularly the officers of the General Staff, owe their high efficiency in mobilization and strategic movement .... That complete preparedness against all probable contingencies is the ultimate aim of this institution; and in the absence of an American General Staff, naval officers are here to determine beforehand what an enemy must or would be likely to do in attacking us by sea, and what, under each set of circumstances, is the best way to repel him."

In his annual report Captain Taylor wrote: "The war game has been useful to a degree far beyond my most sanguine anticipations." Captain C.F. Goodrich, President of the College said in his closing address to the 1897 class: "I am confident … that you have derived much benefit from the tactical games, which have at least taught you some things which a fleet should not do …. The single-ship game has made a distinct step forward, through the introduction of the torpedo as a weapon. Experience and study will improve as well as the other games, so that they may more nearly represent the conditions of actual warfare. It should be borne in mind, however, that a reasonable approximation is the best we can hope for. This much is undoubtedly true, that he who is expert in manoeuvering fleets and ships on the boards of the College will possess a marked advantage afloat, in the more serious game, over his competitor who has been less fortunate in preliminary training …. In the strategic game, fifteen situations have been played during this session. Much interest has been shown and many conclusions of former years verified …. Naturally, because of the imperfection that must necessarily exist in this mimic warfare, its results can not be accepted in their entirety, but must be analyzed and digested before they can be made the basis of future campaigns."

The duel and tactical games were conducted on a "game board." At first, this was simply a piece of paper with a grid drawn on it. The grid was lettered and numbered to assist in preparing records of the games for subsequent study. The records were necessary because some of the early War College games were analytical games and were used to evolve strategies, devise tactical doctrine, etc.*

The term "game board," as applied to the gridded sheets of paper, was probably derived from the military chess type of games that had been popular in Europe in the first part of the 19th century. However, the term soon became a literal one, for the grid was painted on a board with a scale of 10 inches to the mile. The board was mounted on low sawhorses. Following World War I the game board became too small and the grids were painted on the deck of a room with a scale of 4 inches to 1,000 yards. The title, game board, however, remained, and the room itself was called the game room. An early newspaper article had this to say of the paper game board: "By a little checkerboard with miniature war ships as the checkers, naval games by the big bugs of the American navy have been played at the Naval War College at Newport, R.I., during the past three years, and on a vast scale. Every

* As a result of studies and games conducted in 1895, the College pointed out the strategic value of a Cape Cod Canal.[23]

naval campaign which it is possible to conceive that the United States might be called upon to undertake has been anticipated on this little board."

The first ships used on the game board were cut from cardboard and colored by hand. Later the ships were fashioned from wood, and then metal.

Following the summer session of 1896, it was noted that "Great advances have been made in the means and methods of playing the (tactical) game. Officers have undertaken to decide by it certain questions of fleet tactics, so far as they can be proven in this way, at the same time using the game as a professional exercise for themselves; and, systematically played, it has proved to be of much interest. It is not too much to say that we discern now the beginning of a true study of naval tactics .... Vagueness and confusion as to the tactics of steam fleets will, we hope, soon give place to logical methods ...."

In 1900, in order "To study the operations of landing parties and to gain the soldier's point of view"[23] games simulating land warfare were introduced.

Strategic games were conducted on maps and charts. It was a common practice to start a game on a chart and when the forces came into contact, to transfer them to the game board. The newspaper article mentioned above describes such a game in which the opposing forces represented Spain and the U.S. During the Spanish-American War, a British officer lecturing before the Royal United Service Institution remarked that in America at the Naval War College "... I found the officers working out imaginary campaigns in those very waters where they are putting theory into practice."

During a 1902 lecture on scouting at the Naval War College, Captain C.F. Goodrich said: "... more can be learned (about scouting) from patient playing of our game of strategy than in any other way of which I have knowledge." He also appears to have anticipated the invention of radar, but not its limitations: "When a future Marconi or a Becquerel shall devise a means for seeing as far as the wireless message may be heard, the game of scouting will be vastly simplified and secrecy of movement on the high seas a thing of the past."

"The principle of the concentration of the fleet ... was the direct result of a strategic game ..."[3] conducted in the summer of 1903. "Dissemination had been our rule for years, i.e., the ships were divided more or less impartially among the stations 'to show the flag' as the expression was; and at that time the same rule was general with other nations. At the beginning of the game most of the conference (class) had never entertained a suspicion that the custom was not perfectly correct; but at the end there was but one voice, and that strong and outspoken for concentration. But this view, which required but the time of one game thoroughly to capture the entire conference (class), took many a weary month before by mere argument it could convince all of those of our naval authorities who had not had the privilege or opportunity of 'seeing with their eyes.' It was some time after this that England adopted the same principle."[3]

A game conducted at the College (The Double vs the Triple Alliance). "... caused those who had taken part in it to have little doubt, at the outbreak of the Russo-Japanese War, of the outcome of that conflict .... When the news came of the battle of August 10, and every one was wondering why at sunset, seemingly at the very crisis of the engagement, the Japanese battle squadron withdrew and apparently yielded the field, and all sorts of reasons were being advanced to account for it, we here at the College recognized at once an old friend, and laughingly exclaimed: 'Hello! they have hit upon our retiring search curve!'"[3]

During a lecture at the Naval War College on June 10, 1911, Captain Little noted that "The temptation for the commander-in-chief, when he has nothing to do in his own sphere of action, to interfere in the *area of discretion* of his subordinates, is very great, and is moreover very dangerous, because it tends to make the commander-in-chief believe that it is his proper business, it tends to dull in the subordinate his sense of responsibility, and, when the commander-in-chief really has got something of his own to do, it seriously, if not fatally, interferes with his freedom of mind properly to attend to it. The only cure for this is proper war game training." Captain Little then went on to quote from a lecture delivered in 1910 at the Army War College by Captain W.L. Rogers, USN: "Strategy and tactics are intimately bound up with organization and administration. Matters of organization are avowedly subjects of study here (A. W. C.); but administration, as it seems to me, is not acknowledged, although it is actually a subject of instruction in one particular direction where constant iteration must produce an effect in wider fields. I allude to the map problems which professedly are tactical and strategic studies, but besides are daily made to teach the supreme administrative lesson of 'minding one's own business.' Let us take the case of a regiment to assume outpost duties, and the problem is for the colonel to issue the order. If a solution undertakes to go beyond the battalion commanders and give directions to individual companies, the writer is sure to be reminded that he can command three battalions efficiently, but that twelve companies are too much for anyone."

Until the introduction of the so-called "long course" in 1911, the College courses lasted only a few months of the summer and early fall. During the winter months, the staff often played analytical war games. For example, during the winter of 1906–07, "Tactical games were played regularly ... Battle Plan No. 1, as modified on account of the increased range of torpedoes, was perfected and sent to the Fleet for trial."[23] The game board was also used to demonstrate historical actions and tactical concepts. Thus, in 1914 Admiral Fletcher used the board to demonstrate the "... Fletcher Tactics of the battle line."[23]

In the early 1900's the term war game apparently fell into disfavor at the College and the names "board maneuvers" and "chart maneuvers" were substituted for tactical and strategic games, respectively. The duel game which appears never to have attained the popularity of the other two types was discontinued.

During a lecture to the students in 1914, Captain V.O. Chase of the College staff said: "Observe the distinction between the problem and the maneuver. The stated problem sets forth the conditions of a situation requiring action. You study the situation, conceive your mission, form your decision and make your initial moves. As the maneuver proceeds new situations develop, presenting other problems, and these in turn require new estimates and subsequent decisions. In one maneuver, therefore, you will often have to deal with several problems as they arise."

In 1916, Captain N.C. Twining of the College staff told the officers at the Naval Academy that the maneuver (game) board was devised to meet the need for constant, inexpensive and instructive tactical work, and that it " ...serves its purpose remarkably well if we keep its limitations always in mind and do not forget that its results flow from the assumptions made."

A rather unusual (in those days) feature of War College games was the employment of civilian personnel to assist in the plotting and conduct of the game, the drawing of maps and charts, the preparation of material for the critiques, and to provide a continuity of gaming "know how." One of the earliest and perhaps one of the best known of the civilian gaming personnel was George J. Hazard, co-author of *Jutland*.* Mr. Hazard was one of the three men to have had the now extinct Civil Service title of War Games Expert.**

Admiral William S. Sims, World War I commander of U.S. naval forces in European waters was a staunch advocate of the all big-gun battleship. As postwar President of the Naval War College, however, and a keen and constant observer of the war games there, he soon became aware of the advantages and potential of air power and the limitations of the battleship. "'If I had my way,' he said, 'I would arrest the building of great battleships and put money into the development of the new devices and not wait to see what other countries are doing.'"***

* H.H. Frost and G.J. Hazard, *Jutland*, U.S. Govt. Print. Off., 1927.

** The other two were Charles H. Ward and John H. Wilson.

*** "Flattops in the War Games," *Naval Aviation News*, August 1962, p. 22–27.

Concerning the war games, Admiral Sims wrote: "The principles of the war game constitute the backbone of our profession .... At the Naval War College our entire fleet with all of its auxiliaries, cruisers, destroyers, submarines, airplanes, troop transports, and supply vessels, can be maneuvered on the game board week after week throughout the college year against a similar fleet representing a possible enemy—all operations being governed by rules, based upon the experience of practical fleet officers, and upon the immutable principles of strategy and tactics that the students are required to learn. There is no other service in the career of a naval officer that can possibly afford this essential training. In no other way can this training be had except by assembling about a game board a large body of experienced officers divided into two groups and 'fighting' two great modern fleets against each other—not once, or a few times, but continually until the application of the correct principles becomes as rapid and as automatic as the plays of an expert football team."*

During the years between the two world wars, the circular dispositions used in the second were developed on the game board and carried into the fleet by graduates of the College. Aircraft and carriers in the games provided future commanders with an insight into the potential of integrated sea and air power. The role of the submarine received increasing attention and, for a short time, the ill-fated rigid airships appeared in the games. Island-hopping Pacific campaigns similar to those of World War II were played repeatedly. Referring to these games in a lecture at the Naval War College on 10 October 1960, Fleet Admiral Chester W. Nimitz said: "The war with Japan had been re-enacted in the game room here by so many people and in so many different ways that nothing that happened during the war was a surprise—absolutely nothing except the Kamikaze tactics toward the end of the war; we had not visualized those."

When Pringle Hall was completed in 1934, the areas now occupied by the lecture hall, coffee mess and offices to its north formed one large maneuver or game room. The deck of the game room consisted of a game board with a scale of 6 inches to 1000 yards. The present offices to the west formed the control room. Just above and to the south of the game room was the drafting room in which the war gaming personnel were housed, and which contained the necessary facilities for preparing and reproducing maps and charts, and for producing and maintaining the records of war games. Phone communications and pneumatic tubes extended from the control room to many offices in Pringle Hall. Together, all of these facilities constituted what was at that time perhaps the most modern war gaming center in the nation, if not in the world.

---

* *World's Work*, September 1923.

The Pringle Hall Game Board

Figure 2–3

Life Magazine, in an article published October 28, 1940 described the board games as "a fantasy carried into the strictest reality," and said of the players that "... they fight the war that is not yet written into the history books."

The game board was also used to analyze and demonstrate historic naval engagements such as the Battle of Jutland, and the more recent amphibious operations of World War II. It was also used to illustrate and solve search problems. An interesting deviation from the usual straightforward movement of forces on the game board occurred during simulated night attacks by surface forces on huge circular convoys. Due to the size of the formation, the convoy flag remained stationary, and all forces were moved in relation to that ship.

In 1945 the College initiated a request for an electronic display system that would eventually replace the game boards then in use. This system, later called the Navy Electronic Warfare Simulator or NEWS, was not completed until 1958. During this period there was a gradual decrease in the number of board games and a shift toward less rigid and faster techniques.

Pringle Hall Control Room

Figure 2–4

During 1953 studies were initiated to develop a strategic game with a range of command levels from the theater to the national. With this study, the term "war game" returned to the College. This high-level strategic game, as distinguished from the earlier concept of a strategic game as a naval campaign, has been conducted annually since 1955. It has employed the NEWS spaces and communications facilities since 1961.

The Navy War Games Program was established in May of 1958. One part of this program consists of the examination of current fleet and force exercises and plans by means of NEWS gaming.[31] The first game conducted under this program was played in October 1958. A one-week war gaming course for fleet officers was initiated in 1960 in order to acquaint fleet commands with the potential and limitations of fleet gaming on the NEWS. This course was conducted twice a year during 1960 and 1961, and has been conducted annually since 1963.

A War Gaming Department was established at the Naval War College on 11 June 1959. It was assigned a mission of maintaining the NEWS, coordinating, conducting, and supervising war games, and developing gaming facilities and techniques.

A remote-play type of fleet game was conceived and played in February of 1962. The players were the Commander Fleet Air Quonset and his staff. During this game the players were stationed in their own Operations Control Center at the Naval Air Station, Quonset Point, Rhode Island; the control group operated in the NEWS. Players and control group were linked by "secure" communications lines.

During a five-day period in October of 1963 the first large-scale remote-play game was conducted. Known as the Canadian–United States Training Exercise (CANUSTREX) 1-63, this game involved six East Coast Fleet Operations Control Centers and the war gaming facilities of the NEWS and of the Trainer of the Canadian Joint Maritime Warfare School. Some two years later (September 1965) the War Gaming Department designed and conducted the first remote-play game for U.S. and Canadian Pacific Coast Commands. In this game the players were located in their Operational Control Centers on the West Coast and in Hawaii.

Chapter III
Rules, Procedures, and Data

In chess, as in many non-operational type games, the situation, forces, their initial dispositions and relative values are unvaried from game to game. The mission is clear, the same for each side. It is evident to all if black wins, loses, or draws. In a war game, however, the situation must be devised, opposing forces and their characteristics described, and missions expressed or implied. It may not be easy, or even desirable, to pick a winner.

The Conflict Situation. The situation selected for a war game may be real or hypothetical. It may be chosen specifically for a game, or it may be selected initially in order to prepare plans to cope with the situation, to provide students with practice in the use of the military planning process, etc., and later chosen for examination by gaming techniques. In the first instance the situation is generally contrived with some regard for simulation limitations; in the second, obviously, it is picked without any such considerations. Since many situations are chosen for examination, but few gamed, the selection of the conflict situation is not usually thought of as part of a game, but as a pregame activity.

Pregame Procedures

(When the Conflict Situation is Selected Specifically for a War Game.)

When the conflict situation is devised especially for gaming, the purpose, scope and level of the game are determined and the simulation equipment considered. Then, except in the relatively rare instances where the situation is chosen for the express purpose of designing the rules, the existing rules of the game are taken into account and a situation fashioned that meets as nearly as possible the needs of the activity conducting the game, and requires few modifications to existing rules and a minimum number of new rules. "Dreaming up" such a situation, one that is adequate, unbiased, and plausible, and that includes the area of operations, the allocation of forces and weapons and a description of their capabilities, is frequently a rather formidable task. This fact has been long recognized by practitioners of the art. For instance, in discussing the main problem for 1906, Knight and Puleston made the following comment in their *History of the Naval War College*: "The framing of the problem was as difficult as the solution, and much care was taken by the staff to produce a reasonable problem."[23]

The selection of the conflict situation and other pregame procedures have remained practically unchanged since the days of von Reisswitz. The director, assisted by his staff, devises the conflict situation. In the most common type of game, the two-sided, he prepares what is known as the "general situation" and issues it to both sides. He also prepares a "special situation" for each side, i.e., a Red Special Situation and a Blue Special Situation. Depending upon the complexity of the situation, the general and special situations may be brief or lengthy, presented orally or in writing.

The general situation (sometimes called the scenario) contains background and general information that would be known to both contestants in a similar real-world environment. For example, it might describe briefly the events leading to a hypothetical war and a series of imaginary military actions that presumably preceded and led to the situation under consideration. In some instances the general situation may contain the criteria for determining a winner;* in others, this may be done in the rules. However, in most games no attempt is made to define the winner, although after a play it is not unusual for the contestants to argue the point.**

The special situation for each side explains the conflict situation from the point of view of that side. It specifies the area of operations, lists available forces and their characteristics, and provides intelligence of enemy forces and activities that each contestant would presumably possess in an actual situation. The special situation includes any assumptions made by the director, for instance, the availability or non-availability of additional forces or support, the amount of fuel and ammunition on hand, assumed absence of specific threats, and so on. It also includes any assumptions that might have been made in the preparation of the rules

* In Strategic Situation No. 2, Naval War College, June 15, 1895, the Red fleet was divided into two detachments, one bound for Halifax, another at that port. If during the game "... Red succeeds (ed) in communicating with Halifax, a detachment equal in size ... (put to sea) ... and a union with this force before encountering the Blue fleet ... (was) ... a victory for the Red." If Blue intercepted prior to the union, they won.

** There are several reasons why it is not customary to state the conditions that one or the other side must fulfill in order to win a game. First, the general purpose of a war game is usually to furnish information or to provide decision-making experience that is applicable to real-world situations, not to pick a winner. Secondly, a side that may appear to be the winner at the close of a game might well have been the loser had the game been continued. Thus, a fleet that has fired all its missiles when the director ends the simulation might appear to come out on top, but what if the game had been played for another day? Finally, the forces assigned to Blue, for instance, may not be adequate for Blue's assigned mission. This fact might not have been realized until the game was played—or the purpose of the game may have been to determine this point. For somewhat similar reasons, some designers of business games do not attempt to define winners.[32]

that would affect the planning process and, when practicable, expresses force and weapons data in terms which are similar to those used in the rules. The correlation of the situation and rules at this early stage tends to simplify the gaming process, and to eliminate planning by the contestants for events that are not intended to be gamed, or that cannot be simulated.

The special situations may spell out the respective missions, or it may allot this task to the players; it may set up the command structure, or direct the players to do so. In analytical games if particular or special doctrines or accounting procedures are to be employed by one or both sides, these are also noted or explained in the appropriate special situations.

The control group may prepare the plans for one or both sides. Usually, however, the players on each side develop their own plans on the basis of the information and requirements contained in the general and special situations. These plans range from brief oral or written expressions of mission, organization, and intentions to exhaustive and formal presentations. They delineate the methods by which the opposing commanders expect to achieve their given or inferred goals during the play of the war game. One interesting variation of this general procedure occurs when the contestants switch sides after the planning phase and game the plans prepared by their opponents.

If plans are generated by a number of opposing student staffs or teams, the director may select two plans to be war gamed, or facilities and time permitting, he may pair off plans for a number of concurrent games or for a series of games. In the first instance the students whose plans are not selected may be absorbed into the game as lower echelon commanders, staff officers, or as members of the control group.

Some adaptations of the selected plans may be necessary in order to adjust them to constraints imposed by such factors as time available for play, number of participants, equipment, facilities, and model limitations, and some changes in or additions to the rules may be required for the conduct of the game. However, when the situation and forces are selected specifically for gaming, such modifications are usually very slight, often not required at all. If needed, changes are made with due regard for the general purpose and scope and level of the game, and in a manner such that they do not affect the concept of operations of either side, or restrict unrealistically the players' plans for achieving their goals.

The forces are located on the game board or map; the simulator or computer, programmed. Gaming personnel are briefed on the rules, and the signal is given: "Make move 1!" "Start the game!" etc.

A generalized model of pregame procedures for a two-sided war game is depicted in Figure 3-1. This serves to illustrate the steps taken when the conflict situation is selected or devised for gaming purposes. Similar procedures are employed for one-sided and n-sided games.

In early war games, and in current games of limited scope in which the personnel, facilities, time for play, and so on have been tested by previous and similar situations, some of the procedures shown in Figure 3-1 are omitted or varied. For instance, once the general and special situations are selected, the game may be programmed first, and then the players told of the situation and of the forces at their disposal. The players are given a short time to organize and plan, and the game begins.

Pregame Procedures
(When the Conflict Situation is Selected Prior to the Decision to Game.)

In this case the conflict situation exists or is assumed to exist, plans have been prepared by a friendly or Blue Staff or planning agency to meet the contingency, and someone in authority has requested that they be evaluated, rehearsed, or explored by means of gaming techniques. Using the situation and Blue plans as guides, the director and control group determine the general purpose, scope and level of the proposed game, and select the aspects of the situation that are pertinent to the rehearsal or analysis. Plans are prepared for the opposition, for example, the Red side.* As shown in Figure 3-2, the remainder of the pregame procedures follow those established for the simulation of situations that are selected solely for the purpose of gaming. The adaptation process, however, is apt to be somewhat more difficult.

Conduct of the Game. When a war game is set up or programmed, the forces might be compared to the pieces arrayed on a chess board. They are ready to be employed according to the rules of the game. Unlike chess, however, which has been played under the same rules for many years, the rules for war games vary from place to place and from time to time in order to reflect local objectives, available simulation equipment, and the ever changing tools and concepts of warfare. Thus, early Naval War College games were conducted to develop tactical doctrine and to study the strategic employment of naval forces; the rules were based on the use of manual techniques and on the weapons of the day, the gun, the torpedo, and

* When possible opposition plans should be prepared by personnel trained to think and act as officers of the nation or nations represented.

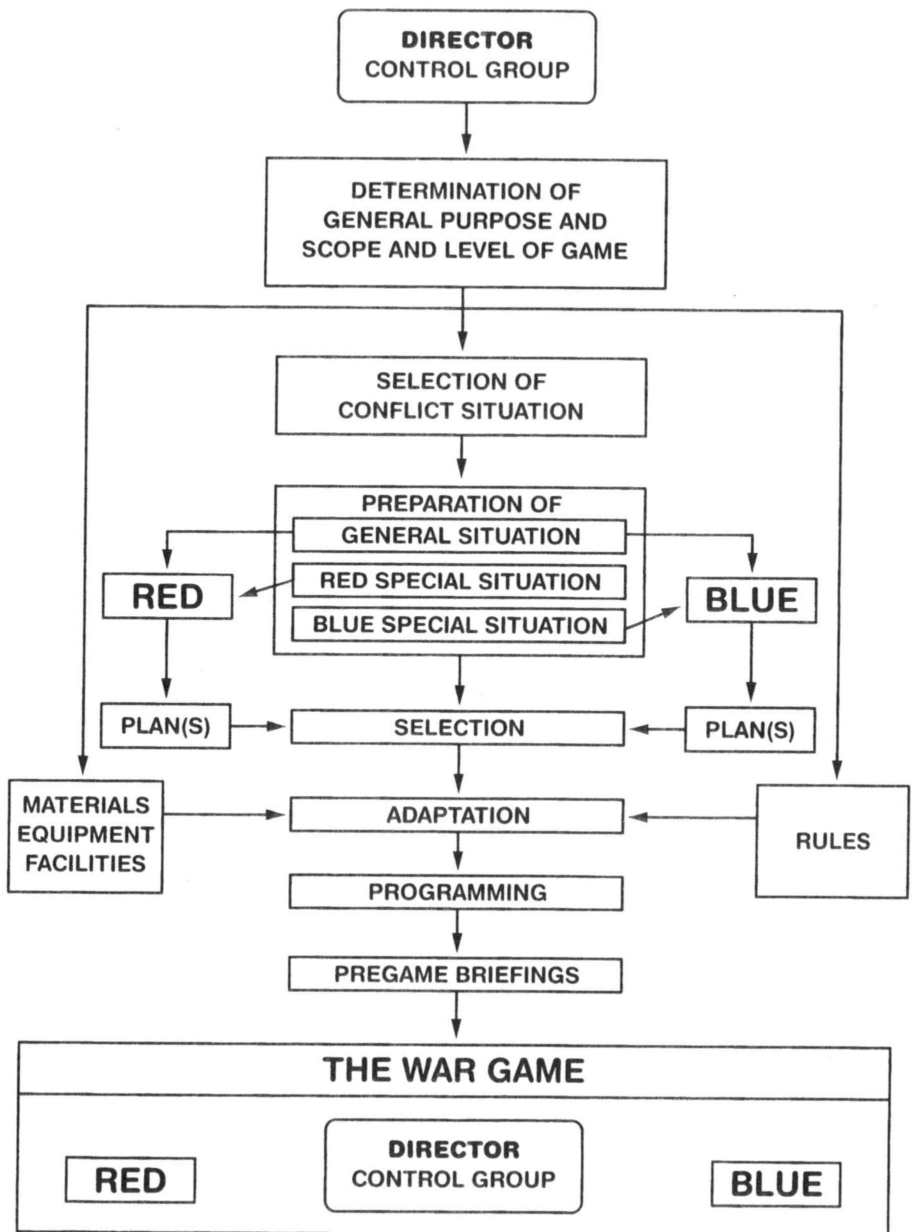

PREGAME PROCEDURES FOR A TWO-SIDED GAME

(When the conflict situation is selected specifically for a War Game.)

Figure 3-1

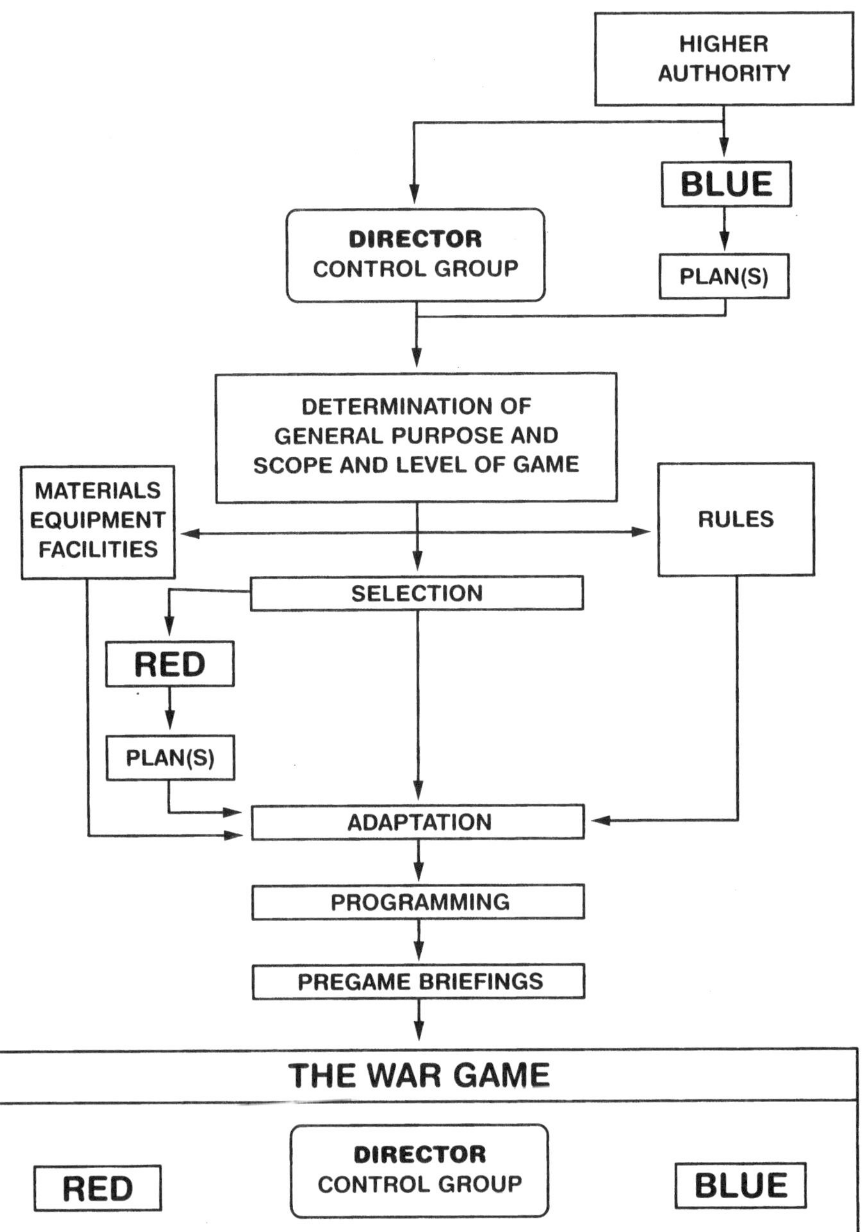

PREGAME PROCEDURES FOR A TWO-SIDED GAME

(When the conflict situation is selected prior to the decision to game.)

Figure 3-2

the ram. Current Naval War College games are chiefly educational in nature, and the rules reflect the weapons systems of today and tomorrow, the greater scope and diversity of military activity, and the introduction of machine simulation.

Kinds of Rules. Roughly, the rules cover three general areas: (1) Description of the game; (2) Player activities; and (3) Control group activities. The rules dealing with all three regions are made available to the control group. In the case of players rules, practices differ. In some games they are provided with all the rules; in others, with only those that they need for play. The latter practice is somewhat preferable. The players have less material to peruse, are more apt to concentrate on their roles, less inclined to concern themselves with evaluation processes.

The description of the game usually includes a brief and general explanation of the methods, equipment, and type of moves. If the game is designed so that one of the sides may emerge as the winner, the method of picking that side is explained, or, as noted earlier, this may be done in the general situation.

While it is evident that no clearly defined line of demarcation is possible, the rules for the players can be classified under two categories, operational rules and implementation rules. The first type describes approximately the selected real-world features; the second explains the methods and procedures employed in the game-world. The operational rules tell the players what can be done; the implementation rules how to do it.

The rules for the control group may also be divided very roughly into two parts: one, those describing the methods of evaluation; and two, the procedures required to utilize such assessments in the game. The former, for example, might explain the methods for determining contacts and damage, and generating intelligence and so forth; the latter, what forms to employ, what phones to use, what information to collect for the critique, etc.

Amount of Detail. Due to local needs, gaming concepts, capabilities, and personnel, the rules for different simulations vary widely in both form and content. The rules for some games are bound in a single cover, those for other games consist of or appear in two or more publications. Some games are guided wholly or in part by detailed rules; others, by rules that are general in nature. Certain compilations assume that the players and the control group will apply the rules in their proper sequence, others include procedures for their step-by-step application. Some sets of rules take it for granted that the control group knows how to translate a given probability into a hit or a miss, a yes or a no, a success or a failure; others specify the equipment and procedures. In computer games where human judgment cannot be applied to the choice or interpretation of the rules or model during the simulation process, all rules are explicit, all complete.

The strategic manual game formerly conducted by the Command and Staff Department of the Naval War College was an example of a game in which all the rules were general in nature, and in which all evaluations were made by the free method. It was a two-sided educational game at the strategic level and involved the joint and combined operations of all services and several nations. Playing time was four days; game time about twenty-six. The level of experience of both players and control group and the objectives of the game made it entirely feasible to use general rules; the compression of time and the number and diversity of forces practically compelled their use.

Since the NEWS incorporates many simulation features, relatively unsophisticated NEWS games employing non-aggregated forces require a minimum of rules. However, in NEWS games employing aggregated and constructive forces certain features cannot be programmed into the system and such games require both general and detailed rules. Computer games are based on well defined models. Manual games such as the Marine Corps' Landing Force Game are conducted according to many detailed rules and procedures.[33] And while little unclassified information is available on the use of games used to assess the results of massive nuclear exchanges, it can be assumed that they require detailed rules and methods of evaluation.

Models. As noted in Chapter I the rules and procedures for the control and conduct of a game, for the acting-out of the conflict situation on a game board, a chart, a machine, or a computer, are also known as the model of the game. While the term "model" appears to more aptly describe the rules and procedures of computer games, its use has certain advantages in other type games, particularly when a number of different kinds of conflicts are simulated, and it is convenient to prepare compatible rules and procedures for each kind of engagement. Thus, a game simulating a naval engagement might include a set of rules and procedures, that is a model or submodel, for an antiair simulation, a second for a surface action, and a third for submarine activities, pro and anti. The outputs of a submodel, for instance the antiair model, would then serve as inputs to the surface action model, and so on.

Basic Game Cycle. In a two-sided war game the Blue and Red Players make the decisions appropriate to their assumed command levels and take the actions necessary to implement their decisions, or if a computer is simulating some or all of the command functions, the computer makes a "Monte Carlo" choice from among a limited number of programmed courses of action. The movements, actions, and interactions of the opposing forces are monitored and evaluated by the control group, or by equipment or computer routines that take over some or all of the functions of the control group, and the results transmitted to the commanders. These reports generate new decisions, new actions, and the cycle starts again. The basic game cycle or generalized model of a two-sided game is depicted in Figure 3-3. The structure of one-sided games is illustrated in Figure 3-4; that of an n-sided game (when n=4), in Figure 3-5.

Moves. In parlor games such as chess each player (side) moves, in turn, a single piece. The moves do not represent an interval of time. The moves made in war games, however, represent definite periods of real-world time, and all forces can be moved simultaneously. The length of a move is the interval of time for which decisions and evaluations are made.

Moves are used in manual and computer games. Two basic methods are employed for determining the length of time represented by the move. In the first, the smallest practical period of time is chosen, and all moves in the game are of that length. At the end of each move evaluations are made, and status of forces updated, and the cycle started anew for a similar interval of time. The second method provides for an examination of future interactions and the selection of a time period that will jump the game up to the time of the next event. In computer parlance the first is called a "time-step" game; the second, an "event-store." These terms are applicable to manual games, the former when regular time intervals are used, the latter when the director estimates the time of the next critical event and calls for a move of corresponding length. Manual gaming, however, permits variations of these two basic cycle-time techniques. Thus, although the rules for a particular game specify five-minute moves, the director can call for two or more moves to be made at one time, thus lengthening the time for which decisions are made. Again, if the rules permit him to specify the length of time of a move, he may, after a move is made, provide some players with intelligence of events that occurred part way through the move and allow them, if they so desire, to modify their moves.

As far as machine games are concerned, time is usually continuous. Thus, when active NEWS forces are employed, there is no requirement for making moves. A player sets the course and speed of his force and it sails or flies at that course and speed until he decides that a change is necessary, or until its speed is reduced by enemy action; he throws an automatic firing switch and a selected weapon fires and continues to fire at a selected target until he releases the weapon,

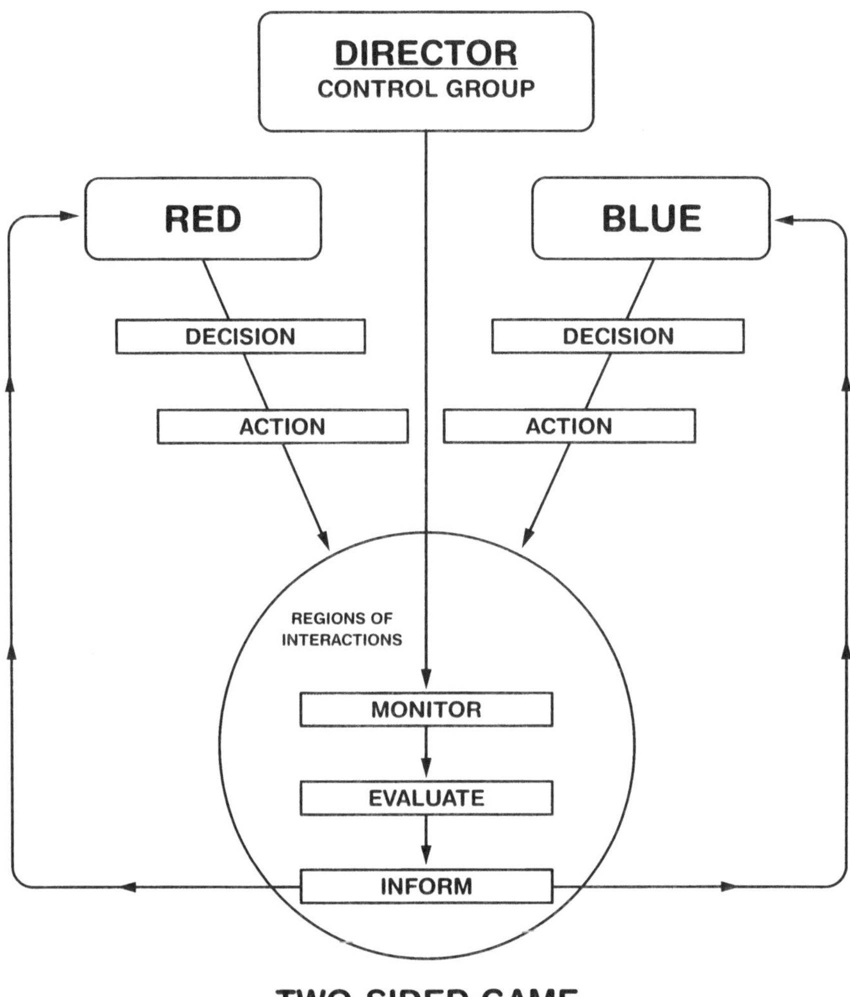
DIRECTOR
CONTROL GROUP
RED
BLUE
DECISION
ACTION
DECISION
ACTION
REGIONS OF
INTERACTIONS
MONITOR
EVALUATE
INFORM
TWO-SIDED GAME

Figure 3-3

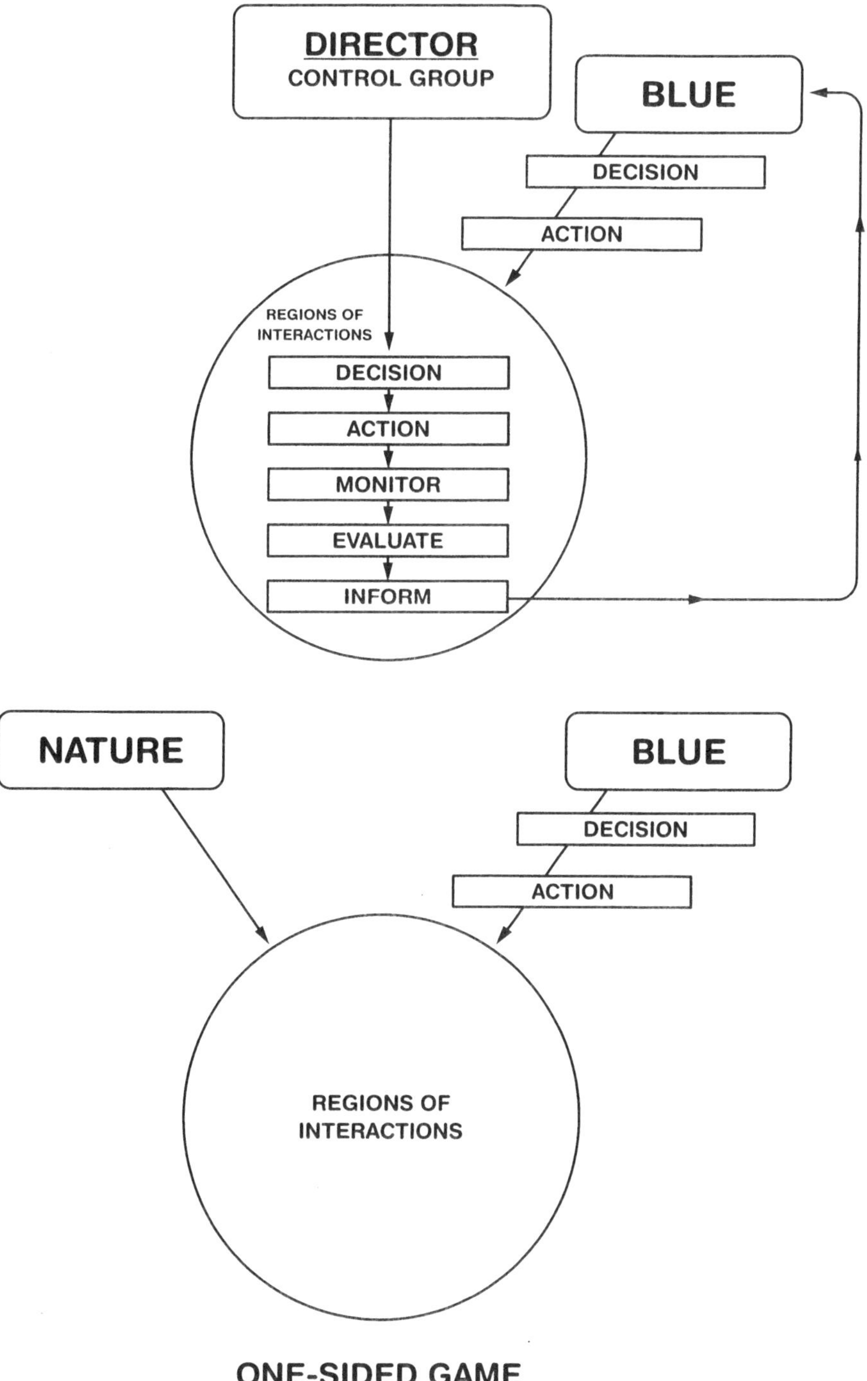

ONE-SIDED GAME

Figure 3-4

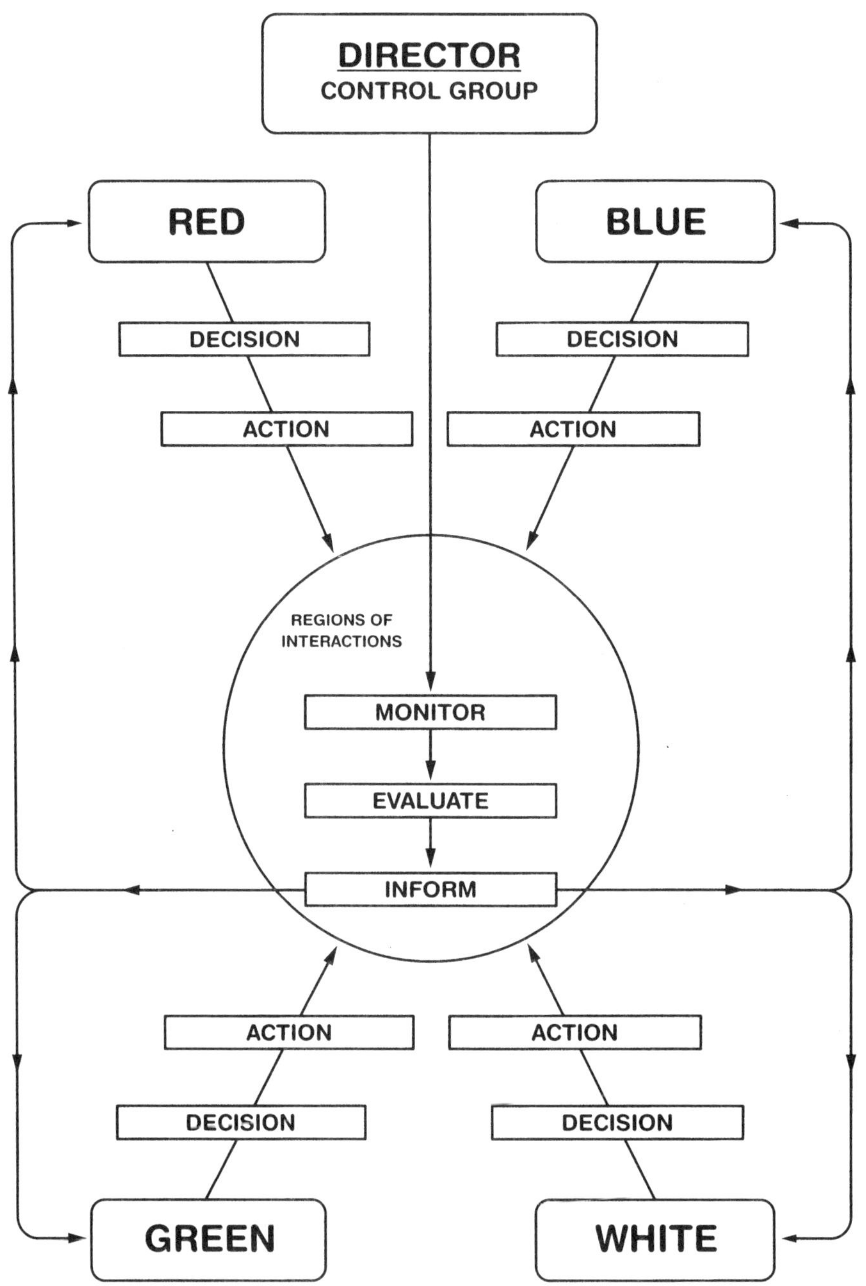

FOUR-SIDED GAME

Figure 3-5

runs out of ammunition, or is destroyed by enemy firepower. If manual techniques are employed in conjunction with the machine simulation, the forces represented by hand-moved symbols are moved for discrete time intervals.

Function of the Rules. The rules of a game model the real world to the extent that commanders or simulated commanders are able to react as they would in a similar actual situation, and that their successes and failures depend not only upon their own skill but upon the decisions and actions of opposing commanders and on the vagaries of chance. Ideally, there should be few enough rules to make a game playable, sufficient to provide realism.*

Evolution of the Rules. Normally, the rules for an operational game are devised to meet the requirements of a particular organization: a college, perhaps, or a research activity. The approach to the problem reflects local needs, personnel backgrounds and preferences, and the kind and amount of simulation equipment available. In all cases, however, the preparation of the rules and procedures for a game is largely a matter of judgment and experience plus a certain amount of trial and error, and in most instances begins by answering or seeking the answers to such questions as: What sort of conflict situation is to be simulated? For what purpose or purposes? What is the possible range of command levels? What service or services are involved? What type or types of operations? How many sides?

A crude analysis of the answers discloses the possible extent and nature of the forces, weapons systems, communications, and area of operations, and delimits to some degree the pertinent command decisions, implementing actions, and the sort of intelligence required by the decision-makers. It provides an insight into possible aggregations and a gross selection of real-world processes and interactions. This initial choice includes all forces, weapons, events, processes, and so on that appear essential to the selected conflict situation and to similar situations so that the rules can be designed to cover as broad a range of activities as possible. For example, as observed by Commander Davis and Dr. Tiedeman, in an article in the *U.S. Naval Institute Proceedings*, "... in an ASW game, refueling of DDs from the carrier of

---

* For gaming purposes the word "realism" means many things to many people. Perhaps the best working definition is an outgrowth of the University of Michigan's 1955 Conference on War Games: "The approach to realism must be qualitative rather than quantitative; the objective of realism is to provide an environment that will elicit from the subject (student) the same response or decision as would be elicited by the corresponding real-world situation. Once this condition is satisfied for responses or decisions which are pertinent to the purpose of the given simulation, all useful realism (perhaps validity is a more appropriate term here) has been achieved." Thomas and Deemer observed: "We should deplore the tendency to introduce trappings and ornaments in simulation to gain the 'appearance' of reality when it is the 'essence' which we need."[13]

a HUK group may be important."[31] This process would, therefore, be listed in the preliminary crude analysis of this type of situation.

The processes and interactions isolated by the early analysis are examined more closely to determine whether or not the proposed simulation is feasible in view of the "state of the art," and the equipment and personnel available. Should the conflict be treated as a whole, or separated into its component sub-conflicts and the rules or a model prepared for each? At this stage is it better to attempt the simulation of a selected major phase, say the ship to shore movement of an amphibious operation, and to prepare the rules for the overseas movement, advance force operation, and other phases at a later date? What assumptions can be made that will simplify the rules and that are acceptable for the purpose of the game? Thus, can all ships be grouped into a limited number of classes for damage assessment purposes? Can surface-to-air missiles and surface action weapons be ignored in an ASW game? Is the refueling of the DDs from the carrier sufficiently important to be included? "Unfortunately, the game designer is continually confronted with choices. If he fails to insert in his model such details as DD refueling, he may produce a game adequate for the problem in hand but inadequate for other similar problems .... Great savings accrue if many possible uses are considered early in the model building process."[31] However, simulation time, personnel, and equipment capacity delimit the scope and application of the possible uses that can be designed into the rules.

Concepts are developed for the simulation of the processes, forces and weapons systems, detection and communication systems, and the types of interactions finally selected. For instance, if the preceding analysis had established the need for simulating DD refueling, how should this be done? By keeping track of the ships' fuel expenditures? How? Using average consumption rates? Or would refueling at regular intervals suffice? In a computer game the first method might use a large amount of computer storage capacity; in a manual game it would be somewhat time consuming. The second method is simpler, quicker. Which concept is best suited to the purposes of the game? For the level of command? If a game is conducted on the NEWS does the number of forces exceed the capacity of the system? If so, is the problem best solved by reducing the number of forces, by aggregating certain forces, or by supplementary manual techniques?

How are weapons employed? Will individual commanders specify weapons and targets, or is it assumed that when opposing forces come within range they will open fire? Is it necessary to provide accounting procedures for ammunition expended by all weapons simulated, or only for missiles or torpedoes? Can some weapons be aggregated? Can it be assumed, as it is in many games conducted on the NEWS, that even though forces are within range a commander will not employ his weapons until he is in the correct firing position, or should such an assumption be made for a percentage of the engagements?

Within certain distances the probability of a radar detecting a target varies inversely with range. Should these probabilities be cranked into the game, or should a detection always be a "yes" proposition at a predetermined range? The first concept is usually used in computer games. Due to the design of the system the latter method is employed in NEWS games. Depending upon the price the analyst wishes to pay in terms of complexity and game time, either concept can be used in manual games.

Is it practicable to separate all commanders of friendly forces, to insert communications delays and difficulties? Should all communications be perfect, or should compromises be made?

Must evaluation procedures be rigidly prescribed as in most computer games and in cases where experienced umpires are not available? Does the purpose of the game indicate that rigid methods are preferable even though experienced personnel will be employed as umpires? Is the time for play sufficient for detailed assessment techniques? Should the director or other members of the control group be permitted to modify or set aside evaluations made by a computer or by umpires working in accordance with established rules and formulas? Are some interactions more amenable to free umpiring, others to rigid, or are the objectives of the game best attained by employing free methods of evaluation in all instances?

Should the game be conducted by the time-step method, or should it employ the event-store technique? Is it necessary or desirable to spell out each procedure, or can the players and the control group apply the rules without detailed instructions?

The selected processes, as modified by the assumptions, are described in accordance with the evolved gaming concepts, and these descriptions constitute the model, or the rules and procedures of the game. Thus, if prior analysis and study had determined that refueling of the DDs from the carrier should be included in the game, and that this process would be simulated by the players actually plotting the movements of the ships, then the rules of the game would specify that this process would be carried out and would furnish or refer to tables that provided the necessary data. (The special situation would describe the assumed initial fuel levels.) Other rules would tell the players how to move their ships and, when applicable, the length of moves and how to use the plotting devices employed in the game.

A rule might state that a certain per cent of the total aircraft on a field or carrier are operational. Another, that if a player wants to send off a strike he must prepare a flight plan to a specified scale and indicate the number and types of planes and weapons. Other rules provide for umpire checks on the number of aircraft, the planned radius of action of each type, and weapons availability and loadings. Additional rules may stipulate the methods for computing aborts, losses from aerial combat and surface-to-air missiles, the amount and kind of damage inflicted on the various targets, and the types and flow of intelligence.

Depending upon the simulation concepts, the rules may cover each pertinent feature or aggregate some of the events. For example, if each of the major steps in an interceptor versus bomber interaction are to be considered, the rules may state that when a fighter approaches to within 12 miles of a bomber it has an 80 percent probability of detecting the bomber; if it detects the bomber, a 90 percent probability of attaining a launching position; and should it reach that position, a 70 percent probability of destroying the bomber. If only the overall interaction is to be played, the rules would state that the fighter has a 50 percent probability of destroying the bomber.

The rules may tell the umpires to use the given numbers, or to use or not use them as they see fit. If the free method of evaluation is specified, data are not usually furnished although, if possible, the data should be available in case an umpire wishes to refer to them.

In either a step-by-step or less detailed case, the rules may call for the use of random number tables and explain their use, or they might specify the use of a pair of ordinary dice, a pair of 20-sided dice, or leave to the umpire the method of translating a probability into the occurrence or nonoccurrence of an event. Sometimes, when a pair of regular dice, for instance, are called for, the tables of data may not mention probabilities, but merely say: if a 2, 4, 5, 6, 7, 8, 9, or 12 is rolled, the fighter detects the bomber, and so on.

In some instances when evaluation procedures are applied by members of the control group they need not be described in the rules. For instance, consider the play of a NEWS game in which two planes of an aggregated force of four are armed with nuclear weapons; two with conventional. The force suffers a loss of fifty percent en route to the target. Which planes are lost, the two carrying the big bang, the two with the iron bombs, or one of each? An experienced member of the control group does not need rules to find the answer. As shown in Appendix B, he simply makes a decision based on the appropriate probability distribution.

Since such parameters as detection, conversion, and kill probabilities may differ from play to play, and since these variations can occur, at least within limits, without affecting the structure of the rules or the model, the data are often furnished separately, and the rules refer to the proper tables or graphs. This method is more realistic, more flexible, and sometimes permits the rules to be published under a lower security classification than would be possible if the data were included.

The preparation of the rules or the model is facilitated in many instances by flow charting the selected processes and events. Rules are also developed by actually trying out portions of the game, a type of activity sometimes termed "design play." Another method is the use of or modification of rules from other games. For example, many of Livermore's rules were based on the works of German authors; some of Little's rules were adapted from an Italian game.

The rules or model may take the form of a verbal, graphical, or mathematical description, or combinations of these forms. The rules are often tested in an "exploratory play" or a pregame rehearsal in order to find and to eliminate the bugs that inevitably appear in spite of the analyst's care and regardless of his experience.

In general, the initial rules for a game should treat only the bare essentials. Other features may be added as experience with the game points out their need and feasibility,* and as new systems and concepts develop. Increases in the number of processes simulated tend to raise the complexity of the game and the time required for play. Hence such changes cannot be made haphazardly, or at the whim of every newcomer to the game, but only after careful consideration of their value and effect on the game as a whole. New rules should be integrated with the old, and some of the latter discarded or modified to keep the game from becoming unmanageable or too time consuming. Otherwise, as has happened so often in the history of gaming, the number of rules and the amount of detail contained in the rules increases until the game becomes too unwieldly or too lengthy for the purpose and personnel for which it was intended.

Data. Where do the planning factors, hit probabilities, attrition factors, and other data come from that are used in the special situations, the rules, and in the adjuncts to the rules? They are derived from a variety of sources: historical records, analyses of past actions, the experience and knowledge of military officers, lesser scale war

* It is interesting to note that the first set of rules for Naval War College games required four pages; the last complete set published in 1950 and used during the early 50's, 80 pages plus fire effects tables and other data. Currently, no single set of rules cover the broad spectrum of the College's games.

games,* military periodicals and books, and from classified material such as intelligence reports, contractors' estimates, operational specifications, reports, tests, field experiments, and studies of future weapons systems concepts and capabilities. Their collection, analysis, and adaption to gaming is a never ending endeavor, a constant challenge to the skill, ingenuity, and perseverance of the analyst. The tables of visibility and of recognition employed in the first Naval War College games were copies of those used in an earlier game, the maximum speeds of the ships were obtained from past records, and the numerical expressions of their combat values were based on the judgments of experienced naval officers.** Since, additions to and revisions of the data have been made on an almost continuing basis to reflect, or to anticipate, the increased speeds, ranges, and lethal effects of vehicles and weapons, and the changing methods and concepts of war and of the simulation of war. Every available source of information has been and continues to be culled for the best possible data.

A great deal of basic data such as maximum speeds, rates of march, fuel consumption, personnel strengths, replacement rates, construction times, transportation capacities, rates of travel of messengers, and so on can be obtained or extrapolated from classified sources and from material compiled "For Official Use Only"; for instance, FM 101-10, Staff Officers' Field Manual, *Organization, Technical and Logistical Data*. A surprisingly large amount of information can be found in unclassified periodicals and publications: *Jane's all the World's Aircraft, Jane's Fighting Ships, Handbook on the Soviet Army,**** Fahey's *Ships and Aircraft of the U.S. Fleet*, etc. When data are not available on the equipment of other nations it is customary to use similar "own" side information.

In addition to classified sources, press releases, magazines, and the records of budget hearings provide cost estimates of weapons and delivery systems. The publications of the Bureau of the Census, the United Nations, the Industrial Conference Board, etc., and standard reference works, periodicals, and newspaper items furnish information on populations and their age and occupational distributions, gross national products, indexes of production, and on other factors useful for high level games.

* "... in practice the smaller details are treated in small games, and the results form the basis for conventional rules or summary decisions of the umpires when they arise as incidents of the higher games."[3]

** "The rules ... were adapted from ascertained facts when possible, and from the best obtainable opinion when actual data could not be had."[23]

*** *Handbook on the Soviet Army*, Department of the Army pamphlet No. 30-50-1, 1958. For sale by the Superintendent of Documents, U.S. Government Printing Office, Washington 25, D.C., Price $2.00.

What are the effects of terrain, time, and weather; of communication and production delays; of damaged transportation and production facilities; of equipment, ammunition, and food shortages? Examinations of peacetime maneuvers and production schedules and the records of past battles and campaigns provide an insight into these problems. Interrogations of military leaders, economists, and other authorities result in numbers and qualitative information, often in the nature of educated guesses.

Quantitative information on the reliability of systems and weapons, detection and hit probabilities, the effects of enemy countermeasures, and the amount and effects of damage caused by hits of different weapons on different targets are difficult, ofttimes impossible to obtain. If test or experimental data are available, the analyst is confronted with such questions as: Were the conditions under which the tests were conducted truly indicative of operating conditions?* Did the personnel have the degree of skill and experience in the maintenance and employment of the weapon or system that could reasonably be expected from wartime military personnel, or were they highly trained manufacturers' engineers and technicians? Should the results of the tests be degraded to reflect field conditions and, if so, by how much? The analyst may derive the answers from his own experience; more likely he would question experienced officers. When no data are available he must seek the numbers from experienced personnel, and translate the qualitative information and educated guesses that they furnish into numbers and mathematical functions. This latter method which was particularly valuable in the early days of gaming is, and will continue to be, useful in those areas where there are simply no quantitative information. This is also true for other types of operational games. In an article in the August 1957 issue of *Operations Research*, Bellman and others describe in detail how the formulas for a business game were designed to reflect qualitative information.[32]

Information concerning the overall effects of a week or a month of a given level of Blue shipping and ASW effort versus a specific Red subsurface threat, or the effect on people and production of a massive nuclear exchange are far more difficult to obtain than data on the possible outcomes of the interactions of individual units and weapons. Some information may be gleaned from the histories, reports, and analyses of past wars, for example, the reports of Fleet Admiral King,** or the analyses contained in *Methods of Operations Research* by Morse

* This problem is one of long standing. Thus in 1908 Sayre observed: "Many of us have formed exaggerated ideas of the effectiveness of firearms from our observation of the effects of firing on the target range."[4]

** *U.S. Navy at War, 1941–1945*, Official Reports by Fleet Admiral Ernest J. King, USN, United States Navy Department, 1946.

and Kimball,* and updated to reflect current or future operational conditions. For newer and untried weapons and systems the outcomes of analytical games of a tactical nature provide inputs to higher level simulations. Or again, the knowledge of broadly experienced military officers, or of experts in other fields, may be utilized.

The data furnished for the game should be consistent with the concepts of simulation. If the rules are based on average values, these should be provided; if on the employment of distributions, tables or graphs. For example, should past records of mechanical breakdowns of a piece of equipment reveal the distribution shown in Figure 3-6, then in the first instance the average value of 660 hours would be furnished and used in the game, and all such equipment operated for 660 hours without undergoing a specified maintenance period would suffer a breakdown. In the latter case the graph or a table would be provided, and a chance device employed. If detections during a simulation are certain at fixed distances, or between a known range of values, then these numbers should be provided rather than probabilities of detection, for they are the numbers that are valid in the game world. Again, if a player is provided with 0.5 hit probability for a shipboard missile, he should also be told whether or not this figure includes the reliability of the system. Otherwise he can assume only that the probability holds for each attempted missile launching in the game, and should this not be the case, he may end up playing a game in which the probabilities are far different from those which he had been led to expect.

Umpires. The members of the control group who make decisions affecting the course and outcome of a game are called umpires, sometimes referees. If one such individual measures the slant range between a missile-firing ship and a bomber, consults a table of probabilities, refers to a table of random numbers or some other chance device, and comes up with a decision, he is said to be "umpiring" the game. However, if a computer is used, the term umpiring is not employed even though the computer may, in effect, take the same steps, and come up with the same answer. If a member of the control group measures the range, but does not make the hit-or-miss decision, he is not, strictly speaking, an umpire.

Umpires have three basic duties. The first is to monitor the actions of the players and to enforce the rules of the game, or if no rules cover the situation, to keep the players from acting unrealistically. For example, if the rules state that it takes 16 hours to construct a bridge, then the umpire will not permit a player to send tanks across before that time has elapsed. If the rules do not consider this contingency, then the umpire does not permit the commander concerned to put up a bridge in

* Philip M. Morse, and George E. Kimball, *Methods of Operations Research* (New York: The Technology Press of MIT and John Wiley & Sons, 1951).

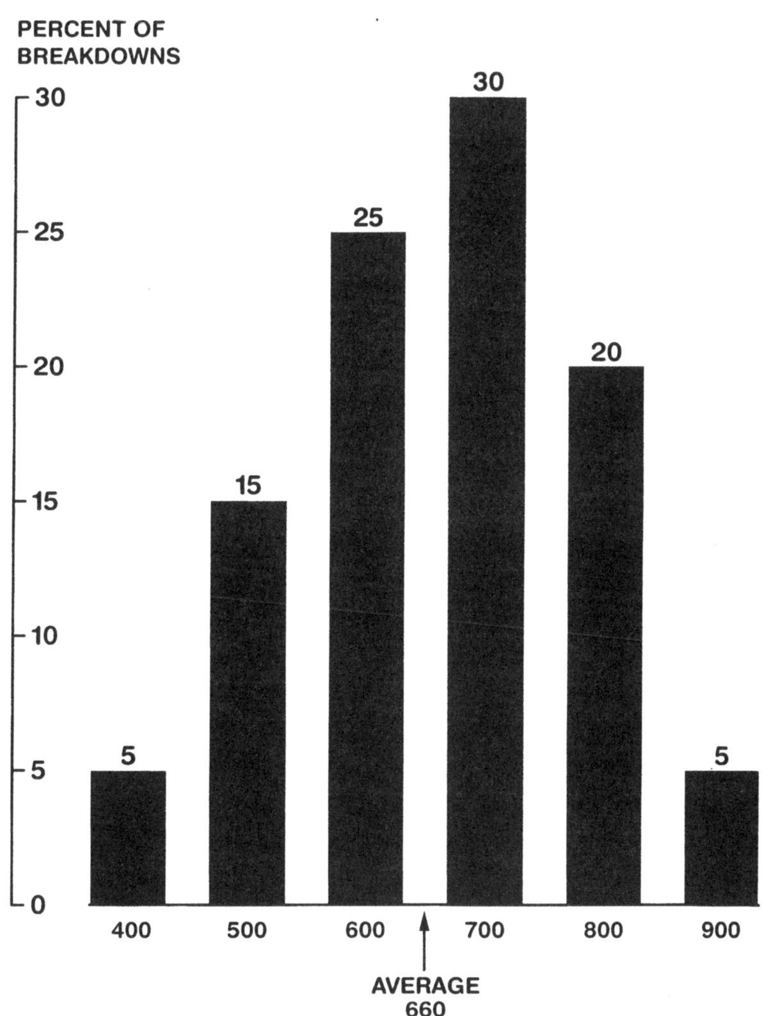
PERCENT OF
BREAKDOWNS
30
25
20
15
10
5
0
5
15
25
30
20
5
400
500
600
700
800
900
AVERAGE
660
HOURS SINCE LAST MAINTENANCE PERIOD

Figure 3-6

an unrealistically short period of time, or he tells him how many hours (according to the umpire's judgment) it will take to bridge the river. Should a rule state: When a ship loses 40 percent of its effectiveness its radar search capability is destroyed; then, if that amount of damage occurs, the umpire takes the steps necessary to implement that rule.

The second major function of the umpires is the evaluation of interactions in accordance with the methods and data prescribed by the rules of the game.

A third duty of the umpires is to provide the players with the amounts and kinds of information and intelligence that would be available under similar circumstances in the real world. This task usually requires a high degree of military experience and, in games conducted for educational purposes, a high degree of imagination.

The organization of the control group and the duties of its various members, including the umpires, are described in the rules of the game. Depending on the complexity of the game, and the equipment available, the organization of the control group varies from the extremely simple to the very complicated; its membership from one to perhaps ninety or more. Based upon the real or assumed familiarity, or lack of familiarity, of the umpires with umpiring techniques and chance devices, the umpire rules and/or briefings vary from the detailed to the general. Additionally, the umpires should be briefed on, or have an opportunity to study, the plans and intentions of the opposing sides.

The difficulties inherent in the application of the control procedures have in the past more or less dictated a requirement that the key positions in the control group be filled by personnel with prior gaming experience. The current trend appears to favor the establishment of permanent or at least semi-permanent control organizations. Such groups, because of their experience with the rules of the game and with umpiring data and devices, are usually able to keep the game moving smoothly and at a reasonable pace. Permanent or semi-permanent control groups are particularly useful when the rules for the control of the game are involved, when an understanding of complicated simulation equipment and procedures is necessary, or "... when analysis and objective quantitative data tell the tale."[34]

Probability. More likely than not, probabilistic notions are required in the compilation of the data, the preparation of the rules, and the implementation of many of the control procedures of a war game, for as was correctly observed in the description of one of the earliest naval war games, "In actual war a thousand mishaps occur, a thousand cases which vary the result to modify the decisions of a Commander, etc."* More recently, Admiral Morison noted the tremendous influence of chance in warfare, particularly naval warfare.**

If an event can happen in h equally likely ways, and fail to happen in m equally likely ways, then the chance or probability of success, p, is expressed by the following formula:

$$p = \frac{h}{h+m} \quad \text{, and}$$

the probability of failure, q, by:

$$q = \frac{m}{h+m}$$

Since the event must either happen or not happen, $p + q = 1$, or certainty.

A probability is expressed as a common fraction, a decimal fraction, or as a percent.

An event that is certain to happen has a probability of occurrence of one; an event that cannot possibly happen, a probability of zero. If the occurrence of an event is neither impossible nor certain, the probability of its occurrence is some numerical value greater than zero and less than one (or one-hundred percent). The greater the probability of an event, the more likely it is to occur; the smaller the probability, the less likely. Thus, the capture by the Allies of a permanent bridge across the Rhine during World War II was possible, but the probability of such an event happening was so slight that neither side even considered such a contingency in the preparation of their plans.*** (If it had been a war game instead of a war, a simulation in which the analyst had translated the remote possibility into a low probability, what would have been the reactions of the director and of the players if, as the Ninth Armored reached the Rhine, a roll of the dice had ruled that the Ludendorff Bridge at Remagen was intact?)

Many of the probabilities employed in war games are derived from field tests and experiments. For example, should a gun shooting at a target at a given range

---

* A. Colombo. "A Naval War Game." *Rivista Marittima*, December 1891. (Translated by William McCarty Little, 1892.)

** Samuel Eliot Morison, *History of United States Naval Operations in World War II* (Boston: Little, Brown, 1947)" I, p. x.

*** Ken Hechler. *The Bridge at Remagen.* (New York: Ballantine Books, 1957).

score 423 hits out of 846 firings, its single shot hit probability (SSHP), p, experimentally determined for that range and target is:

$$p = \frac{423}{846} = 0.5$$

The larger the number of trials, the greater the reliability of the determination.

If an unbiased coin is tossed there are two equally likely ways in which it can fall, heads or tails. The theoretical or mathematically determined probability of tossing a head is, therefore, 0.5.

When a large number of rounds are fired under similar circumstances, or many coins are tossed, the average or expected number of hits, or heads, E, can be predicted with a fair degree of accuracy by:

$$E = p \times n$$

where n equals the number of trials. Thus, if 500 rounds, each with a single shot hit probability of 0.5, are fired, or 500 coins tossed, the number of hits, or heads, would be approximately 0.5 x 500, or 250.

In any particular firing, or toss, only one of two possible events can occur; but which event will happen cannot be predicted. However, in a war game, the firing of a weapon can be simulated by a chance device that is known to have the same probability of success, a method known as the "Monte Carlo" technique. For a weapon with a single shot hit probability of 0.5, the chance device could be a coin: tails, zero hits; heads, one hit; and a toss determines the value of the random variable, N, the number of hits, which in this case would be either 0 or 1.

The number of hits resulting from a few or many firings of a gun, or the number of successes of other events having known or estimated probabilities of occurrence, can be determined by a corresponding number of tosses of a coin (when the probability of success is 0.5) or by the use of other suitable chance devices. These devices include ordinary 6-sided dice, 20-sided dice, and tables of random numbers. They are discussed in Appendix A.

The compound or overall probability of success of an operation consisting of two or more events, the probability of success of each event being known or estimated, can be computed by multiplying the probabilities of occurrence of the various events. Thus, in a fighter versus a bomber interaction, if the fighter's probabilities of detection, conversion, and kill are: 0.80, 0.90, and 0.70, respectively, the overall probability of the fighter destroying the bomber is: 0.80 x 0.90 x 0.70 = 0.504, or for practical purposes, 0.50 (See Appendix A). A four component system, each of which has a reliability of 0.80, has an overall probability of success of 0.80 x 0.80 x 0.80 x 0.80, or 0.4096; not 0.80. If the hit probability of a shipboard missile is

0.50, but the probability that the missile will be launched successfully is 0.50, then the overall probability that the missile will hit is 0.50 x 0.50, or 0.25.

The probabilities associated with the occurrence or nonoccurrence of chance events are usually injected into rigid and semirigid games in one of two ways: as average values or as random variables. As noted in Chapter I, when the rules specify the use of averages, the model and the game are referred to as expected-value or deterministic; when the rules specify the use of a chance device to determine whether an event occurs or does not occur, the model or game is known as a stochastic, probabilistic or Monte Carlo model or game. Some games employ both the expected-value and the stochastic techniques.

Expected-Value Models. In games employing the expected-value technique, if a chance event arises, the expected or average result is assumed to occur. For instance, if a weapon in a game is fired five times, each with a single-shot hit probability of 0.20, then the average or expected number of hits is 5 x 0.20, or 1, and one hit is scored. If the same weapon is fired under the same conditions later on in the game, a single hit will again be obtained. This procedure is followed even though the number of firings is small as in the above example, or large, say 500 firings, in which case a value of 500 x 0.20, or 100 hits would be obtained.

Expected-value models use average rates of fire, average consumption rates, and so on. For example, if the data provided in Figure 3-6 were used in a game, the average value of 660 hours rather than the distribution would be employed, and the rules would specify that after 660 hours without maintenance, the particular equipment in question would suffer a mechanical failure. None of this equipment (in the game) would fail before 660 hours; none would operate longer than 660 hours.

Expected-value games often yield fractional results, 1.75 hits, 3.28 aircraft destroyed, and so on. When it is desired to round-off such values, either simple arithmetic or random rounding procedures are used to decide whether 1 or 2 hits are scored or 3 or 4 aircraft destroyed. The latter technique employs a chance device in the same manner as in a stochastic game. For example, if a random number table is used as a chance device, a number from 01 to 28 determines that four aircraft are destroyed; a number from 29 to 00, three aircraft (see Appendix A).

Stochastic Models. In models using the stochastic or probabilistic method, the occurrence or nonoccurrence of chance events in the game are determined by chance, i.e., by a chance device such as a pair of dice or a table of random numbers. If a weapon is fired five times, it may score 0, 1, 2, 3, 4 or 5 hits, the exact number depending upon the throw of the dice or the entries in the random number table (see Appendix A). If the same weapon is fired again, it is likely that a different number of hits will be scored. Should the weapon be fired a large number of times during the game, then the number of hits scored will approach the expected number.

The rules for stochastic games specify the use of distributions rather than averages. Thus, if the data furnished by Figure 3-6 were used in a game, a chance device would be used to determine the length of time that each piece of equipment would function without a breakdown. Depending upon chance, one piece of equipment might require maintenance after 900 hours, a second after 500 hours, and so on as shown in Table A-2, Appendix A.

Choice of Models. Whether or not a game designer selects an expected-value or a deterministic model is based upon a number of factors including the preference of the designer. In general, stochastic models are used when games are to be conducted a number of times (as in computer simulations) and it is desired to obtain a distribution of results; expected-value models when the game is conducted once or a small number of times, and it is desired to eliminate the possibility of a run of either good or bad luck. Thus, a 1922 Naval War College Publication (*Construction of Fire Effect Tables*) noted: "It is possible by dice or other mechanical means, to apply in the Tactical Maneuver a previously evaluated chance factor. This was done at one time. The fault in this method is that in a limited number of trials the minor chance may turn up every time, and false conclusions may be drawn as to what is on the average to be expected. In a sufficiently long series of trials the chance factor would be eliminated. As time is not afforded in the college course to make repeated trials of each situation, it is considered better to eliminate the chance element, and to apply what we estimate to be average performance, so that under a given set of conditions a given result will always follow."

Stochastic models sometimes use average values to represent a few of the less significant (for the particular model) distributions. For instance, a game employing chiefly probabilistic techniques might use average acquisition times for missile batteries, thereby reducing the complexity of the model and the time required for play. On the other hand, expected-value models sometimes rely on chance devices to round-off fractional values, or to determine the outcome of one or a small number of trials. Thus, some of the rules for Naval War College games specified the use of average or expected values for determining the results of gunfire, and the use of chance devices for evaluating the effects of torpedo fire.

Chapter IV
Manual Games

From 1824 until computer and machine gaming were introduced in the late 1950's, all war games were hand-played, that is, they were conducted by manual techniques. The games of von Reisswitz and von Verdy, of Livermore and Little, and the later games developed and conducted by military schools and staffs in England, in the United States, in Germany, and in Japan, were manual games. When conducted without bias, war gaming history attests to their efficacy—both as educational aids and analytical tools.

With the beginning of computer simulation, some analysts, beguiled by the prospects of many replications in short periods of time, looked forward to the end of manual games. When the Navy Electronic Warfare Simulator was installed, a few officers believed—and understandably so—that the use of manual gaming techniques at the Naval War College would no longer be necessary. As is not surprising, neither of these expectations materialized. Despite their many advantages, computers and simulators lack some of the flexibility of manual techniques, and are presently less adaptable to the play of high-level educational type games, although they may be valuable adjuncts to such games.

Manual methods are currently employed—either alone or in conjunction with other techniques—by many activities for the simulation of military and other types of conflict situations, and undoubtedly will continue to be used for many years to come.

Advantages. Manual games can be played by organizations that cannot afford, or do not want, computers or other simulation devices. The equipment is inexpensive. Existing offices and other available spaces usually can be adapted to gaming needs. Almost any number and type of forces can be represented. Time may be compressed or expanded to meet best the immediate requirements of a particular facet of the overall play. Forces may be shifted quickly (in terms of real time) from one part of the area of operations to another. The overall area of operations may be at one scale; the regions of interactions, at a larger scale. If unforeseen events expand the area of play, additional maps can usually be procured without too much difficulty. In certain types of manual simulations, game time can be faster than real time—for example, the Electric Boat Company's Submarine Tactical Game,* or the Naval War College's Strategic War Game.

Manual games may be educational or analytical. They can encompass any desired range of command levels, include one, two, or three military services, simulate any type or types of operations, and embrace any area of operations.

Manual games may be one, two, or n-sided, and may be played either open or closed. Evaluations can be free, rigid, or semirigid.

At this stage in the art of simulation, manual techniques are somewhat better than other simulation methods when the physical and military characteristics of terrain are important considerations. They are also useful for illustrating the overall progress of a military operation, a picture that is almost impossible to obtain in the real world. For instance, at the Marine Corps Educational Center the Amphibious Assault Trainer "... can be used as a stage upon which the air, sea, and land aspects of combat can be graphically displayed by placing upon it the ship, aircraft, and terrain models required for the operation. Here the student can see an entire amphibious operation in miniature ..."**

Manual games are useful for determining and gaining an insight into the processes that are to be simulated on a computer, and for these reasons, some computer games "... are handplayed prior to translating to machine (computer) language, ..."[31] "Out of a large number of combat variables, the (manual) game serves to highlight the critical ones."[35]

Manual games are useful tools for teaching war gaming techniques. For example, when a war gaming course (War Gaming, N706) was established at the U.S. Naval Academy in the spring of 1965, manual war gaming was included as part of the course. Manual war gaming is also part of the course "Introduction to War Games," which is required for all students enrolled in the Operations Analysis/Systems Analysis Curriculum of the U. S. Naval Postgraduate School, Monterey, California.[36]

* "A considerable savings in time results from the use of this game as compared to real operations. A twenty-four-hour transit can be completed in about three and one-half hours of game time. This saving results from the use of a compressed time scale in the game and from elimination of the necessity for forces to get into position, as they would have to do in a sea exercise."[35]

** D. C. Wolfe, "Sand, Sweat, and Scholars," *Naval Aviation News*, May 1960.

Limitations. With some exceptions, as were noted earlier, manual games in general proceed much slower than clock time. This is particularly true when many forces are involved and when evaluations are made according to the rigid method. After the players make a move they wait a long time for the control group to assess interactions, transmit intelligence, and call for the next move. During this waiting period the players may have little or nothing to do (at least as far as the game is concerned), or they may be "... planning ahead—planning with time that would be non-existent on the actual battlefield."[37] As the history of war gaming reveals, these periods of "dead time" between moves have caused more dissatisfaction with war gaming than any other feature, and led to the introduction of the free method of evaluation and other techniques aimed at shortening the period between moves.

The slow pace of manual games also cuts heavily into the curriculum time of military colleges. This became particularly noticeable when "World War II and subsequent developments ... expanded manyfold the fields with which a high commander must be familiar. In the (Naval) War College the problem of providing adequate time ... (was) met in part by such steps as reduction of time-consuming game board problem plays and chart plot problem plays ..."[*] However, it should be noted in passing that a fast game, or even a game conducted at real-world time, is not always desirable. A somewhat slower pace in a simulated action may provide the serious players with an opportunity to consider the various courses of action, to weigh alternatives when there is time so that they can make the proper decisions when there is little or no time.

While some members of the control group learn as much from a game as the players (and a few may learn even more), there are usually some control group duties that are purely war gaming functions, or that are more or less routine computational, bookkeeping, clerical, or drafting tasks. If officers or executives are assigned such tasks, they gain neither decision-making experience nor decision-making information—a definite weakness in a game, from their perspective. However, by using war gaming and supporting personnel to perform some of these tasks, this limitation has been minimized in Naval War College games. Many other war gaming activities also employ gaming personnel for evaluation procedures and the application of purely gaming techniques, officers for the handling of military forces.

Although a limited number of replications may be possible, it is generally not feasible to replay a rigidly controlled manual game a large number of times in

* Frank Virden, "The Naval War College Today," *U.S. Naval Institute Proceedings*, April 1953, p. 366.

order to obtain results that are of statistical significance.* Such a series would require an unreasonable length of time. The players, unlike computers, would either become bored, and neglect to follow closely the course of events, or unwittingly inject into the game knowledge gleaned from earlier plays.

Simulation Requirements. In accordance with the rules of play, the simulation equipment employed in a war game enables the players to exercise their command functions, and the control group to carry out its monitoring and evaluation duties. For most military games, equipment, devices, and materials are needed to simulate or represent the area of operations, forces, interactions, and communications.

In the real world, a force usually has under its immediate surveillance a portion of the area of operations. The information obtained from surveillance activities is processed and correlated by the force's staff personnel and, as evaluated data, is constantly available to the commander. A force also has maps and other visual displays (polar plots, for example) of the area of operations—or, portions of it—on which its own intelligence as well as that obtained from higher echelons, friendly forces, and reconnaissance elements is plotted or recorded. As the command level rises, the commander is more concerned with the overall picture, less with that obtained from the surveillance pattern of a single force. Thus, the evaluated data that a ship commander receives reflects the type and level of decisions that he is required to make; the data that the fleet commander gets, the type and level of decisions that he must make.

In some manual games, a commander gets the information that he needs by viewing a part of a replica of the area of operations; in most, by reports from friendly forces and the control group. A player is usually furnished maps and plotting devices so that he, or his staff, can keep track of the location and movements of his own force or forces as well as other forces of which he has knowledge.

The control group requires a model of the area of operations—a game board, a map, a terrain model, a group of related plots—with the correct locations, movements, and regions of surveillance of all forces. The scale of the model is inversely proportional to the scale and level of the game. The more tactical the game, the larger the scale of the model; the higher the command levels, the smaller the scale. To simplify gaming processes, and to reduce the number of requirements for maps

* In some cases, repeated plays of manual games have been conducted. For instance, 120 tactical games were played at the Naval War College during 1896 to evaluate the effects of superior speed. As a result, it was concluded that "the value of 20 per cent superior speed to a fleet of ships of the line of battle is less than one-twelfth of its total tactical force."

and other graphical aids, the practical needs of the players and the control group are sometimes combined.

Forces in a manual game are simulated by models, blocks, pins, or symbols. Status boards, forms, or other bookkeeping devices are furnished, so that each commander or an assistant can maintain a record of the status of his force and other pertinent information. Such records are based on the aspects of the situation that are specified in the rules. Thus, for a company of infantry, the number of personnel available for duty might be recorded; for a missile battalion, the number of available launchers and the number and type of missiles. The status of a ship might include its "effectiveness" or "per cent of life remaining," maximum available speed, and unexpended ammunition and fuel. The control group needs similar accounting devices to maintain a record of all forces in order to evaluate interactions and to monitor the decisions and actions of the players, to keep forces from moving faster than weather, terrain, and damage permit, to insure that guns without ammunition do not fire, etc.

While current games usually use status boards and accounting forms, in some earlier games bookkeeping procedures were incorporated into the design of the pieces or models used to represent the forces. Thus, in Livermore's game, the side of a piece that was turned up indicated the effectiveness of the piece (force). The pieces of Totten's game had slated surfaces for record purposes. In some naval games rings were placed on the mast of a ship to indicate its current effectiveness.

A commander's decision to move a force, institute a search, fire weapons, replenish fuel, etc., may be expressed verbally, on forms, or on tracing paper or acetate overlays. The actual moving of the forces on the representation or representations of the area of operations may be handled by the players or by the control group. The plotting of these movements usually requires scales, protractors, turning cards, and other measuring devices. If weapons employment is to be displayed graphically, arrows or under-attack symbols are needed.

Control group inputs for evaluation procedures are obtained from the players' decisions and moves, and from the use of measuring tools. Detections, hits, and damage are determined by one of the three methods of evaluation, and chance devices, tables, graphs, and computing forms may be necessary. Following the assessment of interactions, the control group's record is updated, and intelligence transmitted to the players either verbally or on forms designed for that purpose.

Game communications are designed to furnish practicable approximations of the communication channels normally available to military commanders; to enable the control group to monitor, inject delays, or to deny player communications in accordance with the rules of the game, and to provide means for transmitting information between the players and the control group. In manual games, these functions are accomplished by person-to-person contacts, messengers, pneumatic tubes, phones, or by various combinations of these methods.

Historically, the simulation requirements of the players and the control group resulted in the development of the so-called "one-map," "two-map," and "three-map" games. In a one-map game all forces appear on a single large map, terrain model, or game board. A two-map game allots one representation of the area of operations to each side. In this type of game, there is no single complete delineation of the area of operations and all forces. The players on each side have the picture of their respective sides, plus a display of any enemy forces of which they have knowledge. The control group moves from map to map to correlate the dispositions and actions of the players. Three-map games employ three representations of the area of operations, one for each side and a third for the control group.

Commanders of the various forces in a real-world area of operations are usually physically separated from each other, although they may be able to see adjacent forces. Two basic concepts have been developed to simulate these conditions. These might be called the "viewers' concept," and the "command center concept." In the former, the players are allowed to see a representation of the area of operations, or portions of it; in the latter, they gain their knowledge of the location and composition of adjacent forces from intelligence obtained from other players and from the control group.

Generally speaking, two-map and three-map games use the viewers' concept; one-map games, either the viewers' or the command center concept, or a combination of both.

Using the viewers' concept in a one-map game in which the area of operations is a large floor-type game board, the forces and their commanders are separated, insofar as possible, by screens, and the players see only those forces that they would normally see in the real world. If the game is conducted on a map, small game board, or terrain model, then the control group covers or removes the forces that the Blue players, for instance, cannot see, and the players move to the replica of the area of operations to gather intelligence and make their moves.

In a two-map game, all commanders on the Blue side, for example, have access to the map that represents, from Blue's point of view, the area of operations and locations of Blue and Red forces. Blue players make their moves in the presence of each other. The rules of the game prescribe the method or manner in which they may communicate.

The method of conducting the three-map game is similar to that for the two-map, except that after the Blue and Red players have made their moves, these moves are transferred to the control group's representation of the area of operations. Because three rooms are usually required, one for each side and a third for the control group, these games are often called "three-room" games.

When the command center concept is employed, force commanders—as far as practicable—are located in different rooms. They transmit the movements and employment of their forces to the control group. The forces are moved on the control group's simulation of the area of operations. Evaluations are made and information sent back to the command centers.

The Duel Game. The single-ship or duel game simulated a conflict between two battleships. It was played at the Naval War College from 1894 to about 1905. This was one of the simplest of manual games, and serves to illustrate some of the basic manual simulation concepts.

In some instances, the general purpose of the duel game was educational; in others, analytical. In the former, the specific purpose was to provide an officer with experience in fighting a single ship; in the latter, "... to test the value of a 20 per cent superiority in speed, ... to test the value of a smaller turning circle, ..." etc.[1]

The area of operations was an unspecified area of the sea, about three miles long by two miles wide. It was a two-sided game, and employed rigid methods of evaluation. Two players and one director were required.

The rules of the game changed from time to time to reflect the impact of new weapons and of increased experience with gaming techniques. Thus, torpedoes were introduced into the game in 1897, and new rules were needed for their simulation. The length of a move was originally one minute. This was later reduced to half that time. After an initial period of experimentation, the rules covered about six pages.

The duel game was a one-map game and the players remained in view of the model of the area of operations. This model was simply a plain or gridded piece of paper stretched out on the top of a table. The scale was one inch to one hundred yards. A ship was represented by a rectangular transparent stencil with a scaled cutout along the longitudinal axis. The stencil had compass lines radiating from the center of the ship, and scales along the edges. Other plotting equipment included a turning card and a transparent card for plotting torpedoes.

The mechanics of the game were simple, but representative of manual games in general. The director called for a move. The players wrote their decisions on slips of paper which were monitored by the director. When the director called for the move to be made, the players plotted their forces, drew in the outlines of the ships at the end of the move, wrote down the move number, and drew short lines to indicate the guns that were being employed.

The life or "fighting endurance" of a ship was measured in points. The effects of gunfire were determined by measuring the range between the firing ship and the target ship and referring to a table or a "range wand" to find the loss of life of the target in points. This figure and the cumulative loss were recorded next to the move number so that a complete history of the game—moves, guns employed, and damage sustained—appeared directly on the paper which represented the area of operations.

When a player fired a torpedo, he plotted its course on a torpedo card. The probability of a successful launching was 0.50, and a die was thrown to simulate the firing. If the launching was successful, a hit was scored if the track of the target ship intercepted the plotted torpedo track. A ramming was considered successful when the ram struck the side or stern of the enemy vessel. If the ramming took place while the ships were on opposite courses, or if the stern struck the stern, the result was ruled a draw. A vessel successfully ramming another was considered motionless for two minutes or more.

Naval War College Board Games. From 1894 until the academic year of 1956-57, naval tactical games at the Naval War College were conducted on the game board. These games were known by various names: fleet tactical games, board maneuvers, tactical maneuvers, and board games. They were designed to simulate the tactical interactions of the individual ships of opposing fleets, either in specific or unspecified areas of open water. However, they also included "Problems in Interior Waters," board games played in "... proximity to shore or outlying shoals ..."[1]

Board games were characterized by detailed rules that approximated closely the conditions of naval warfare, and by the relatively large scale of the ships and the board, although the scale was smaller than either the duel or the coast artillery game. Each individual ship in a conflict was represented by a scaled model. There were no aggregated units. However, in computing the effects of gunfire in the later games, a division of destroyers in close formation was considered as a single firing unit and as a single target.

The first board games were relatively simple one-map games concerned chiefly with the interactions of opposing fleets of battleships and cruisers. Moves represented two and one-half minutes of real time. The games required five participants: two fleet commanders, a director or arbitrator who also acted as recorder, and two movers. Sometimes an additional officer served as recorder. When forts, destroyers, torpedo boats, and submarines were involved, additional players were assigned to act as their commanders. If the conflict turned into a melee the game was stopped, or additional players were assigned to act as the commanders of the individual battleships and cruisers, and the game was continued under the rules of the duel game. The ships in the game were represented by model sailing vessels with red hulls for one side, blue for the other. Different colored sails were used to represent the various types of ships. A careful record was kept of the positions and status of all ships at the end of each move for subsequent study and discussion.

Over the years there were many variations in the board games, numerous changes in the rules. Many ingenious devices, forms, and methods were developed to facilitate the play. Their basic pattern, however, remained unchanged.

When the game board was transferred to the floor, portable screens were used to restrict the fields of view of the players to those portions of the area of operations that corresponded approximately to real-world conditions. The introduction of submarines into the game made it necessary to use command centers for submarine commanders and to maintain a supplementary plot for submarine operations. This plot evolved into a master plot, a portrayal of all activities—surface, subsurface, and air—that occurred during the play, and procedures were developed to collect and display all the necessary information. As the number and range of aircraft increased, the master plot was supplemented by a separate air plot. With increases in the number of participating forces—and, consequently, with the number of players on the game board—the rules were changed to permit the players to move their own forces. For ease in plotting, moves were lengthened to three minutes. (A ship making 20 knots travels 2,000 yards in three minutes; one moving at 30 knots, 3,000 yards, and so on). Aircraft moves, however, were called for separately, and were usually one-half hour or more in length.

In the early days of naval war gaming a point system was used for assessing damage. Thus, around 1900, a battleship was assigned a "life" or "fighting endurance" of 1000 points; an armored cruiser, 500 points; and a protected cruiser, 170 points. If a ship received a number of points equal to its fighting endurance, it was considered to have sunk, struck, or lost all its offensive capability. A battleship that was hit by a torpedo lost 500 points and all of its speed; other type ships were generally considered sunk. If a ship received a number of points equal to 30 per cent of its total fighting endurance, its offensive power was reduced by one-half; a 60 per cent loss of life resulted in a 75 per cent loss of offensive power.

The offensive power or capability of a battleship for a two and one-half minute period, in terms of broadside fire, was expressed in points as a function of range.

Table 4-1 illustrates the point values that were used around 1900. The point values were based on the assumption that the full and undiminished broadside fire of a battleship would sink or put out of action a target that was another and similar battleship in fifty minutes (20 moves) at a range of 2,500 yards. These values were changed from time to time to reflect improvements in ship construction, accuracy of fire, and longer ranges. Generally, the tabular values were transferred to range wands so that the number of points of damage inflicted on a target could be read directly as range measurements were taken.

Table 4-1

DAMAGE INFLICTED BY THE BROADSIDE FIRE OF A BATTLESHIP DURING A TWO AND ONE-HALF MINUTE MOVE (circa 1900)

Range in Yards	Points	Range in Yards	Points
262	480	1,465	120
565	320	1,810	90
725	240	2,275	60
890	200	2,912	40
1,120	160	5,480	10

The broadside fire of an armored cruiser was assumed to be one-half that of a battleship; that of a protected cruiser, one-fourth. An "end-on" battery inflicted one-half the damage caused by broadside fire. Differences in the position of the target in relation to the firing ship were not considered, i.e., broadside and end-on targets were assumed equal.

A gun in a fort was considered equal to four guns afloat. If a fort received 300 points during a move, its fire for the succeeding move was reduced by one-half; if it received 500 points, its guns were silenced during the next move.

The point system of assessing damage was superseded by one in which the life or "resisting power" of a ship was expressed in terms of 12-inch hits. Thus, a dreadnought battleship was assigned a life of twenty 12-inch hits; a predreadnought battleship, a life of fifteen 12-inch hits. A 10-inch hit was assumed to have two-thirds the effectiveness of a 12-inch hit, and an 8-inch hit one-half the effectiveness.

All ships of one type were considered to mount the same number and caliber of guns. For example, for game purposes, all dreadnought battleships carried ten 12-inch guns; all predreadnought battleships, eight. The hit probabilities for the major caliber guns are shown in Table 4-2.

Table 4-2

HIT PROBABILITIES FOR MAJOR CALIBER GUNS (circa 1916)

Range (Yds.)	12-inch	10-inch	8-inch	Range (Yds.)	12-inch	10-inch	8-inch
1,000	1.00	.95	.85	11,000	.14	.12	.10
2,000	.95	.85	.68	12,000	.12	.10	.08
4,000	.68	.51	.38	14,000	.08	.06	.03
6,000	.38	.30	.25	16,000	.03	.025	.02
8,000	.25	.21	.17	18,000	.02	.01	.005
10,000	.17	.14	.12	20,000	.005	—	—

The results of several replications of a duel-game between two ships of the same type were used to illustrate the effects of chance. The rules for the tactical games also provided for an "even chance of smoke interference when the funnel smoke and powder gasses drift(ed) down the formation or between it and the enemy," and a one-sixth chance of a spray penalty.

In 1922 a new and more sophisticated system for assessing damage was devised, a system based on actual armaments and actual ships. Known as the "War College Fire Effect System," it was designed to lead "to sound tactical conclusions when used in connection with game board problems," and to furnish "a means of making substantially accurate relative strength comparisons of ships and forces" as illustrated in Figure 4-1 and Table 4-3. As far as was known, this was the only system at that time to "give the relative effects of all naval weapons including planes, bombs, torpedoes, etc., against all enemy targets under varying conditions."

In the War College Fire Effect System, the various fleets of the world were assigned color codes: Blue for the United States, Red for Britain, Orange for Japan, Black for Germany, and so on. Based on studies of naval engagements, armor penetration tests, etc., all the ships in the different fleets were analyzed with respect to tonnage, thickness of armor belts, and other pertinent factors, and each ship, or class of ships, was assigned a life value in terms of the number of fourteen-inch hits that it was considered would be necessary to sink it. Thus, the Blue cruiser, *San Francisco*, was given a life of "... between four and five (14-inch) penetrative hits or twice as many non-penetrative ones."* The effects of shells of lesser or greater caliber were expressed in terms of 14-inch hits.

* Bruce McCandless, "The San Francisco Story," *U.S. Naval Institute Proceedings*, November 1958, p. 35.

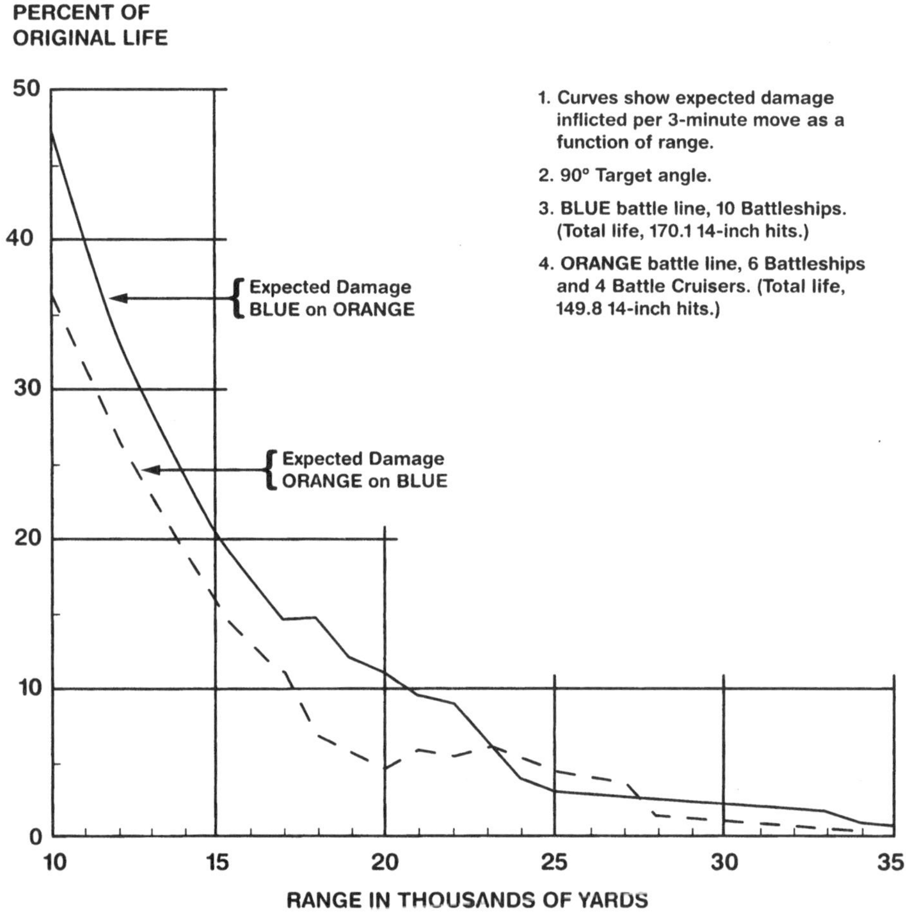

A PREGAME COMPARISON OF OPPOSING BATTLE LINES —1926

Figure 4-1

Table 4-3

SUMMARY OF SURFACE LOSSES IN A 1926 NAVAL GAME

Side	Type Ship	Original		Damage Received in Terms of 14-inch Hits from							No. Lost	Remaining	
							Planes						
		No.	Life*	Guns	Torps	Mines	Bombs	Torps	Ramming	Total		No.	Life*
BLUE	BB	10	170.1	42.5	33.6	—	6.0	19.7	—	101.8	4	6	68.3
	CL	9	35.1	25.8	2.6	—	—	—	—	28.4	4	5	6.7
	CV	5	47.6	13.1	4.7	—	4.7	—	—	22.5	2	3	25.1
	DD	111	144.3	58.3	5.2	3.9	—	3.9	14.3	85.6	64	47	58.7
	DM	9	11.7	3.9	—	—	2.6	—	—	6.5	4	5	5.2
	Totals	144	408.8	143.6	46.1	3.9	13.3	23.6	14.3	244.8	78	66	164.0
ORANGE	BB, CC	10	149.8	51.2	61.2	—	17.8	9.0	—	139.2	7	3	10.6
	CA, CL	28	94.3	54.7	14.8	—	—	—	3.6	73.1	17	11	21.2
	CV	5	49.0	2.8	3.0	—	8.0	12.0	—	25.8	1	4	23.2
	DD	77	93.1	44.7	8.3	—	—	—	7.3	60.3	50	27	32.8
	Totals	120	386.2	153.4	87.3	—	25.8	21.0	10.9	298.4	75	45	87.8

* In 14-inch hits

"Fire effect" tables were prepared for each type of gun versus each type of target (or class of targets). These tables listed as a function of range, target angle,* and type spot (top, kite, plane), the expected per cent loss of target life for a single gun firing for the length of a single move; i.e., for three minutes. The losses were computed or extrapolated from the results of target practice and armor penetration studies, and such factors as rates of fire and angles of impact of hits were carefully considered. Thus, for certain ranges it was calculated that a hit would penetrate the armor of a target; at other ranges, it would not. In the former instance there was more damage; in the latter, obviously less.

Provided that they could be brought to bear,** the number of guns fired at a target was based solely on the number that the commander of the firing unit decided to fire. At this point no consideration was given to any damage that the firing vehicle might have sustained. Hence, the "normal" damage caused by the same size guns of a firing ship during a move was the product of the fire effect of a single gun and the number of guns firing.

The "final" fire effect was the normal damage times an "M" factor or multiplier. If there were no deviations from the assumed normal conditions, the value of M was 1. Its value was reduced by 0.10 for each ten per cent above-water damage or loss of effectiveness to the firing ship. "M" was also reduced during the first move in which the guns were fired, when the fire was shifted from one target to another, when a ship was hit by a torpedo, mine or bomb, if the sea was rough or heavy, and so on, for all of the various conditions that affected adversely the effects of gunfire on a target. Fractional values were added to "M" when the firing ship was not under fire, and when the target was silhouetted during twilight hours.

Damage to ships was classified as above-water and below-water; total damage, as the sum of the two. Above-water damage degraded the offensive capability of a ship in direct proportion to the damage sustained. The maximum speed of a ship was reduced according to the amount of under-water damage received plus an additional amount for above-water damage in excess of 30 per cent. A loss of specific shipboard equipment was correlated with damage. This information, together with losses in gunfire effectiveness and speed, were printed on the damage reports that the ship commanders received after each move was evaluated. Thus, they not only knew how much numerical damage their force had received, but

* The target angle was defined as the angle between the line of fire and the keel line of the target ship. A limited number of target angles were recognized—for example, 90, 45, and 0 degrees—and angles were measured to the nearest of these values.

** If the line of fire was within 30 degrees of the bow or stern, only bow or stern guns could be brought to bear. Otherwise, all guns of the broadside could be fired at the target.

also what this meant in terms of mobility, offensive power, communications, and intelligence facilities.

Aircraft losses from aerial combat were computed from formulas which considered the number and type of attacking and defending planes. Aircraft lost from the gunfire of surface ships were based on so-called standard fire units (SFU). One standard fire unit represented the antiaircraft firepower of a destroyer. Other vessels were assigned standard fire-unit numbers in proportion to their antiaircraft firepower as compared with that of a destroyer. The number of standard fire units that would be expected to oppose an air attack was the sum of the fire units of the ships which were able to fire at the raid. These ships were determined from the formation and direction of attack. If the latter were not specified, it was determined by rolling a single regular die and multiplying the number turned up by 60 degrees.

The total number of standard fire units opposing the attack was converted into effective fire units (EFU) by use of a multiplier with a normal value of 1. The value of the multiplier was increased or decreased by an amount that equaled the algebraic sum of the numerical values that were assigned to conditions that might prevail just prior to and during the air attack. Thus, if the surface force was under gunfire, a factor of -0.2 was specified; if the aircraft was coming in for a torpedo attack, a factor of 0.6. Provided that these two factors adequately described the conditions of the attack, the algebraic sum would be 0.4, and the value of the multiplier 1.4. The number of effective fire units, then, would be 1.4 times the total number of fire units opposing the attack.

A table was entered with the number of effective fire units and the number of aircraft in the attack, and the number of planes destroyed prior to attaining the attacking point was read out. If different types of aircraft took part in the raid, losses to each type were apportioned in accordance with their relative strength. Losses to aircraft during retirement were assumed to be a fixed per cent of the approach losses.

The number of hits obtained by the aircraft was based on target size, type and altitude of attack, and number of weapons released. This number was modified in accordance with the speed and evasive tactics of the target. Armor penetration curves showed whether or not the damage inflicted was penetrative or non-penetrative, and tables indicated the per cent of life lost per penetrative hit or non-penetrative hit for each of the target types.

The procedures that were employed in board games from the time the game was transferred to the floor until the immediate post—World War II period are illustrated best by a brief description of a game conducted in the Pringle Hall game room. On this board, the scale usually used was six inches to 1,000 yards.

Individual surface forces were represented by model ships—carriers, battleships, battle cruisers, heavy and light cruisers, and destroyers—constructed to the scale of the board. Aircraft were represented by paper cutouts of planes mounted on sticks according to altitude. Small black screens indicated smoke screens. Units that were out of sight of each other were separated by curtains or portable screens. Surface force commanders operated from the game board. Subsurface and air commanders were assigned rooms away from the game room, but connected to it by phones and pneumatic tubes.

The rules of the game were published under one cover and were entitled: *Maneuver Rules and Rules for Aircraft Maneuvers on the Maneuver Board.* They were supported and supplemented by data furnished in such other publications as the *Fire Effect Tables, Aircraft Damage Assessment Tables*, descriptions of the capabilities of ships and aircraft, and so on. The rules were divided into ten sections covering the general description of the game, speed and logistics rules, contact rules, communication rules, and so on. About twenty forms were employed ranging from aircraft casualty sheets to the umpires' communication records.

The control group included the director, move, damage, air, and communications umpires and their assistants; liaison and plotting personnel, and a historian. Their duties were defined in the rules of the game.

The director called for one, or, if he thought nothing much would happen, for several moves. The players filled out move and gunfire forms which were checked by the control group. At the signal, "Make move 1" (or, "Make moves 1, 2, and 3," etc.), the players commanding surface forces advanced their ships on the game board and drew in the tracks with chalk; those off the game board sent in tracings (flimsies) of their moves via the pneumatic tubes. The movements of all forces—surface, air, and subsurface—were transferred from the board and from the flimsies to the master plot. The tracks of torpedoes were plotted on the master plot.

Intelligence was generated from both the master plot and the game board. If the move resulted in additional forces coming within sight of each other, the screens were rearranged.

From the ships on the board, umpires measured ranges and target angles, and then computed the gunfire damage that accrued during the move. Damage from torpedoes, mines, bombs, and aerial torpedoes was assessed and added to that received from gunfire. Aircraft losses from surface weapons and aerial combat were computed.

When all damage had been assessed and all intelligence disseminated, the director announced the next move.

A Post-World War II Board Game

Figure 4–2

Board games were played usually for a part of the day. After each day's play the final positions of all forces were transferred to a new master plot for use on the following day. Then the essential information and tracks from the old master plot were fitted, with the aid of a pantograph, to a standardized sheet of drawing paper. This was photographed and a slide produced for use during the critique. When the game was finished, all the drawings were bound together to serve as a graphical history of the game. Included with the history were comparisons of the relative effectiveness of opposing fleets and of damage sustained during the game. (Figure 4-1, Table 4-3).

From about 1950 until the installation of the NEWS, Naval War College board games were conducted in accordance with the command center concept. The players were stationed in offices around the building and transmitted their decisions over phones to "talkers" in the game room. The talkers passed the information to the board plotters who made the moves on the game board, that is, they moved the ships and drew in the tracks. Arrows were placed near the ships to indicate gunfire, and the tracks of torpedoes were drawn on the game board. The umpires evaluated contacts and damage, recorded the results, and the data were transmitted to the players. The players maintained their own plots and kept a record of the status of their own forces.

Damage computations were progressively simplified. This was due to three basic reasons. First, less curriculum time was available for war gaming. Secondly, at this time it was thought that detailed damage assessment procedures appeared to emphasize the analytical rather than the educational aspects of the games. Finally, uncomplicated assessment methods speeded up the game and provided more opportunities for the players to practice decision-making.

Various methods were employed to simplify the damage assessment techniques. The number of fire effect tables was reduced by grouping targets into fewer classes. The computation of the value of the M factor was shortened. Chance damage and sinking factors were introduced. Thus, if for a single move the computed damage was due to non-penetrative hits and amounted to, say, 20 per cent, a table was entered and a value that may have been greater or less than that amount was read out. That was the damage actually assessed for the move. If the hits were penetrative, a chance sinking table was used.

Manual damage computers in the form of circular slide rules were also used to facilitate damage computation. These were based on earlier fire effect tables, but they did not specify whether the damage was due to penetrative or non-penetrative hits. Chance damage tables, consequently, were not used. However, chance sinkings were considered. When a ship lost 60 per cent of its effectiveness, its probability of sinking was one-third, and this probability was increased by one-sixth for each additional 10 per cent damage received. A regular die was used as a chance device. In computing damage, the value of the M factor was based solely on the effectiveness of the firing ship.

Most of the post—World War II games were played for the entire working day. Little or no attempt was made to record graphically the moves for future references, or to prepare carefully edited drawings and slides illustrating the progress of the play. In general, critiques were conducted a short time after the last move, and the tracks on the game board were used in lieu of slides.

Submarine Tactical Game.* This manual war game was developed by the Research and Development Department of the Electric Boat Division under contract with the Office of Naval Research. "Through this contract, research assistance is provided to Submarine Development Group TWO in support of its task of developing new tactics for the submarine ASW mission."[35]

---

* Electric Boat has developed a gaming facility for submarine games which combines manual and analog computer (machine) techniques.

Initially, the general purpose of the game was analytical—to investigate the parameters of submarine tactics. It has also been employed as a training device. "In this capacity it is particularly useful for training the reserve officer who seldom has an opportunity to exercise at sea. It enables him to become familiar with tactical problems and to practice solving them. Similarly, a commanding officer can prepare himself, at least on the theoretical level, for an operation before he embarks on it."[35]

The submarine game is a two-sided closed game. It simulates a conflict situation in which the submarines of one side are attempting to penetrate a barrier maintained by the submarines of the opposing side. Each of the players represents a submarine captain. The area of operations is an unspecified ocean area, 100 nautical miles by 100 nautical miles. The rigid method of evaluation is employed.

Usually, there are five players: two command transiting submarines; three barrier submarines. Two of the barrier submarines are SSK's. These act as listening platforms, and their movements are restricted by the rules of the game. Their job is to detect the transiting subs and to vector the third barrier submarine, a nuclear boat (SSN), in for a kill. The mission of the transitors is to penetrate the barrier. The game ends when the transiting submarines accomplish their mission, or the barrier submarines fulfill theirs; that is, they detect and destroy the penetrators.

The area of operations is represented by a gridded chart or game board which is divided into 20 by 20 large squares, five miles on a side. These are subdivided into 100 smaller 1,000-yard squares.* Moves are generally 7.5 minutes in length. A boat making four knots travels one-half mile, or one square in one move; one moving at eight knots, two squares, etc.

Certain assumptions and restrictions are made in order to simplify gaming procedures. Thus, it is assumed that passive sonar is in continuous use by all forces, and that the SSK positions are constantly covered. SSN's may use speeds of 0, 4, 8, 12, 16 or 20 knots only; transitors, 0 or 4 knots. Sonar communication ranges are indicated by squares rather than circles.

The rules of the game are divided into four parts. One part is a general description of the game. The other parts are: rules for the control group, rules for the barrier submarines, and rules for the transiting submarines. The players are presented with the general description and the procedures for their respective roles. The rules include communication, detection, and weapons data, the latter two in the form of probabilities. The data and/or the rules can be changed "... and the effect of such changes on the outcome of the game ... observed."[35]

* The Naval War College game boards were gridded in a similar fashion.

The game is a one-map game; that is, the area of operations is simulated by the control group's grid, or master plot. Each player has a chart of the area of operations for "... plotting his own position, and, when possible, the other ships' positions."[35]

The players are physically isolated from each other. Sound-powered phones and a control-group-operated switching device permit communications between the players and the control group and, when the rules allow, monitored communications between players. The forces, on the control group's master chart, are represented by symbols; their tracks, by lines. These symbols reflect the state of the submarine at any time during the game. For example, a cross may indicate a snorkeling boat; a small open circle, a submerged submarine, etc. Asterisks show where a boat was detected; an arrow, the source of a torpedo. Thus, the master plot can be used directly for the "post-mortem" discussion or critique as well as for a history of the game.

Interactions are evaluated by the control group in accordance with the rules of the game. Tables provide the probabilities of detections and hits at various ranges, and a table of random numbers provides the "yes" or "no" answers. Communications are allowed between submarines at specified ranges and under well-defined conditions. For example, if two submarines are at periscope depth, they may communicate at 50 miles or less. "One move is required to surface and communicate; a second move is required to return to listening depth."[38] Thus the game, like many others, is partly probabilistic, partly deterministic.

Prior to the game, the players are briefed on the general purpose and applicable rules and are provided with charts and plotting tools. In accordance with the rules, the initial positions of the forces are selected in part by chance, in part by the decisions of the players. For instance, one transitor is assigned a chance position near the northern edge of the chart; the second may pick any position—within stated limits—that he wishes. Initial battery life is handled in a similar fashion. One transitor has a random choice of any number between 0 and 4. This number "... represents the number of hours of battery life remaining before his batteries are 50 per cent depleted and he must snorkel. The second transitor may select, at his option, from 0 to 8 initial battery hours."[38]

When the players are familiar with the purpose and rules of the game, and know their initial positions and battery hours, they are allowed about ten minutes to discuss their plans and communication procedures. The players then go to their own rooms (command centers) and the umpires call for the first move. Each player plots the movement of his own sub on his plot. By means of sound-powered phones, he reports his speed and the coordinates of his position at the end of the move. He states if he is proceeding on the surface, submerged, or at snorkel depth, and whether he is using sonar, radar, or radio. If he fires torpedoes during the move, he indicates the time of firing and the coordinates of a target area.

The umpires monitor the moves and intentions of the players, evaluate contacts and torpedo firings, and notify the players of the outcomes, if any. If a torpedo is fired and no hit is obtained, the umpire tells the player when the running time of the torpedo (assumed to be five moves) has elapsed.

Hexagonal Grid Systems. The game boards used in the games that have been described employed square grid patterns. When this grid system is used for generalized games in which the forces are permitted to move only from one square to an adjacent square, a force may move in any one of eight directions. However, if it moves diagonally, it covers about 1.4 times the distance that it does when it moves vertically or horizontally. Hexagonal grid patterns, on the other hand, equalize the length of moves between adjacent hexagons, but restrict the possible directions of movement to six.

The hexagonal grid system has not been used in Naval War College games, but has been employed by the RAND Corporation and other gaming activities.

Naval War College Chart Games. Prior to the post-World War II era, strategic games at the Naval War College were concerned chiefly with naval campaigns. These games simulated the strategic employment of naval forces rather than the detailed tactics of naval battles. When the main bodies closed to engage, the game was ended, or the forces were transferred to the game board and a tactical game was played. In some games, senior students commanded the divisions and squadrons during the strategical and tactical plays; junior students, the individual ships during the detailed play.

Strategic games embraced relatively large areas of operations, mainly definite ocean areas and coastal regions in the low and middle latitudes. They were conducted on medium or small scale Mercator charts. This type of projection was normally used by naval officers for navigation and planning, and was the kind of chart most readily available. It was sufficiently accurate for the regions of the world in which the games were played, and possessed the useful property of representing any constant course or loxodrome by a straight line. For the game scales employed, the horizontal parallels of latitude and the vertical meridians of longitude provided a convenient and familiar grid system, and eliminated the need for a game board network. Strategic games became known as chart games or chart maneuvers.

Together with board games, they corresponded to what were known elsewhere as map games.

Chart games were basically one-map games, with the control group's map serving as a replica of the area of operations. With the exception of scouting elements, the forces were aggregated. Forces were represented by symbols. The kinds of symbols and track lines that were used were specified in the rules of the game. Fuel capacity and expenditures and other planning data were included with the rules or issued separately. Rules for detections and communications were the same as for tactical games. The director was allowed to select weather conditions, but the rules noted that the simplest method was to use the actual weather conditions prevailing at the College.

During the planning phases the players prepared large-scale diagrams of the cruising formations, battle formations, etc., that they expected to employ during the game. Copies were furnished to the control group to assist in the evaluation processes.

The chart game was conducted according to the command center concept. Commanders of aggregated forces (and their staffs) were located in individual offices. The director announced the length of a move—six hours, twelve hours, or whatever number of hours he thought appropriate. The players made tracings of the intended movements of their forces and sent them via liaison officers, pneumatic tubes, or messengers, to the control group. The intended movements were plotted on the control group's representation of the area of operations. The umpires correlated the movements and intentions of the opposing forces. If a contact or other event occurred that might cause a change in the movements or intentions of a force or forces on either or both sides, the game time was advanced to the time of the interaction, and evaluated intelligence transmitted to the proper players. These players then made any modifications to their moves that they desired, and notified the control group of their decisions. The director advanced the game time to the next event, and so on, until it was time for the next move.

If a player—perhaps as the result of a message from a friendly force, or for any other reason—wished to change his move, he contacted the control group. The game time was advanced to the time of the proposed change, and the modification made.

In the chart maneuvers which were conducted in the early days of College gaming, the results of engagements between detached squadrons were decided by the following sort of set-piece evaluations: If two forces with relative strengths of 2 to 1 engaged, the inferior force was removed from the game. When the odds were 3 to 2, the lesser force lost one-half his strength. With odds of 4 to 3, the superior force defeated his adversary, but was considered incapable of carrying out any large operations during the remainder of the game. The length of time required for an engagement was determined by the umpires. The rules covering actions between lesser units and scouts read: "If armored vessels come within 2,000 yards, or unarmored within 4,000 yards, of each other, and remain within these distances for more than an hour, the action will be decided, at the option of the umpire, by the relative number of points at which each vessel is valued."[1] The fighting values of the various ships were similar to those shown in Table 4-4.

Table 4-4

FIGHTING VALUES OF SHIPS[(1)]

Type	Class	Fighting Value in Points
Battleships	A	20
Armored Cruisers	B	10
Cruisers, first class	C	4
Cruisers, second class	F	3
Monitors	M	10*
Gunboats	D	2
Fast Scouts	E	2
Destroyers	V	—**
Torpedo Boats	t	—**
Torpedo Gunboats	g	—**

* The fighting value of monitors at sea is 3.

** Torpedo destroyers have a maximum value of 7 (night or thick weather), and a minimum value of 2 (day and clear weather). The maximum and minimum values for torpedo gunboats are the same as for torpedo destroyers; the values for torpedo boats are 7 and 1, respectively.

With the introduction of fire effect tables and the representation of the life values of ships in terms of 14-inch hits, tables of fighting values in terms of points were no longer compiled. Umpires assessed damage in strategic games by assuming that the commanders of opposing forces employed optimum tactics and applying the damage assessment rules of the tactical game, or by the free method of evaluation.

Following extensive curriculum and organizational changes during the early 1950's, College chart-gaming techniques were updated independently by each of the three academic departments (Command and Staff, Naval Warfare, and Naval Command Course*) to meet their own specific requirements. One of each of the resulting departmental games is described briefly in the following three sections.

* The Naval Command Course Department was established in 1956. This department conducts an annual course for approximately twenty-five senior naval officers of allied nations. In April 1965 the names of the Naval Warfare Department and Command and Staff Department were changed to School of Naval Warfare and School of Naval Command and Staff respectively.

These descriptions are followed by brief discussions of a few of the many manual games conducted by other activities.

Command and Staff Department Manual Game. This game constituted the final phase of the last Command and Staff Department's operations problem of the academic year. It was a two-sided—Green versus White—strategic game involving the joint and combined operations of all services and several nations.

Initially, the students were divided into three groups: a Green Staff, a White Staff, and a small Problem Intelligence-Center Group. The first two groups prepared the operational plans for their respective sides. During the real-world time span represented by this planning phase, the two opposing staffs could, within the restrictions imposed by their directives from higher headquarters, order certain force movements, initiate reconnaissance flights, submarine patrols, etc. The members of the Problem Intelligence Center monitored and recorded such force movements and intelligence activities, and furnished information that was compatible with the reconnaissance and anti-reconnaissance efforts, and that stimulated decisions and furthered the purpose of the game. The problem director acted as the next higher command for both sides, and ruled on any player's requests for additional forces and support.

When the plans for both sides were prepared, some students from each planning staff and the members of the Problem Intelligence Center were assigned to the control group. (Their detailed knowledge of concepts, plans, and pregame activities greatly facilitated the conduct of the game.) The remaining students in the planning staffs were organized to play the game.

The control group was headed by a director and two assistants, one responsible for White, one for Green. Other members were organized into four umpiring teams: naval, air, land, and logistics; and an administrative section. The naval, air, and land teams evaluated interactions in their respective spheres of interest, prepared intelligence and operational summaries, recorded the history of each move from their viewpoints, and noted any lessons revealed by the game. The logistics team monitored constraints imposed by logistic factors, and recorded the effects of logistic considerations upon the decisions and actions of opposing sides.

The administrative section received the intelligence and operational summaries, the histories, and the "lessons learned" from the four umpiring teams. Its members eliminated duplications and resolved discrepancies. They prepared, produced, and distributed consolidated operational and intelligence summaries to the players, and maintained a history of the game and a record of the lessons that its play disclosed. This group maintained a record of the message traffic between player staffs and between the players and the control group. In addition, some of its members recorded the information on the large maps that were displayed as appropriate.

The game was a three-map game. The auditorium of Sims Hall was used as the game room. Three identical large maps of the area of operations were fastened to the sliding panels at the rear of the auditorium, one each for Green and White, and a third for the control group. Medium-scale paper maps and small-scale transparencies of the area of operations were issued to the participants. The players on each side were assigned different rooms in accordance with their respective command organizations.

The Green players assembled in the game room, and the commander-in-chief and his subordinate commanders briefed the control group on their concepts and plans. Then the Green players returned to their rooms, and the White side had their turn at presenting concepts and plans. The opposing concepts and plans provided the director with the information that he needed to determine the length of the first move. When this was announced, the players indicated the movements of their forces on the paper maps and on the transparencies. These were sent to the game room. The transparencies were projected from an overhead projector, and the moves plotted on the maps of the respective sides. Then the Green side entered the game room and each force commander, or a member of his staff, described his intentions. During this period the large map showing Green's intended movements was displayed. After the briefing by Green, that side returned to its rooms and the White side assembled in the game room and presented its case.

The control group correlated the movements for the opposing sides by laying the paper maps over each other. They considered the soundness of the plans, the means used to execute them, and attempted to arrive at creditable outcomes that would serve best the objectives of the game.

Following the umpire evaluations, the tracks and actual locations of the forces at the end of the move were plotted on the control group's map. Intelligence and operational summaries were prepared and distributed. The former contained information of enemy forces and activities; the latter, own-side losses and gains, and the situation as it existed at the end of the move. Upon receipt of the summaries, the players made a new estimate of the situation and prepared for the next move. The game cycle began again.

This manual game was adapted to play on the NEWS and conducted on that simulator until 1965. In 1966 a new planning exercise replaced the operations problem on which the game was based. It is planned to conduct two separate one-sided NEWS games, each in a different area of operations, in support of this planning exercise.

The School of Naval Warfare Strategic Game. This game simulates a global political-military environment in which two major powers, Blue and Purple, are attempting to implement and support conflicting national aims and policies. It is a two-sided educational game with the emphasis on decision-making at the national level. The players represent the heads of the two governments, key cabinet posts, and high-echelon military commanders; the control group, other Blue and Purple government agencies and military commands, other national governments and the United Nations.

It is a manual and, in general, a continuous-time game. One hour of real time usually represents a day of game time. A game lasts about three working days, and covers approximately three weeks of game time. The area of operations is depicted on an outline map of the world. Map sections, overlays, and forms are provided to facilitate the mechanics of game; data cards and information about various countries, treaties, etc., to assist in its conduct and control.

Initially, the game was called the Naval War College Strategic Game, later, the Strategic War Game (SWG). The first play took place in May of 1955. Since, one or more plays have been conducted each year. These plays were conducted in Pringle Hall until 1960. The 1961 and following games utilized the spaces and communication facilities of the NEWS.

For the 1956 play, a comprehensive set of rules was prepared. The set was divided into three models: the ocean model, the theatre model, and the zone of the interior (the Blue and Purple homeland) model. The latter was further divided into three submodels: a combat submodel, an economic submodel, and a military forces and facilities submodel. Each model and submodel considered the possible major types of military actions within its own sphere of interest. The control group was organized into two divisions, administration and umpiring. The umpiring division was subdivided into four sections, ocean, theatre, zone of the interior, and logistics. A punched card system was employed to assist in record-keeping and in the making of moves.

In the 1956 and 1957 games, the high-speed computer of The George Washington University's Logistic Research Project was used to test the logistic feasibility of student plans and to determine residual capabilities. These are the only times that the College used computer assistance in its games. The College and the research activity were connected by a paper-tape-to-paper-tape system operating over leased lines.

Following the 1957 game, greater emphasis was placed on the political aspects of the game,* and the rules were replaced gradually by general procedures covering cold-war political and military maneuvers, and limited and general war situations. While there have been various changes in control group organization and procedures and the number of games conducted each year, the general concept of the game, as described below, has remained fairly consistent.

During a strategic planning study that lasts for two and one half months, the students of the School of Naval Warfare are divided into a number of Blue and Purple Staffs. Each staff, utilizing previously developed student National Strategy Papers which set forth national policy and goals, prepares a Joint Strategic Capabilities Plan and supporting plans for cold, limited, and general war.

At the end of the planning study, four sets of opposing plans are selected so that an equal number of independent games can be conducted by four different teams of opposing Blue and Purple players. The Blue and Purple plans that are chosen and matched for play are picked to provide the participants of each game with a maximum number of situations requiring decisions at the national or near-national level. Students from the planning staffs are either assigned to a Student Government or to the control group. An independent control group is organized for each game.

The Director of the Strategic Planning Study selects one student from each of the four Blue gaming staffs to act as President, and appoints one in each of the four Purple planning staffs to an equivalent position. The student heads of state organize their groups of about ten students into skeletonized top-echelon governmental structures—civilian and military—that reflect similar structures in the countries that they represent. Thus, each Blue President appoints personnel to cabinet posts, the National Security Council, and Joint Chiefs of Staff. This sort of student organization helps insure full participation by all players in all decisions. In addition, one officer from each playing team is assigned as the secretariat of that team to check all incoming and outgoing messages. The personnel in these jobs are changed daily.

A control group consists of two officers from the faculty of the School of Naval Warfare and approximately fifteen students. It is composed, essentially, of four sections. One section consists of the two faculty officers and students from opposing student-planning groups. This section is concerned with the overall control

---

* One of the purposes of political gaming, as noted by Dr. Bloomfield, "... is to demonstrate in a fairly unforgettable way the variety of factors, subtle and unsubtle, which go into the formulation of strategic decisions." He then goes on to observe that "This is of particular value to a military officer whose environment in the course of his training and in the earlier years of his career does not often reveal the actual weight of political, economic, and other non-military factors in decision-making or assign to them a dominant role in the national policy structure."[29]

and conduct of the game. Each of the members of a second section is assigned an area of the world, and the responsibility for monitoring and assessing the situations and interactions that occur in that area. The third section handles message traffic, and a fourth maintains liaison with the opposing student governments.

The general situation describes developing hypothetical world situations to a point two years in the future. These situations are designed to allow student governments to implement their previously prepared policies and plans. Each control group also develops and issues additional special situations to further stimulate decisions and actions by their respective opposing student governments.

Two of the four games are conducted simultaneously, and then, upon their completion, the second two are played. For each set of two games, each of the four student governments involved are assigned three NEWS command-center spaces, one of which serves as a communications center. The NEWS umpire area is divided into two sections, and one is assigned to each of the two control groups. A send-and-receive teletype machine is installed in each student government's communications center and in each control group's work area. Opposing student governments can only communicate with each other through their control group.

During the play of the game, the student governments act and react to the changing world situation in accordance with their previously established national objectives, policies, and plans. The control group monitors and assesses the opposing strategies and actions, furnishes the results in appropriate terms and, if necessary, initiates additional situations to keep the game moving. At the end of play, each game is critiqued by both faculty and students.

Naval Command Course Manual Game. The Naval Command Course conducts several war games each academic year in support of its curriculum for allied naval officers. These games, with one exception, are played on the NEWS. The exception is a manual game which serves to introduce the students to gaming techniques that may be of use in their countries. It is played in the office spaces and auditorium of the Naval Command Course.

Gaming equipment includes game clocks for the control group and players, an intercommunication system, and the usual plotting devices, forms, and status boards. Moves are submitted on special plotting sheets which are converted to viewgraph transparencies by a photo copier for projection on a Master Plot in the Umpire Area located in the Naval Command Course Auditorium. The rules are general in nature, and are explained verbally to the players. Umpire evaluations are in accordance with the free method, although the control group is provided with certain data that can be used as a guide.

The play of the game is usually divided into two phases, a movement phase which ends when the major forces are within striking distance of each other, and an engagement phase during which the major forces are in action. In the former, time is treated as a discrete variable, and both player decisions and umpire evaluations are of the set-piece variety. The lengths of moves are determined by the director. In the engagement phase, time is considered both as a discrete and as a continuous variable, and set-piece and encounter type decisions and evaluations are made. All moves are for twenty-four-hour periods of game time.

Upon receiving the opposing plans, the control group analyzes them and determines the probable length of time it will take the major forces to get into action. The director divides this period into two or three convenient moves, and calls for the first move. The commanders submit plotting sheets and supporting data to describe their intentions. Opposing moves are analyzed by the control group, interactions evaluated, and the results made known to the players in the form of reconnaissance reports, losses, damage inflicted, etc. The commanders modify their directives, if necessary, and make the second move. This cycle is repeated until the movement phase is completed.

For the second phase of the game, the commanders submit their moves, and about 0900 the game clocks are started at eight times real-world time. The control group issues certain intelligence—for instance, information on the progress of land battles—on a periodic basis, perhaps once every eight hours of game time; information on other events, at the time of their occurrence. If the flow of intelligence indicates to either commander the need for a re-estimate of the situation, game clocks may, at the discretion of the director, be either slowed or stopped to allow the commander and his staff sufficient time to reach a decision. Should such a decision result in modifications to the original plans, the players inform the control group of their new intentions by means of the intercommunication system, and send revised moves via messengers.

When the game has progressed through a twenty-four hour period, the play is ended for the day. The control group prepares summaries of the game-day's operations and brings the master plot up-to-date. The summaries are issued to the players, and discrepancies, if any, between player and control group records are adjusted. The commanders and their staffs prepare their plans and moves for the next game-day, and submit them to the control group. Play begins again about 0900 of the next day.

JCS Politico-Military Desk Games. For a number of years between the two world wars, political-military games were conducted in Germany. The participants in those games included representatives of the Wehrmacht, political institutions, business, the armament industry, and the Propaganda Ministry.[8] Based upon techniques developed at the RAND Corporation, a political-military game was conducted at the Massachusetts Institute of Technology in 1960.[39] The players in this game included senior specialists in and out of government.* Similar games are conducted by the Cold War Division of the Joint War Games Agency of the Joint Chiefs of Staff. They are referred to as JCS Politico-Military Desk Games.[40]

JCS Politico-Military (PM) Games are initiated by the Cold War Division of the Joint War Games Agency or by officials from the White House Staff, Department of State, Department of Defense, Joint Chiefs of Staff, and other departments and agencies. They are played in the Pentagon to assist in the analysis of national policies and plans, and to provide the participants with an insight into possible future contingencies.

The general situation or scenario is prepared by the war gamers in the Joint War Games Agency with inputs and assistance from all interested agencies. The scenario is designed to provide a plausible sequence of events building-up to a future crisis situation, one that will lead to an examination of national objectives, stimulate new ideas, and so on.

The participants are civilian and military officials, analysts, economists, and others involved in actual day-to-day political-military problems. Sometimes non-governmental experts from various fields participate as players or as members of the control group. The participants are divided into a control group and two or more teams of five or six players. The player-teams discuss possible strategies, then confer with teams of more senior officials who can devote only a short period daily to the game. The moves are written-up by the players and passed to the control group. The control group evaluates the actions of the opposing teams, updates the situation, and provides intelligence to the players. A game lasts about four to six days and is followed by a critique. The scenario, messages, and other material compiled during the game and critique are distributed to the players for further analysis.

The games are purely manual games although the Computer Branch of the Cold War Division is developing submodels to provide computer assistance. Some games have utilized a remote-play technique similar to that used at the Naval War College for Fleet games. These games permit concurrent participation by officials in Europe and Washington.[40]

* Student participation games are also conducted at MIT and other colleges in the teaching of foreign policy, strategy and international relations.

Landing Force War Game (LFWG). This game is conducted by the War Games Division of the Marine Corps Landing Force Development Center, Marine Corps Schools, Quantico, Virginia. It is the only game conducted by the Marine Corps.[33]

The Landing Force War Game is a hand-played game. It is a two-sided—Red vs. Blue—free-play closed game. This game differs from all those previously described in this chapter in that it is concerned chiefly with the details of ground warfare and, from most of them, because it is strictly analytical in nature. It is similar in many respects to the tactical type of educational games used to train army officers, but employs more detailed rules and rigid assessment procedures. The Marines call it a research game.

Basically, it is a three-room game, and large scale (e.g. 1:25,000 or 1:50,000) maps are used. Forces are normally represented by map pins of various sizes, shapes and colors. It is a time-step game. Moves, or game intervals, usually represent thirty minutes of real time. Due to the many details that are considered and evaluated in accordance with rigid rules and procedures, a single move may take a day or longer to complete.

A game is conducted by two opposing teams and a control group. The customary pregame procedures are followed, i.e., a conflict situation is devised, and general and special situations prepared. The control group examines carefully the detailed rules and, when desirable, adapts some of them to the specific purpose of the simulation. Thus, rules covering aspects of the simulation that are not pertinent to the particular situation may be aggregated; those dealing with pertinent aspects might be revised to include more detailed procedures than had previously been compiled, and additional or updated data provided.

There are two player teams. The Blue team represents the commanding officers and staffs of a Marine Corps force. Depending upon the problem, this force might be an infantry battalion, an amphibious force, etc. The Red team acts as the commanders of an opposing military organization. When appropriate to the problem being analyzed, the Blue team uses Marine Corps doctrine; the Red team, insofar as practicable, the tactics and organization of the force they represent. However, as in a real world, opposing commanders are granted the same latitude in making decisions as they would have in a similar real-world situation.

A single player may represent a number of echelons of command. For instance, he might act as a regimental commander, several battalion commanders, a number of company commanders, and so on. Playing so many separate and distinct roles requires imagination and mental discipline on the part of each player, and careful monitoring and assessment by the control group. Thus, if a player, in his role as a battalion commander, possesses intelligence that a platoon commander would not receive for two hours, then as a platoon commander, he acts as if he did not possess this information. An order that a player issues as a division commander might not reach him in his capacity as a battalion commander for a number of hours that is specified by the control group in accordance with the rules. Hence he does not respond to the order at the lower level until the appropriate time has elapsed.

A game is not played to the bitter end; it is stopped when it is considered to have achieved its purpose, and sufficient data have been compiled for analysis and study and the preparation of a report. In general, a game is played but once, although portions of a game may be replayed several times in order to provide more meaningful information or a range of possible results.

TACSPIEL Control Board–the Director is checking the location of a piece which represents a Blue counterfire radar.

(Reproduced by permission of the Department of the Army and the Research Analysis Corporation.)

Figure 4–3

TACSPIEL and THEATERSPIEL.[41,42] TACSPIEL is concerned with the details of ground warfare. It is an analytical, two-sided, three-room, computer-assisted game played at the Army division and lower levels. Moves usually represent one-half hour of real time, and require about eight hours to make, assess, and disseminate the results. The area of operations is represented by 1:25,000 scale maps; forces are simulated by pieces of various shapes, sizes, and colors. As in some of the earlier manual games, the "... task of learning the required shorthand is formidable."

This game was developed by the Research Analysis Corporation as a research tool for evaluating tactical situations, and as an experimental game for devising and testing tactical gaming methodologies. The military ingredient is injected into the game by retired military officers who act as consultants and players. Civilian analysts design the models, act as assessors, and conduct the post game analyses.

THEATERSPIEL is a theater-level computer-assisted manual game. It was also designed by the Research Analysis Corporation. The purpose of this game is to "... study selected problems concerning the employment, strength, structure, and support requirements of Army forces at the theater level and in varying conflict situations." It is a three-room game, and each of the gaming rooms is equipped with rear view projection screens for displaying the game situation on maps and overlays.

Schematic of THEATERSPIEL 3-room set-up. Computer is used for bookkeeping and most of assessments.

(Reproduced by permission of the Department of the Army and the Research Analysis Corporation.)

Figure 4–4

Monopologs.[43] Monopologs is a manual game that was designed to simulate a part of the Air Force supply system. In this game a single player acts as a spare-parts inventory manager. If a group plays, a number of games may be conducted simultaneously, with each person playing the role of the inventory manager in his own individual game. In Monopologs, a player's mission is not to exert political or economic pressure or to deploy military forces or engage an enemy, but to satisfy a fluctuating demand for a specific spare part at the lowest cost. It is a military game only in the sense that it deals with a military supply system. Actually, Monopologs "is concerned with the universal problem of inventory as a whole, both military and non-military: how to put the right supplies in the right place at the right time, and at a minimum cost."[43]

The game was developed about 1955 by the Logistics Department of the RAND Corporation as a by-product of a study aimed at building a mathematical model of the Air Force supply system. It has undergone several simplifying revisions, but its basic purpose and framework have not been altered. It has been played by military officers, industrial employees, and RAND personnel.

The game is one-sided, and is conducted chiefly for educational purposes. It is concerned with one depot and five identical two-wing bases. The depot is the wholesale distributor; the bases, the consumers. A rigid method of evaluation is employed.

The spare part with which a player deals is a hypothetical high-value airframe component known as a "widget." There is one widget in each of the bombers located at the five bases. It is necessary to replace widgets when they wear out, or if they prove to be defective. In the latter case, they can be repaired at the depot.

Prior to the game, a player is supplied with the rules of the game. These specify the cost of widgets—$1,000 apiece, plus a fixed fee of $1,000 for each order placed—and a lead time of nine months. An order may be speeded up, or an emergency order placed, but such decisions incur increased costs. The price of repairing widgets in three months time is $400 each, plus a set-up cost. An additional $800 cuts the time to one month. Transportation charges for shipment from base to base are $100 per spare part; transportation time, one month. Storage at the depot or at a base is $40 a month for each serviceable widget; $20 for each that can be repaired. If a player cannot meet the widget requirements for any of the bases for which he is responsible for procurement, repair, and distribution, he is assessed a penalty of $1,000 per month per spare part until the demand is satisfied. This penalty is "... an attempt to assess the cost incurred when a part is not available upon demand, and the resultant loss in military worth of the system."[43]

In addition to the rules, a player is provided with planning data based on hypothetical limited experience with widget demand. Thus, he has a rough idea of the number of spare parts that may be needed over a long period of time, but no idea of how demand will fluctuate from month to month.

The only equipment needed to play the game are the forms required to record the decisions of the player and to keep the scores, and a demand table or a "spinner."

Moves (i.e., decisions) are made by months. At the start of the game there are no spare parts in the system, and all of the bases are inactive. Bases are phased-in according to a schedule which is known to the player. Thus, the first base is activated at the end of the tenth month; the second, at the end of the seventeenth month, and so on. A player usually places his initial order during the first game-month of play since procurement lead-time is nine months, and it takes another month to ship parts from the depot to the base.

When a base is activated, its requirements for spares to replace worn-out and repairable widgets is based upon a random demand which fluctuates about a mean value. The player does not know the exact value of the mean, but the planning data provide an estimate. The demand is revealed by a table—which may be uncovered, month by month, as the game progresses—or the spinner may be used to generate demands. The values obtained with the spinner are based on the same distribution as the table.

At the end of 31 months, the game is ended. A player computes his costs and compares them with scores obtained in contemporary or previous plays. "The score is important, of course, but no more so than the player's skill in evaluating the problems that crop up during the play, and his perception of how his decisions have contributed to the total score."[43] Should the player or players replay the game, a different demand pattern may be created by the use of the spinner, or the same demand pattern may be employed again to allow the players to test a different strategy.

Other Manual Games. The games discussed in this chapter emphasize those that are — or were — played at the Naval War College. The Submarine Tactical Game, the JCS Politico-Military Game, the Landing Force War Game, TACSPIEL, THEATERSPIEL, and Monopologs are included to indicate roughly the scope and diversity of manual gaming. Other manual and computer-assisted manual games are conducted by activities such as the Warfare Systems School of the Air University, the U. S. Army Strategy and Tactics Analysis Group, the Canadian Army Operational Research Establishment, and the RAND Corporation.[27]

Chapter V
The NEWS and NEWS Gaming

The Navy Electronic Warfare Simulator (NEWS) is a large and complex system that was designed for the specific purpose of providing students of the Naval War College with an "... opportunity to gain significant combat experience in a realistic setting and under the press of real time."[44] It was conceived as a replacement for the game boards at the College, and planned and constructed as a two-sided electromechanical war gaming system. The NEWS enables players to maneuver forces, receive intelligence, employ weapons, and communicate with friendly forces and umpires. Subject to umpire control, the system also provides means for the automatic monitoring and evaluation of pertinent aspects of the employment and interactions of opposing forces.

The NEWS occupies the three-story center wing of Sims Hall, Naval War College, Newport, R. I. War games played on this simulator are conducted under the direction and supervision of the War Gaming Department of the College. This department is also responsible for the programming and maintenance of the NEWS.

History of the NEWS. During World War II, the Naval War College relied heavily on traditional board games in carrying out its time-honored mission of preparing officers for higher command. While every effort was made to keep the game rules and data abreast or even slightly ahead of the rapidly changing methods and concepts of naval warfare, it was recognized that the simulation techniques of the game board left much to be desired. Consequently, when the Bureau of Ships noted in early 1945 that a combat information center (CIC) trainer developed by the University of California might assist in the conduct of War College games, representatives of the latter institution viewed it with interest. Although the trainer proved to be too limited in scope for gaming purposes, its principles appeared applicable to the College's war gaming requirements, and thus was born the idea of constructing a system or device for the simulation of naval warfare.

In June of 1945 the Naval War College forwarded a request to the Chief of Naval Operations that steps be taken to design and build a warfare simulator. Five months later the Bureau of Ships was directed by the Chief of Naval Operations to develop a simulation system, and the Bureau assigned the responsibility for its planning and construction to the Navy Electronics Laboratory at San Diego, California.

Originally, it was envisioned that the simulator would employ electromechanical means for moving forces, establishing contacts and disseminating intelligence, and would include appropriate communication facilities. Thus, it would eliminate such cumbersome board techniques as filling out move forms, plotting moves, juggling screens and curtains, etc., and permit time to be handled as a continuous rather than a discrete variable. At this early date, no thought appears to have been given to replacing time-consuming manual damage computations with faster and more modern techniques. This serious deficiency (for the types of games then played) was soon recognized, however, and the War College requested that a computing device be included which would automatically evaluate engagements and reduce the speed and firepower of damaged forces.

The unique nature of the overall undertaking required numerous conferences between interested naval activities, a great deal of original research and experimentation and the design and construction of entirely new components, and it was not until 1957 that the system—with the exception of the damage computer—was completed. During the Academic Year 1957–1958, the Command and Staff Department of the College conducted games on the NEWS without the benefit of the damage computer. Although these games were successful, damage computations (employing manual techniques) were difficult to handle, and the games proved the wisdom of the earlier decision to include an automatic damage feature. The damage computer was completed in 1958, and as Rear Admiral Charles H. Lyman* observed: (freed) "... umpires from the backbreaking job of damage evaluation."[37]

While the simulator was conceived initially for War College use, it became apparent—even during the design and installation phases—that the NEWS was a valuable tool for exploring actual naval operations. Hence, when the Navy War Games Program was established, it included NEWS gaming.[31]

At first the NEWS was called the Electronic Generator and Display system (EGDS); later, the Electronic Maneuver Board System (EMBS). After it became operational the name was changed to the Navy Electronic Warfare Simulator. This title is not intended to imply that the system simulates electronic warfare, but that it employs electronic means to simulate warfare.

---

* Chief-of-Staff of the Naval War College, May 1957 to February 1959.

A number of modifications and improvements have been made to the NEWS since its completion in 1958 and in the latter half of 1962 a major modification resulted in the addition of new equipment and the construction of two additional player spaces known as command headquarters.

The responsibility for the NEWS and for NEWS gaming was assigned initially to the Command and Staff Department. Upon the organization of the War Gaming Department, this responsibility was assigned to that department.

The initial cost of the Navy Electronic Warfare Simulator was approximately $7,250,000. Subsequent modifications and improvements have increased the total to approximately $10,000,000.

The War Gaming Department. This department operates and maintains the NEWS. It develops and conducts the College curriculum games that employ the facilities of the NEWS, and provides war gaming services to Fleet Commands in support of the Navy War Games Program. The department develops and presents naval warfare demonstrations on the NEWS, and conducts short annual war gaming courses for each of the academic departments of the College and for officers from the Fleet.

The War Gaming Department consists of a Director, an Assistant Director, an Administration Section and two Divisions, as shown in Figure 5-1. The Operations, Evaluation and Research (OER) Division consists of fourteen officers and two civilians. One officer heads the division; five are assigned to the Gaming Development Branch, five to the Operations and Programming Branch, and three to the Evaluation and Research Branch. One of the civilians is the operations research analyst for the division and department; the second is assigned to the Operations and Programming Branch as a visual aids specialist for preparing, procuring and maintaining the graphic materials required for games, presentations, and lectures.

There are two officers in the Engineering and Maintenance Division; one heads the Division, the other the Maintenance Branch. The Engineering Branch consists of two engineers and four electronic technicians, all civilians; the Maintenance Branch includes forty-five Navy enlisted personnel. The Administration Section consists of three enlisted personnel; the Director's secretary is a civilian.

General Description of the NEWS. The Navy Electronic Warfare Simulator was designed for the play of a two-sided one-map game at speeds of one, two, and four times real time. The system is composed of three major subsystems: maneuver and

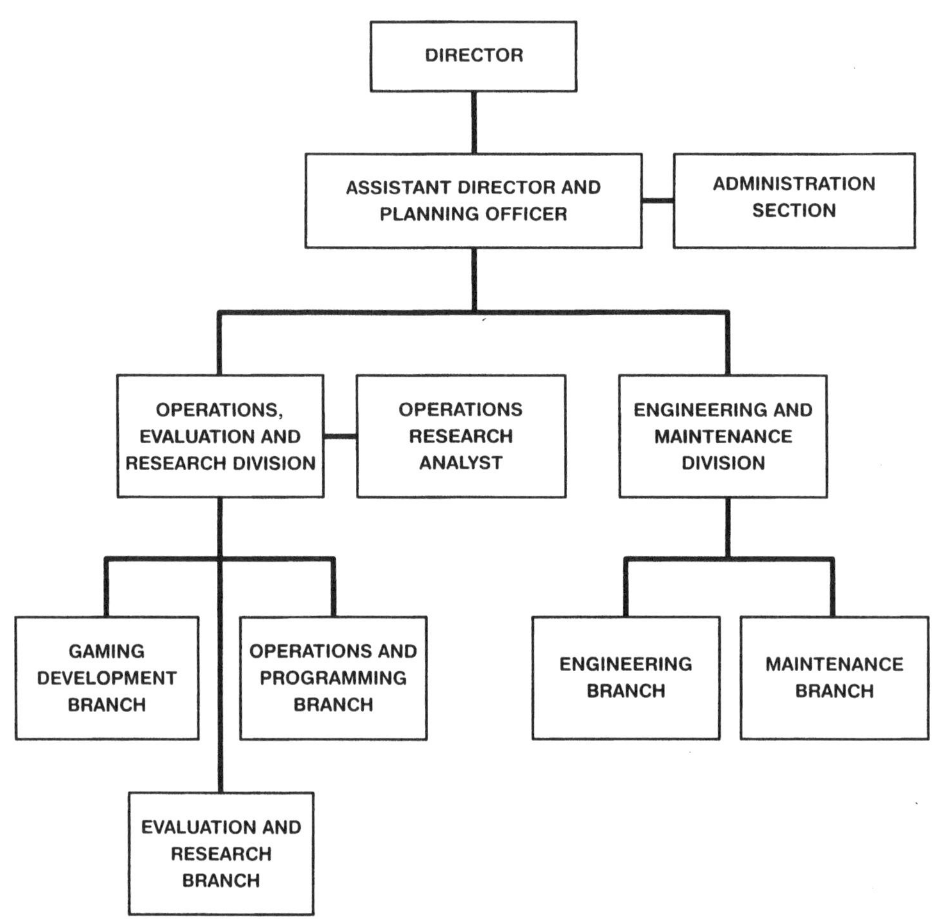

ORGANIZATION OF THE WAR GAMING DEPARTMENT
NAVAL WAR COLLEGE
MARCH 1966

Figure 5-1

display, weapon and damage computer, and communications. The first subsystem is a modern substitute for the game board and its associated model ships, forms, and plotting devices. The weapon and damage computer subsystem takes the place of weapons employment forms, measuring wands, and all of the formulas, tables, and forms needed to manually assess, record, and disseminate the effects of weapons employment. The communications subsystem furnishes the facilities for simulating and monitoring interforce communications, and for communications between members of the control group and between umpires and players.

Elements of the three subsystems are located in the various player rooms and in the control group area. Since the system was designed for two-sided war gaming, half the player spaces were planned and equipped for the players on one side; half for the players on the other side. Similarly, appropriate regions and equipments in the control group area were equally divided between two sides. Following war gaming custom, the spaces and equipment for the opposing sides were designated by colors, Green for the opposition, White for the "friendly."

Twenty player rooms known as command centers are located on the third floor (See Figure 5-2). They are grouped into two sections, one consisting of ten Green command centers, the other of ten White. A larger player room is located on the second floor. This is referred to as the White command headquarters. A similar command headquarters for the Green side is located on the first floor. The command headquarters and centers contain the equipment and controls required by the players for the command and control of assigned force in a NEWS war game.

The control group area is divided into four parts: umpire area, communications room, control room, and equipment room. As the name implies, the umpire area is the room which contains the equipment and facilities that enable the umpires to observe the actions and interactions of forces and weapons, inject professional judgment into the control of the game, and initiate changes and modifications to the automatic monitoring and evaluation functions of the simulator. It is dominated by a large master plot screen which depicts the area of operations, and upon which is projected the moving images of all active forces, Green and White. The umpire area contains equipment which permits the umpires to project themselves into any command center and to "see" the forces—friendly and enemy—that the players in that command center have under their immediate surveillance, to "listen in" on the communications between the command centers on either side, and to know what damage has been suffered by each and every force.

Above the umpire area is a balcony with seating arrangements for approximately ninety. During a game the balcony is used by spectators to observe the play

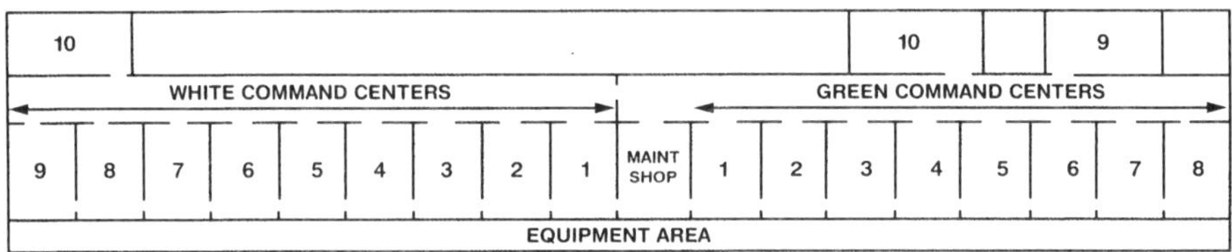

THIRD FLOOR

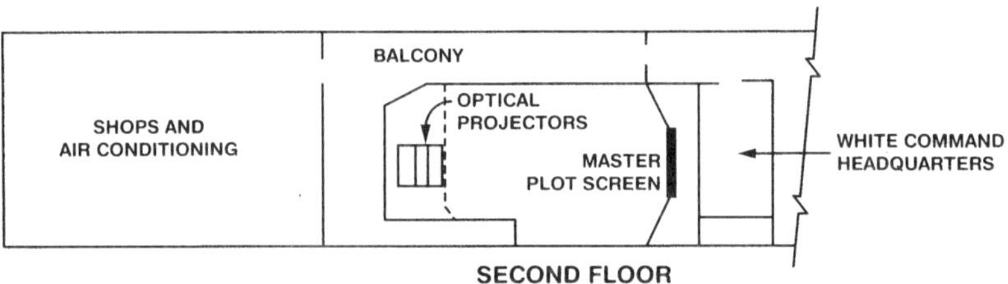

SECOND FLOOR

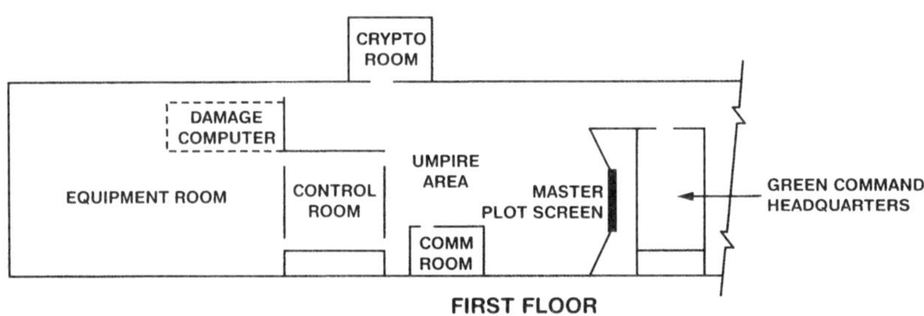

FIRST FLOOR

SCHEMATIC OF NEWS AREAS

Figure 5-2

as it unfolds on the master plot screen and on matrices of lights that signal the employment of weapons. During and after games players may be assembled in the balcony or in the rear of the umpire area for briefings and critiques.

The communications, control, and equipment rooms (plus some areas on the third floor) contain much of the equipment required for getting the system ready for the play of a game (programming), for operating the system, and for making programming changes during the conduct of a game.

Area of Operations. The NEWS has a design capability of representing four ocean sizes or areas of operations: 40 by 40, 400 by 400, 1000 by 1000 and 4000 by 4000 nautical miles.* Positions within an area of operations are identified by a fixed grid that is independent of the size of the area. The origin of coordinates of the NEWS grid is at the lower left, and it has 4000 horizontal or east–west (EW) units and an equal number of vertical or north–south (NS) divisions. Thus, if the coordinates of a position are 1000 EW and 2000 NS, it is 10 miles to the grid east and 20 miles to the grid north of the lower left corner of a 40 by 40 mile area of operations, 100 miles east and 200 miles north in a 400 mile area, 250 miles east and 500 miles north in a 1000 mile area, and so on.

Forces. The NEWS system has 48 active forces; that is, 48 forces which may be maneuvered by the players. Those numbered from 1 to 24 are permanently assigned to the Green command centers; forces 25 to 48, to the White command centers. Since there are more forces on a side than command centers, some centers have more than one force. Thus, on each side, four command centers contain 1 force each; two, 2 forces; and four, 4 forces (See Table 5-1).

The Green command headquarters contains controls and indicators for force 1; the White command headquarters, controls and indicators for force 25. As with many other gaming practices, the assignment of forces to the command headquarters and centers is a compromise between the real-world systems represented and the constraints imposed by space and equipment limitations. It permits the use of more forces in a game than would be possible if only one force was assigned to a command center.

The 48 NEWS forces can also be maneuvered by control group personnel stationed in the control room. This control of forces may be exercised whether or not there are players in the command centers. If players are in a command center and the force or forces assigned to that center are maneuvered from the control room,

* Other sizes may be used. See the section Scaling Factors and Other Gimmicks in this chapter.

Table 5-1

DISTRIBUTION OF NEWS FORCE AMONG COMMAND CENTERS			
Side	**Command Center Number**	**Number of Assigned Forces**	**Force Numbers**
GREEN	1	1	1
	2	1	2
	3	2	3,4
	4	4	5,6,7,8
	5	4	9,10,11,12
	6	4	13,14,15,16
	7	4	17,18,19,20
	8	2	21,22
	9	1	23
	10	1	24
	GREEN Command Headquarters	*	*
WHITE	1	1	25
	2	1	26
	3	2	27,28
	4	4	29,30,31,32
	5	4	33,34,35,36
	6	4	37,38,39,40
	7	4	41,42,43,44
	8	2	45,46
	9	1	47
	10	1	48
	WHITE Command Headquarters	**	**

* Controls and Indicators for Force 1.
** Controls and Indicators for Force 25.

then the players may be given or denied a readout of the course, speed, and altitude or depth of the NEWS forces assigned to their command center.

A NEWS force may be used to represent a single ship, aircraft, submarine, and so on, and in some instances, aggregations or combinations of such units. Each force is projected on the master plot screen as a single image. The shape and color of a projected image reflects the nature and side of the real-world or hypothetical force represented, and both the shape and color of an image may be changed manually from game to game, or during lunch or other breaks, as the situation dictates. Each NEWS force may also appear as a single blip on radar-type scopes known as azimuth range indicators (ARI's) which are located in both the player and control group spaces. All blips are approximately equal in size, and the size of a blip is independent of the nature and composition of the unit or units represented. For instance, if NEWS force number 7 is used to represent a single bomber and NEWS force 25 an Attack Carrier Striking Force, the blips depicting force 7 and 25 on the ARI's are equal in size.

In addition to mobility, a NEWS force can simulate the sensor systems and offensive capability of its real-world counterpart, and its vulnerability to attack by enemy weapons. The command center to which a NEWS force is assigned contains facilities for simulating the communications capabilities of the actual forces represented.

Once it is determined what a NEWS force will represent during a particular game, or for part of a game, then that force is programmed with the pertinent characteristics of the unit or units which it represents. The characteristics that may be assigned (or denied) to a NEWS force are: maximum speed, rates of ascent and descent (if the force represents aircraft or a submarine), detection and intelligence gathering capabilities under various player-selected sensoring options, and the conditions and ranges at which the force can be detected and recognized by other forces in the system. Other characteristics which may be assigned or denied are weapons capabilities and the capacity to sustain damage from enemy weapons and to suffer a degradation of maximum speed and offensive capabilities as a result of such damage.

In addition to the 48 movable forces, the NEWS contains 14 forces that are known as fixed forces or fixed targets. These forces are included for the purpose of representing navigational aids, landmarks, and so on. They can be manually positioned from the control room and assigned to any desired coordinate positions in the area of operations. The fixed forces may be displayed on the ARI's, and may be detected by the simulated sensor systems of active forces. They cannot be projected on the master plot screen, but may be displayed on that screen by hand-applied symbols. Fixed forces cannot be controlled by the players, or assigned mobility or detection capabilities. Neither can they inflict or sustain damage.

Command Centers. The command centers contain the basic facilities for the command and control of assigned forces. A command center may simulate a flag plot, combat information center, operations control center, command post, and so on. If desired, the facilities of two or more command centers may be combined by the use of interconnecting doors.

Figure 5-3 shows the forward section of a typical command center. In the front part are the azimuth range indicators. Each ARI has a range selector switch. This switch enables a player to select at will any one of six range scales: 320, 160, 80, 40, 20, and 8 miles. A force associated with an azimuth range indicator appears as a blip in the center of the scope. Other forces, friendly and enemy, that come within

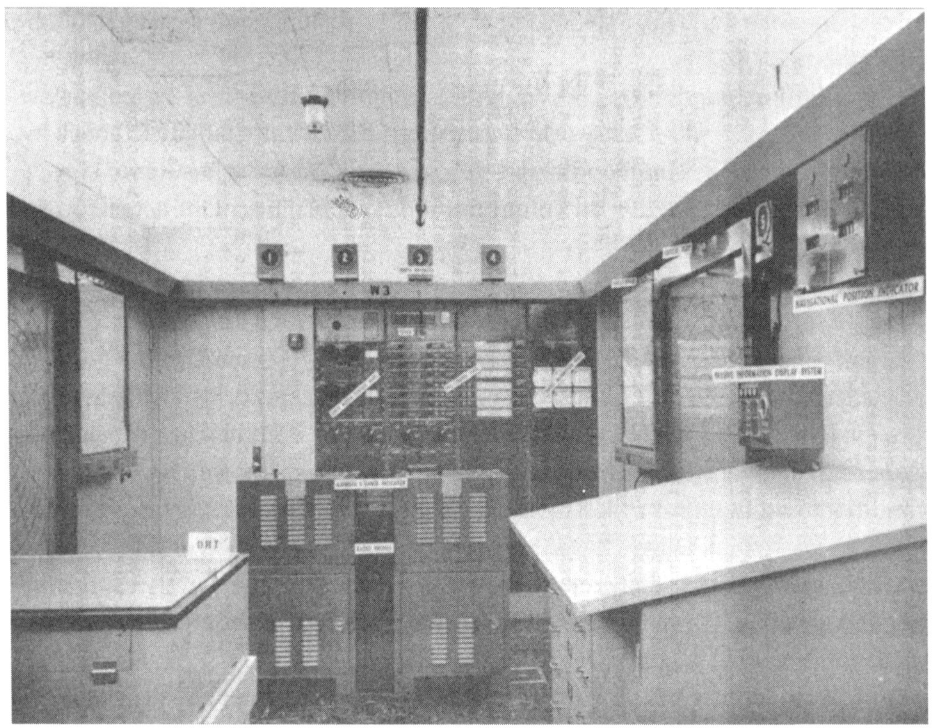

A NEWS Command Center

Figure 5-3

the detection ranges of that force, appear as blips on the scope, and the range and bearings of the blips may be read directly from a polar plot inscribed on the face of the scope. A hand-operated light-sensitive probe provides a means of interrogating any blip. When a blip is interrogated, up to six items of evaluated intelligence of the force represented by the blip may be indicated on a target information panel at the right front of the room. Additionally, if so programmed, the course and speed, and/or the NEWS force number of the probed force may be read out.

A NEWS force may be programmed to receive a "remote look," that is, the "look" of a distant force. For example, if force 25 represents the White flagship and force 28 a White aircraft on an air early warning mission, the presentation that appears on the ARI associated with force 28 may also be displayed on an ARI in the command center which houses force 25, the flagship.

Blips appearing on the ARI's provide both bearing and distance information. For passive or "bearing only" intelligence, a panel of the passive information display system (PIDS) is mounted on the right wall of each command center. Passive electronic or sonar intelligence is originated by the umpires, transmitted to the appropriate command centers, and displayed on these panels.

In the front of each command center and to the rear of the azimuth range indicators are force motion control panels (Figure 5-4). These panels contain the knobs and dials for controlling and reading the course and speed of a force. A change in course can be made at a maximum rate of six degrees per second. A speed dial is labeled from 0 to 50, and one of three adjacent multipliers (1, 10 and 100) is used to indicate which of the following three speed ranges is programmed: 0 to 50, 0 to 500, or 0 to 5,000 knots. Acceleration from 0 to the maximum reading on a speed dial requires approximately 30 seconds. The instantaneous location of any force in a command center is displayed in NEWS grid coordinates on coordinate counters mounted on the right walls of the centers. These counters may be covered if it is desired to deny this information to the players. The track of a selected force may be automatically plotted on a dead reckoning tracer (DRT) installed at the rear of each command center. Game time is displayed by a game clock, and an associated indicator reveals the time multiplier or game speed in use: 1, 2, or 4. Game speeds may be changed in the control room as the director desires. When such a change is made the indicator changes to the new game speed, and the motion of forces adjusts automatically to the new speed. If a game is stopped for any reason, the game clocks read the time at which the game was stopped, and the game-speed indicator reads 0.

A force motion control panel also contains push buttons for the maneuvering of its associated force in five numbered and different altitudes or depths. These five, third-dimensional levels (usually referred to as bands) may be programmed to represent any desired altitudes and depths, and the forces may be assigned realistic rates of ascent and descent, that is, realistic times may be programmed for a force to shift from one altitude or depth level (band) to another. The five bands may also be used to permit players to select at any time one of up to five previously determined operating conditions for the sensor systems of their forces. Thus, band 1 might be programmed to represent a condition in which neither active radar nor sonar are employed; band 2, the employment of active sonar; band 3, the use of active radar, and so on. In this case, if a player wishes to employ radar, he pushes the button associated with band 3, and his force is automatically assigned an active radar detection capability.

Fire control panels are located at approximately the front center of each command center (See Figure 5-4). These panels contain the controls and indicators for the employment of weapons. Four NEWS weapons, A, B, C and D, are

Force Motion Control and Fire Control Panels

Figure 5-4

permanently assigned to each NEWS force. A NEWS weapon may be used to represent a single real-world or hypothetical weapon, or an aggregation of such weapons. It may be fired by single salvos, or placed on automatic fire. In either case, the rate of fire is pre-set to approximate the actual or assumed rate. Salvo remaining counters show the initial number of salvos available to each weapon, and automatically record and display ammunition availability at any instant during a game. When a weapon runs out of ammunition it is automatically deactivated.

If an enemy force is read out on a target information display panel, the players controlling the interrogating force may acquire the enemy force with one or more weapons, and if and when they so choose, press the firing key or keys. When this is done, a bell and a visual signal in the target's command center warns the target force that it is under attack. Should a hit (or hits) be made, the system may be programmed so that a light flashes on the firing force's fire control panel to notify that force that it has scored a hit, or the hit signal may be denied. The percent of damage to the target resulting from a hit or hits causes a corresponding drop in the effectiveness remaining meters of the target force. One of these meters is located on the force's motion control panel, another on its characteristics panel in the control room, and a third is located in the umpire area. Effectiveness remaining meters are graduated from 0 to 100 percent, and an undamaged force is assigned an effectiveness remaining of 100 percent.

Each command center contains facilities for inter-player and player-to-control-group communications. Inter-player communication facilities include eight wall-mounted speakers and associated handsets, and a teletype unit. The teletype units provide a means for simulating landline teletypes, radio teletypes, etc. The speakers and the handsets are normally used to simulate voice radio nets such as primary tactical (PriTac), HUK (Hunter-Killer) air common, and so on, and the nets are arranged to conform to the players' communications plans. If umpires in a game are acting as subordinates to the players, the required command and control circuits may be set up between the appropriate command centers and umpire area. Additionally, selected voice radio channels may be patched into loud speakers in the umpire area so that communications between player-commands can be broadcast into that area.

A problem (game) control intercommunication (PCI) system provides for two-way communications between command centers and umpires. This system is intended chiefly for game control purposes and for the transmission of verbal intelligence from umpires to players. An in-house dial telephone system provides a link between players in the command centers and equipment maintenance personnel, and an additional link, if so planned in the rules of the game, between the umpires and players. Each command center also contains switches for the transmission of digital-coded information. This system is called the force operating status indicator (FOSI) system, and it provides a one-way visual communications link from each force in a command center to the umpire area. Outputs are displayed in two-digit form below the respective force numbers at the front of the umpire area. The umpires can acknowledge receipt of information received, but cannot transmit over this system.

In addition to the equipment previously described, each command center contains a drafting table and plotting tools, two three-foot edge lighted status boards, two five-foot edge lighted polar plotting boards, a blackboard, and a bulletin board.

Command Headquarters. The two command headquarters contain much of the same equipment as the command centers. They are, however, larger than the command centers, and are usually assigned to the highest level player-commanders. The command headquarters do not contain NEWS forces but, as shown in Table 5-1, each contains the controls and indicators for one force on their respective sides and the coordinate counters, effectiveness remaining meters, and under attack signals associated with these forces. The command headquarters do not contain controls or indicators for weapons employment, or salvo remaining counters. Each contains one azimuth range indicator console on which is mounted a target information panel. These consoles are not fixed in a position as are those in the command centers, but may be moved about as desired, or even removed from the room.

Umpire Area. The umpire area contains the equipment required for monitoring the employment and interactions of opposing forces, and for controlling the game. At the front of the area is the master plot screen. As noted previously, this screen provides the umpires with a model of the area of operations used in a game. The moving images of active forces are projected on the screen from a bank of optical projectors situated high and to the rear of the room. There is one projector for each of the 48 movable forces. Cameras are located above and to one side of the optical projector rack for taking color or black and white transparencies of the master plot screen for use during critiques; on the other side, slide and overhead projectors for displaying weather and other information on the master plot screen when and as required by the umpires.

The master plot screen is fifteen feet square, and constructed of plexiglass (Figure 5-5). Behind the screen and its adjacent panels are three plotting tiers and banks of ultraviolet lights. Plotting paper is suspended from the rear top of the screen and tracks of ships and aircraft, symbols, etc. are plotted on the paper with fluorescent crayons, yarns, and paper. The plotters work on the three tiers behind the screen, and wear protective goggles to shield their eyes from the ultraviolet lights which illuminate the plot. The screen is coated to prevent the ultraviolet rays from entering the umpire area.

Prior to a game, charts of the area of operations with a superimposed NEWS grid are prepared and issued to the players. These represent the maps that would normally be available to commanders and their staffs for planning and plotting purposes. The original of these charts is photographed and reproduced as a negative slide. This slide is then projected from the rear of the umpire area to the master plot screen, and coastlines, roads, airfields, etc. are plotted on the paper at the rear of the screen.

At some distance to the left of the master plot, the Green command center numbers and Green force numbers (1 to 24) are listed on a vertical bank of 24 panels. At the right of each force number is a polar plot indicator. This doughnut

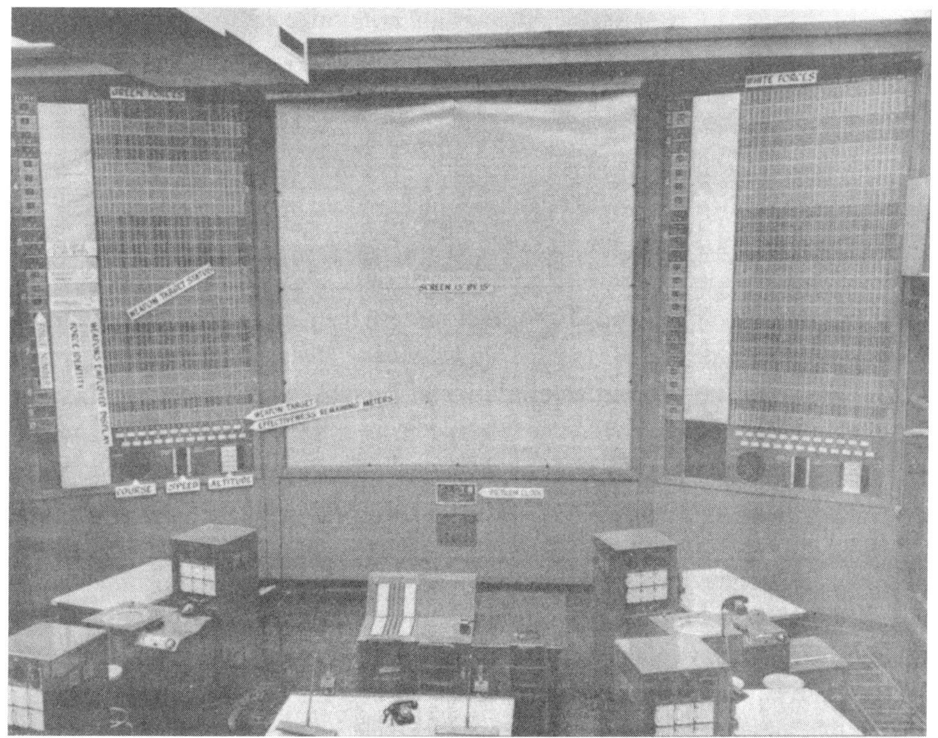

Master Plot Screen

Figure 5-5

shaped indicator illuminates when a polar plot is displayed around the force image on the master plot. Below the force number and polar plot indicator are five band indicators. These indicate the current altitude, depth, or operating band of a force, and whether or not it is in the process of shifting from one band to another.

To the right of the panels containing the force numbers is a vertical plexiglass side panel. This panel is used for displaying the names of the real-world forces and weapons represented by the respective NEWS forces and weapons. The names are lettered on sheets of paper, one for each NEWS force, and the sheets are attached, as required, to the rear of the plexiglass. If the forces represented by a NEWS force are changed during a game, a new name sheet is prepared to replace the old.

Adjacent to the plexiglass panel is a column of 96 weapons employment lights. These lights are arranged in vertical groups of four. One of these groups is directly opposite each of the 24 Green force-number panels, and the individual lights in each group indicate the status of each of the four NEWS weapons (A, B, C and

D) of the respective Green forces. When a light is illuminated, the corresponding weapon is programmed and available for use by the players in the command center; when it is not illuminated, the weapon is inactive, i.e., it is either not programmed or it is out of ammunition.

Alongside the left side of the master plot is a second and parallel column of Green force numbers. Below each is a two-digit readout of the force operating status indicator (FOSI) system. As noted in the section describing the command centers, these readouts are activated from the command centers and enable the umpires to receive digital-coded information from the players. Next to the column of force numbers and digital readouts is a column of "own side" lights, one for each of the Green weapons. These lights indicate the acquisition of a Green force as a target by weapons on the Green side, and the firing of these weapons. If weapon A of Green force 7 acquires any force on the Green side, the own side light opposite the weapon light is illuminated. Should that weapon fire, the own side light blinks. The blinking light signals the firing of Green weapon 7A at a force on its own side. However, it does not indicate which Green force was fired at.

Between the column of own side lights, and the column of weapons employment lights, is a 96 by 24 matrix of lights known as the weapon-target matrix. The 96 rows correspond to the Green weapons; the 24 columns identify the twenty-four White forces or targets. The columns are labeled, top and bottom, with the White force numbers, and effectiveness remaining meters for the White forces are located at the bottom of the matrix.

When a Green force acquires a White force (target) with a weapon, the light at the intersection of the corresponding weapon row and target column of the weapon-target matrix is illuminated. If the Green weapon is fired, the light flashes. Should the weapon score a hit, the effectiveness remaining meter of the White force indicates a reduction in the effectiveness remaining of that force. Whether or not a hit is scored, and the amount of damage resulting from a hit, is determined by the damage computer.

To the right of the master plot screen is a similar arrangement of force numbers, band indicators, weapon-target matrix, and so on for the White side.

Below the effectiveness remaining meters on both sides of the master plot screen are several umpire information readout panels. These readout panels permit the umpires to obtain, at any time, a readout of the course, speed and altitude or depth of a selected force, and its speed and altitude or depth limits. Readouts are activated manually by an operator at the plot console.

The plot console is located in the forward part of the umpire area. By means of push button controls, the operator at this console can, as requested by an umpire, display umpire information readouts, blink any projected force image so that it may be identified on the master plot screen, or project a polar plot about any projected force image. The polar plot enables an umpire to obtain the ranges and bearings directly from the master plot. In addition, the operator can activate the slide projectors which project weather and other environmental information on the master plot.

Up to four azimuth range indicators (ARI's) and associated target information readout cabinets may be installed, as desired, in the umpire area. These ARI's permit an umpire to position any force in the center of the scope, and to obtain the same scope presentation as seen by the player in a command center. An umpire may also select an "umpire look," in which case he sees all forces within the range of the scope regardless of whether or not they appear on the player's scope. Additionally, an umpire may set the center of the scope to any desired grid position within the area of operations and obtain a scope presentation centered on that position.

Four problem control intercommunication (PCI) consoles may be set up in the umpire area. These are part of the problem (game) control intercom system mentioned previously in the section on command centers. The PCI consoles and their associated handsets enable the umpires to communicate with other umpires in the umpire area, and with command centers and headquarters, communications room, control room and damage computer. They also permit the umpires to monitor inter-player voice radio communication nets, broadcast inter-player transmissions throughout the umpire area, and broadcast information from the umpire area to selected areas within the NEWS. Additionally, electric powered headset (EPH) circuits may be arranged, as needed, between umpires, status board keepers, control room personnel, and so on.

The in-house dial telephone system discussed earlier in the section on command centers provides a second system by which the umpires may communicate with the players. This system also enables the umpires to communicate with various control group and maintenance areas, and with the office spaces of the War Gaming Department. The dial phone system can, if desired, be patched into offices in other areas of Sims Hall.

The PCI, EPH, and dial phone systems comprise the complete set of umpire and control group voice communications circuits and equipment that were installed when the NEWS was built. Since that time other communications facilities have been added for the conduct of task group and task force level games in which umpires, acting as subordinates to the player-commanders, maneuver the forces. These facilities include circuits and equipment for the establishment, as desired, of additional umpire-to-umpire communications, and direct voice communications between specific umpire positions and command centers and headquarters. Also, circuits and outlets have been provided in various sections of the umpire area so that teletypes and tape cutters may easily be installed for use during remote-play Fleet games.

When the passive information display system (PIDS) is used in a game, two transmitting panels are set up in the umpire area. One panel serves the Green side; the other, the White side. Passive intelligence is generated by the umpires in accordance with the rules of the game and from distances and bearings obtained from the master plot screen or the azimuth range indicators, and then transmitted manually to the appropriate forces. If the force operating status indicator (FOSI) system is employed, two portable control boxes are placed in the umpire area, one for each side. These boxes enable the umpires to acknowledge receipt of player messages transmitted over the FOSI system.

Three game-time clocks and game-speed indicator units are located in the umpire area; one below the master plot screen and one in each of the two front corners. Above each of the latter two clocks is a sign which indicates whether it is dark or daylight in the game area of operations. These signs are controlled manually from the control room. On the right wall is a panel of lights called the detectability and look indicator panel. This panel consists of 48 sections, one for each NEWS force. Each section contains a NEWS force number and six lights. Three of the lights may be used to indicate the types of sensoring devices that may detect the associated NEWS force; the other three, to indicate the types of sensoring devices currently employed by that force. These light indicators are changed if, as a force shifts from one band (altitude, depth, or operating) to another, there is a change in status. Thus, if a force representing a submarine submerges below periscope depth, the light indicating that it is detectable by radar (or visually), is deactivated. These changes are made manually by personnel in the equipment room.

The umpire area also contains a number of tables, edge-lighted status boards and similar equipment. This sort of equipment is moved in and out of the area as needed, and is arranged to suit the requirements of a particular game.

The umpire area status boards are used for posting task organizations, call-signs, contact reports, and for recording events and the status of aggregated forces, airfields, and so on. These boards are photographed periodically. The information contained on the photographs of the status boards is correlated with the information contained on the photographs of the master plot screen and with the records of the umpires for the post-game analyses, reports and critiques.

Communications, Control, and Equipment Rooms. The communications, control, and equipment rooms, as well as a few other spaces, contain the electronic and mechanical equipment required for the programming, operation, and maintenance of the NEWS. Only a general knowledge of the functions performed in these areas is needed by players and by officers who are called upon to augment the War Gaming Staff for the control of a game.

The communications room contains panels and jacks for the establishment of player voice communication nets prior to the play of a game, and for changing these nets or breaking communications between forces during a game. It also has a panel and jacks for setting up, as required, direct voice communications circuits between designated umpire positions and players. The effects of voice communications countermeasures can be introduced into the simulated voice radio circuits, and the circuits can be bridged so that the players on one side may hear some of the transmissions of their opponents. In-game net changes, communications interruptions, countermeasures, and bridging are manually injected when and as directed by the cognizant umpires.

There are two tape recorders in the communications room. These are used to transmit taped messages or information over selected circuits, and to record communications as desired. In addition, the room contains a teletypewriter with tape perforator and reader for transmitting and receiving selected command center and command headquarters messages, and facilities for establishing one teletype net on each of the opposing sides.

The control room contains 48 sets of panels, one set for each NEWS force. The sets for the Green side, forces 1 through 24, are lined up on one side of the room; the sets for the White side, forces 25 through 48, on the other side. Each set of panels contains two panels arranged one above the other. The bottom panel of each set is the force characteristics panel. This panel contains an effectiveness remaining meter and switches and other controls for inserting certain operational characteristics and controls of the real-world force represented by the respective NEWS force. For example, if NEWS force 7 is used to represent a bomber, then its maximum speed and maximum altitude band are programmed. Also, switches are arranged so that up to six items of evaluated intelligence concerning force 7 are programmed. Then if force 7 appears as a blip on any azimuth range indicator, and the blip is probed, the programmed items of intelligence will be displayed on the target information panel associated with the azimuth range indicator. Additionally, control of force 7 may be given to the players in the command center to which force 7 is permanently assigned (command center 4—see Table 5-1 for the assignment of NEWS forces to command centers), or the players may simply be allowed to read out its course, speed and altitude as displayed on the course and speed dials and altitude indicators in the command center. Or, if desired, both controls and indication can be denied. In the latter two cases, force 7 is maneuvered in altitude by controls on its characteristics panel, while its course and speed are controlled from its navigation computer.

A navigation computer is associated with each active NEWS force. The navigation computer panel for each force is located above the corresponding force's characteristics panel. Each navigation computer contains a NEWS grid coordinate counter and grid-position controls. The latter enables control group personnel to program the initial position of a force; the former, to read out the position of a force in grid coordinates at any instant during a game. Course and speed dials permit the setting of initial course and speed, a readout of course and speed during play or, if desired, control of course and speed. As in the command centers, the speed dials are calibrated from 0 to 50. Adjacent speed range multipliers of 1, 10, and 100 permit the setting of speed range scales of 50, 500, or 5000 knots. For example, a NEWS force simulating a destroyer with a top speed of 32 knots is assigned a speed multiplier of 1, while a force representing an aircraft with a maximum speed of 600 knots is given a speed multiplier of 100. The 0 to 50 calibrations on their speed dials then represent 0 to 50 and 0 to 5000 knots respectively. However, a player cannot drive either force beyond the maximum speeds programmed in their characteristics panels, which in this example would be 32 and 600 knots. Additionally, if so programmed in the characteristics panel, the top speed of a force is reduced automatically in direct proportion to damage sustained. Thus, if the effectiveness remaining meter of the destroyer drops to 75 percent, its top speed is automatically reduced to 24 knots.

At the rear of the control room are switches for setting the size of the area of operations (the ocean scale switch), and for setting and changing, as desired, game time and speed of play. There are also facilities for positioning the 14 fixed forces and, as in the case of active forces, for programming up to six items of intelligence. Other equipment includes an azimuth range indicator (and associated target information panel), and two panels containing position matching switches. These switches enable control room personnel to slave up to three forces on one side to another force (a master force) on the same side. Thus, forces representing aircraft may be slaved to a carrier until such time as the aircraft may be launched.

The equipment room is located to the rear of the control room. This room contains the units for programming the rates of ascent and descent for NEWS forces that are used to represent aircraft or submarines. There is one of these units for each NEWS force. When a NEWS force, say force number 7, is used as an aircraft, eight time delay components are inserted in the ascent and descent unit. Then the realistic times required for that particular type of aircraft to climb from band one to band two, from two to three, etc., are inserted in four delay components; the times required to descend from band five to band four, and so on, in the other four units.

Across from the ascent and descent units are the detectability and look panels, one panel for each force. Each panel contains dials and switches for programming its respective force with that force's real-world susceptibility to detection by specific types of sensoring devices. For instance, if force 7 represents an aircraft, it is susceptible to detection by radar, but not by sonar. This characteristic is called the "detectability" of that force. Each force panel also contains the dials and switches for programming the capabilities of the sensoring systems of the real-world force it represents. This characteristic is called "look." As an aircraft, force 7, then would be programmed with a radar look, but no sonar look.

In order to assign detectability and look characteristics to a NEWS force, three separate and distinct electronic detectability and look circuits are included in the NEWS. These are referred to as busses, A, B and C. If a force, say a submarine, is assigned a sonar detectability on bus C, then only forces with a look in this bus can detect the submarine. The detection and look capabilities and values for each bus are programmed as a function of the altitude (depth, or operating) band. For instance, if a submarine is operating on the surface, it can be detected by a force with a radar or visual look capability, and in turn can detect aircraft and ships. If a player or a member of the control group causes the submarine to dive below periscope depth by shifting depth bands, then the submarine's detectability and look capabilities are changed automatically. The submarine can no longer be detected by radar or visual means, nor can it see forces representing aircraft. However, it can be detected by forces with a sonar capability, and detect surface and subsurface forces with its own sonar equipment.

Below the detectability and look panels for the 48 active NEWS forces are detectability panels for the 14 fixed forces. The dials and switches on these panels permit the assignment of detectability characteristics and values to the fixed forces. Adjacent to the fixed force detectability and look panels is an array of switches. These switches may be used to signal the umpires the current detectability and look status of the forces in terms of programmed busses. Thus, if a force representing a submarine is detectable and has a look in busses A and B, this information may be displayed on the detectability and look panel in the umpire area. When the force shifts to another band which has a programmed detectability and look, say in bus C only, then the corresponding switches are manually activated to display this information in the umpire area.

The NEWS damage computer is also located in the equipment room. This computer is described briefly in the next section.

On the third floor, in the areas to the rear of the command centers, are facilities for programming the rates of fire of each of the four NEWS weapons associated with each NEWS force. In addition, there is some equipment for inserting, under very limited conditions, the time of flight or running times of such weapons as missiles and torpedoes. These various facilities are part of the weapon and damage computer subsystem.

For remote-play games, a cryptographic room has been established on the first floor. This room contains facilities for encoding and decoding six full duplex (simultaneous transmit and receive) circuits. These circuits are connected to commercial landline telephone circuits as needed for a remote-play game and, by secure lines, to outlets in the umpire area. Six full duplex teletypes and three tape factories (facilities for cutting or reproducing paper tapes) are available. The teletypes are usually used to transmit tapes produced by the tape factory, and to receive printed and tape copies. However, keyboard transmissions may be sent if desired.

The NEWS Damage Computer. The damage computer is the major component of the weapon and damage computer subsystem. As noted previously, other parts of this subsystem such as weapons employment lights, weapon-target matrix, and effectiveness remaining meters are located in the umpire area; and components such as weapons controls, salvos remaining counters, under attack signals, effectiveness remaining meters, and rate of fire controls are located in or to the rear of the command centers.

The damage computer is a special-purpose, time-shared, on-line analog computer which follows a fixed and unchangeable sequence of operations. The computer accepts and stores for each weapon-type and target-type combination that may be used in a game the parameters for computing hit probability as a linear function of slant range, and the expected or average percent of target-life lost per hit. Typical weapon-type, target-type combinations are: a surface-to-air missile versus a bomber, a thousand pound bomb versus a cruiser, and so on.

Each NEWS force is assigned an appropriate target type. For instance, if forces 5, 6, 7 and 8 simulate individual and identical bombers, then each is assigned the same target type. Similarly, all NEWS weapons employed in a game are assigned appropriate weapon types. Thus, if weapons A and B for forces 5, 6, 7 and 8 are each used to simulate a one-thousand pound bomb, then each is assigned the identical weapon type.

When a player in a command center acquires an opposing force and fires a weapon, this information is displayed in the umpire area by a light on the weapon-target matrix, and in the target force's command center by an under attack indicator. The damage computer calculates the slant range between the firing and target forces and, using the stored weapon-type target-type parameters for the weapon and target involved, computes the hit probability. Then, by means of a random noise generator (a chance device that is functionally analogous to a pair of dice or a table of random numbers), the computer determines if the weapon hits or misses. Should a hit be obtained, and depending upon programming, the firing force may or may not receive an indication of a successful firing. A hit results in damage to the target force. This loss of life is shown by a corresponding reduction in the readout of the target force's effectiveness remaining meters in the umpire area, characteristics panel, and command center. The percent loss of life may be the expected percent which is stored for the particular weapon-type, target-type combination or, depending upon programming, it may be a value selected at random from a Gaussian distribution with the stored value as a mean.

Damage to a NEWS force (as reflected in its effectiveness remaining meters) can, if the computer is so programmed, result in a reduction in its maximum speed, or a reduction in its offensive capability, or both.

If a player on the Green side should acquire and fire at a Green force, this information is displayed on the own side lights in the umpire area. The Green weapon will expend ammunition, but it cannot inflict damage because the damage computer does not assess interactions between Green weapons and Green forces, or between White weapons and White forces. In these situations the target force does not receive an under attack signal.

A damage computer console enables its operators to monitor the operations of the computer, and modify, as directed by the umpires, stored weapon and target data and the results of automatically assessed damage. The console contains a weapon-target matrix similar to that in the umpire area, and limited facilities for the acquisition of forces and the firing of weapons.

System Capabilities. The subsystems and associated equipment and spaces of the NEWS provide the means for the conduct of two-sided continuous-time machine games in which players maneuver forces, fire weapons, and so on. The system eliminates the need for players making moves for stated periods of time, or for

The Damage Computer

Figure 5-6

back tracking if a critical situation develops in the middle of a move. Detections are made automatically; concomitant intelligence is available immediately. Weapons can be fired by simply pressing keys. Damage assessment is automatic, and practically instantaneous. Umpires are relieved of many tedious and time-consuming details; are free to watch the larger picture, to inject their professional judgment into the game. Time may be speeded to two or four times real-world time when forces are jockeying for position, and slowed when interactions develop. A game may be stopped at any time, started again when convenient, or it may be stopped and then continued in a smaller area of operations.

In certain instances NEWS forces can be used to represent an aggregation of ships or aircraft. Also, a force may be used to simulate a variety of real-world forces during the conduct of a single game. Force 7, for instance, might be used to represent a single bomber on an armed reconnaissance mission in one part of a game, and a flight of four bombers on a strike mission in another part of the game. In each case it would be assigned the appropriate characteristics, weapons, and target type.

While the NEWS was designed for the conduct of two-sided machine games of the type described above, it is readily adaptable to one-sided games. In such a game the umpires, from their vantage point in the umpire area, and using the display facilities, controls and communications at their disposal, can provide the required amount and degree of opposition to meet the purpose of the game. The forces at their disposal can be maneuvered by control group personnel stationed in command centers or in the control room. Additionally, the control room and communications facilities provide the means for the conduct of both one or two-sided games in which the umpires act as lower echelon commanders. In these games the umpires maneuver the forces in response to the orders of player-superiors. The players may be stationed in the NEWS command centers or in their own operations control centers or flag plots.

The NEWS command headquarters and centers, plotting and display devices, game clock, and communications nets also provide excellent facilities for the conduct of manual games.

Equipment Limitations. As designed, the NEWS is capable of representing only four sizes of areas of operations, and simulating 48 forces, 24 on one side and an equal number on the other. Game time may be one, two or four times real time, but changes in game time affect only the horizontal component of the speed of forces. It does not affect turning rates, programmed rates of ascent and descent, or programmed firing rates. For instance, if an aircraft requires six minutes of real time to climb from band 2 to 3 at a game speed of one, it requires an equal amount of real world time (or twenty-four minutes of game time) to make that same climb if the game speed is switched to four.

While the size of an area of operations can be changed during a game, a change of this nature requires the determination of new grid positions for all forces, and the repositioning of forces in terms of grid coordinates. If land areas are involved, charts and slides must be prepared in advance so that a new master plot can be drawn.

The NEWS does not automatically track or record the positions and status of forces. It does not keep a tally of the number of operational aircraft at an airfield or on board a carrier, or contain any facilities (except status boards) for maintaining such records. With the exception of ammunition (salvo remaining) counters, the NEWS does not contain any facilities for simulating or recording fuel consumption or other logistic factors and constraints.

The damage computer calculates hit probabilities as a function of range only. Target angles are not considered, or whether or not a weapon can be brought to bear. In order for damage to be assessed, a hit must be obtained. Therefore, the computer cannot assess the effects of a nuclear weapon detonating at a distance from a ship, or the effects of a near miss by a conventional bomb. Except in a very few cases, the time of flight of a long range or a relatively slow speed weapon cannot be simulated. If a weapon is fired at a force on its own side, the umpires must determine which force was fired at, and then assess the results either by rules or professional judgment.

Scaling Factors and Other Gimmicks. The inherent capabilities of the NEWS are enhanced and some of its limitations minimized by scaling factors, the use of equipment for other than its intended purpose, and manual gaming techniques.

Scaling factors are generally used when it is desired to simulate an area of operations that is different in size from any of the four available selections. The scaling factors may be applied to the speed dials, and to the available game speeds and speed multipliers. In the first instance, overlays calibrated from 0 to 60 might be placed over the normal 0 to 50 scale on the speed dials. Then with an ocean scale switch setting of 1000, an area of operations of 1200 on a side is obtained. Using the second method a game speed of two may be scaled to read one, thus providing a 500 mile area of operations with a 1000 mile ocean scale switch setting. If the speed multipliers of 10 and 100 are changed to read 1 and 10 respectively, then a 1000 mile ocean scale setting results in a 100 mile area of operations. Various combinations of scaling factors may also be used. For instance, a speed dial scaling of 0 to 60 combined with a game speed scaling of two to one, and an ocean scale setting of 1000, results in a 600 mile area of operations.

Whenever one of the four available ocean areas is scaled, the scales on the azimuth range indicators are changed accordingly. Thus, if by means of speed dial scaling, a 1000 mile area of operations is scaled to represent a 1200 mile area, the scales on the azimuth range indicators are changed from their design calibration of 320, 160, 80, 40, 20, and 8 miles to read 384, 192, 96, 48, 24, and 9.6 miles.

Equipment has been added to drive the NEWS game clock at five and ten times its designed speed. This equipment enables games to be conducted at 5, 10, 20, and 40 times real time. In order to employ a game speed of 5, the clock speed switch is set to four, and the speed dials are scaled to 0.8 their normal range. If it is desired to switch game speed to 4, 2 or 1, the equipment which drives the NEWS clock at a speed of five is disconnected, the clock speed switch set at the desired game speed, and the scaled speed dials removed or ignored. Due to the need to use two speed dials in case of game speed changes, game speeds of five times real time are usually employed when the forces are maneuvered by control group personnel.

To conduct games at 10, 20, and 40 times real time, speed multiplier scaling is used. For instance, if a game is proceeding at a clock speed of one, and the decision is made to shift to a speed of ten, then the speed multipliers on the navigation computers are manually shifted to the next higher position. The speed multiplier of 100, therefore, cannot be used at clock speeds of 1, 2, and 4, but must be reserved for shifts of 10, 20, and 40 game speeds. In practice, the game speed of 10 is the maximum useful game speed.

While the weapon and damage computer subsystem was intended for the simulation of the employment of weapons systems, it has, on occasion, been employed for simulating fuel expenditures. In this case the effectiveness remaining meters show fuel states. In some instances NEWS weapons have been used to simulate fighter aircraft. The players pressed the appropriate acquisition key to vector a fighter against an incoming raid and then, after a suitable time delay, the firing key. Another method merely requires the use of the firing key, in which case the time delay is programmed. In either case, the overall bomber kill probability is programmed, and the damage computer assesses the interaction.

Whenever NEWS components are used for functions that differ from their normal or designed functions, their employment is explained in the rules of the game.

Manual Techniques. The machine gaming capabilities of the NEWS are often supplemented by a variety of manual gaming techniques. In general, the higher the command levels represented by the players, the greater the requirement for manual techniques.

Manual methods are used when forces, either before or during a game, are outside the area of operations selected for NEWS play. For instance, if the NEWS area of operations is an area 1200 miles square, and at the beginning of the game a submarine is proceeding toward this area, then that submarine is plotted as in a manual game. When the submarine reaches the edge of the NEWS area of operations, it is then programmed as an active NEWS force. In a similar manner, if a force proceeds outside of the NEWS area of operations, it is deactivated and played as in a manual game.

For a game in which forces are or may be expected to move outside the NEWS area of operations, a game chart is prepared which encompasses a suitably sized area. The NEWS grid (0000 to 4000 EW; 0000 to 4000 NS) is superimposed on that portion of the chart which is displayed on the master plot screen, and then extended as necessary to include the remainder of the chart. This provides a common grid for both NEWS and manual play.

If a NEWS force is used to represent an aggregation of ships such as a carrier striking force, then diagrams of the dispositions which may be used by that force are required by the umpires as they would be in a manual game.

When there is an insufficient number of active NEWS forces to simulate the forces involved in a game, then some forces are represented by manual methods. Forces so simulated may include patrol aircraft flying search patterns, destroyers on antisubmarine patrol stations, logistic support units, airfields, shore installations, ground units, and so on. Search tracks of aircraft are drawn on transparencies and projected, as needed, from the rear of the umpire area; other forces are represented by images and symbols pasted on the rear of the master plot. Ground forces are usually played on topographical maps.

Forces depicted by manual means, and employed in conjunction with active NEWS forces, are sometimes referred to as "constructive" forces. For the most part, they are handled as they would be in a manual game.

The techniques of manual war gaming are used to evaluate interactions between NEWS and constructive forces, and for detections and damage assessment when the azimuth range indicators and damage computer are not used. Manual methods are also used to determine aircraft aborts, to record the status of airfields, aircraft down times, and the like, and to record aircraft availability, status of runways, fuel states, and so on.

Types of NEWS Games. Two general types of NEWS games are played: curriculum games and Fleet games. The former are educational; the latter, analytical in nature, in that they are usually conducted to provide the players with information that is directly applicable to their real-world jobs.

Curriculum or educational games are conducted for the two resident schools and the Naval Command Course Department of the War College, and for the Naval Destroyer School. They have also been played to support the curriculum of the Reserve Officers' Command and Staff Course, an annual two-week course conducted by the School of Naval Command and Staff of the College.

Fleet games are conducted for Fleet Commands who want to rehearse scheduled at-sea exercises, examine contingency plans, "try-out" operational concepts, etc., by means of NEWS gaming. The facilities of the NEWS and the services of personnel of the War Gaming Department are available for such Fleet games from the first of July to the end of December of each year, and at such other times as may be determined by the President of the Naval War College.

Curriculum Games. War College curriculum games are the final phase of a complex operations or planning problem. They provide students with the only possible means of completing the last phase of the military planning process, i.e., the execution of their plans.

There are three general types of curriculum games. These are the unit-level game, the task-group or task-force-level game, and the strategic or national-level game. The levels refer to the lowest player command-levels in a game. For example, in a unit level game some of the players act as commanding officers of ships.

The first College curriculum games which were conducted on the NEWS involved, for the most part, task group plans. Players acted as task group commanders and staffs and as the commanding officers and staffs of ships, submarines, and aircraft (or flights of aircraft). From their flag plots (command centers), task group commanders issued orders and received reports over planned communications nets. Commanding officers of ships and aircraft, stationed in command centers (as illustrated in Figure 5-7), maneuvered their ships and submarines and aircraft, made detections on their scopes (azimuth range indicators), maintained plots, acquired enemy targets, fired weapons, sustained damage, and responded and reported to their game superiors. The subsystems of the NEWS, in accordance with programmed data, determined if and when detections were made, disseminated intelligence, evaluated interactions and assessed damage. The umpires monitored communications and interactions, initiated in-game programming, and compiled information for the critique.

These games were machine games. They employed all of the subsystems of the NEWS: maneuver and display, weapon and damage computer, and communications. Since the games utilized all of the NEWS facilities, relatively few umpires were required. The umpires were usually stationed at the locations shown in Figure 5-8.

One or more unit-level games were conducted annually in support of the College curriculum from 1958 to 1964. Similar games were also conducted for the reserve officers of the Command and Staff Course during the latter part of this period.

In 1962 a one-sided unit-level machine game was devised for the students of the U.S. Naval Destroyer School. A number of these games have been played annually since that time. They are conducted in support of the curriculum of that school.

Soon after the first unit-level games were conducted on the NEWS, task-group-level games were designed and played in support of the College curriculum. In these games the lowest player-command level was at the task group level; the highest extended to the Fleet and Joint and Combined Task Force levels.

The initial task-group-level games utilized all of the facilities of the simulator. In most cases the NEWS forces were used to simulate task groups rather than

A NEWS Command Center
during the Play of a Unit-Level Game

Figure 5-7

individual units. The NEWS forces representing task groups were controlled by their respective group commanders and staffs. Detectability and look values were programmed to simulate, as closely as possible, the composite capabilities of the task groups; weapons were programmed to represent their total offensive capability against various types of targets. The effectiveness remaining meters represented the total life of a group with each ship contributing to the total life in accordance with a predetermined scale of relative life values. When a force was damaged and its effectiveness remaining meter dropped, it was up to the umpires to translate this loss of effectiveness into terms of specific ships sunk or damaged, and so on. In order to do this, the umpires needed formation diagrams of the task groups which were represented by the moving images on the master plot screen.

In addition to formation diagrams, other techniques of manual gaming were introduced to handle the numbers and variety of forces that were involved in

The NEWS Umpire Area
during the Play of a Unit-Level Game

Figure 5-8

task-group-level games. The manual techniques included the projection of aircraft search tracks, the use of paste-on images to represent forces, supplementary plotting and evaluation methods, and so forth.

From these manual-machine games, a more realistic type of task-group-level play evolved, one that places greater reliance on the umpires, less on the machine. With the exception of the School of Naval Warfare Strategic Game, this type of gaming is now used for all War College curriculum games conducted on the NEWS.

The current concept is based upon the realistic notion that task group commanders and their staffs do not drive ships and aircraft; their subordinates do. Hence, for this level of play, the umpires act as the subordinates. The players, stationed in simulated flag plots and operations control centers, (command headquarters and centers), exercise command and control of their forces in the same manner as they do in the real world.

For the conduct of such games, umpires and other control group personnel are formed into modules. Each module contains the people and equipment needed to support a particular task group commander, or to carry out some specific function in the game, e.g., provide merchant shipping, trawler, commercial air, and other inputs.

The module personnel supporting a player-commander and his staff act as the commanding officers of all of the ships and aircraft under the player's operational control. If the player orders a search, the module conducts that search. If, during the course of the search, an aircraft gains a contact, this intelligence is reported to the player in the same manner as it would be if the contact were made by an actual aircraft at sea.

The players also receive orders and intelligence from their player-seniors and information from adjacent player-commands in accordance with their emission control (EMCON) policy and communications plans.

The umpires who act as subordinate commanders have at their disposal a number of NEWS forces which are programmed with certain ship, aircraft, and submarine characteristics. These forces are used as needed during a game. For instance, NEWS force 7 might be programmed as an aircraft. When a search is ordered, an umpire checks to determine if an aircraft is available and then, if it aborts. If an aircraft is operational and does not abort, the umpire contacts the control room and orders force 7 activated and started on its mission. As all forces are controlled by the umpires, there is usually no particular requirement for assigning all Green NEWS forces to the Green side, and all White to the White side. Thus, force 7 (a Green NEWS force) might be employed as a White aircraft.

Because in this type of game the players do not maneuver forces and fire weapons, they do not use the force motion and weapons controls. (The azimuth range indicators, probes, and target information panels are used in some games.) However, as in flag plots at sea or in operations control centers ashore, the players use communication nets and plotting facilities. If required, or desirable, the spaces and facilities of two or more command centers may be combined by means of the interconnecting doors to form a larger flag plot or operations control center.

The problem control intercommunications consoles are removed from the umpire area. Direct voice communications nets are established between the supporting modules and players. Other voice nets are provided to link the modules, the control room, the status board writers, and the plotters behind the master plot screen. If the azimuth range indicators and the target information readout cabinets are not required, they are removed, and the spaces used for other purposes.

In addition to acting as subordinates to player-superiors, members of the modules also perform umpiring duties. For the most part they determine if and when contacts and other interactions occur by utilizing the information portrayed on the master plot screen and on supplementary plots and status boards, and by intermodule coordination. Each module maintains its own status boards. These boards, in conjunction with the master plot, display the true status of forces and contacts. When applicable, they also indicate the situation as it is known to, or evaluated by, the players. For example, antisubmarine forces are working over a false contact. The task group commander is receiving periodic reports from the units on the scene. His current evaluation is: "probable submarine." The true nature of the contact as well as the player's evaluation is displayed on the appropriate status board.

Damage assessments are made in accordance with the semirigid method and, in most cases, are subject to override by the game director. The damage computer is rarely used and, when it is, targets are acquired and weapons fired from the damage computer console. Usually, damage is assessed by a module which is set up for this purpose. Members of this group, known as roving assessors, collect the pertinent information from the cognizant modules. For instance, in a destroyer versus a submarine interaction, they obtain the actions and reaction of the control group personnel acting as their respective commanding officers. The interaction is assessed at the damage assessment module, and the outcome transmitted to the umpire–commanding officers by the roving assessors. The results are then transmitted verbally to the players in the same terms and in the same manner as they would be transmitted by commanding officers in the real world.

The director of the game acts as all echelons of command above the senior player-commanders. A module (usually called the lateral inputs module) acts as all adjacent and parallel commands that are not played in the game. This module also provides any other inputs that may affect the play of the game but are not under the direct cognizance of the players, and hence cannot be handled by the player-supporting modules. If, for example, in the situation simulated, merchant vessels are steaming through the area of operations, then the lateral inputs module injects merchant ship traffic and acts as the skippers of these ships.

These manual-machine task-group-level games, obviously, require larger control groups than those needed for machine games. While the size and arrangement of the control group naturally varies from game to game, Figure 5-9 illustrates a fairly typical control group. This figure shows the control group for 4C-65, a game conducted for the School of Naval Command and Staff in June of 1965. This game was played initially as a manual game, and the original hand-played version is described in Chapter IV in the section titled Command and Staff Department Manual Game.

As mentioned at the beginning of this section on curriculum games, the third type of curriculum game that is conducted in the NEWS is a national-level

The NEWS Umpire Area
during the Play of a Task Group-Level Game

Figure 5-9

military-political game. This is a manual game that uses the player and umpire spaces and the communications facilities of the NEWS. It is described briefly in Chapter IV in the section, The School of Naval Warfare Strategic Game.

Approximately seventy College curriculum games were conducted in the NEWS from 1958 through 1965. Figure 5-10 contains a list of the curriculum games which were conducted during 1964 and 1965.

Traditionally, War College curriculum games have been two-sided. However, as a result of experience gained in one-sided Fleet games and because the situation appeared to lend itself to this type of play, a one-sided curriculum game was devised and conducted in 1963. A similar game, 2F-64, an Escort-of-Convoy Game was played in 1964, and two one-sided games were conducted in 1964, 1F and 1NW. Three one-sided games are planned for 1966, one for the Naval Command Course Department and one for each of the two schools of the College.

Date	Sponsoring School or Academic Department	Game*	Type of Operations Simulated by Friendly Side
12-13 Feb	Naval Command Course	1F-64	Naval Surface
27-28 Feb	Naval Command Course	2F-64	Escort of Convoy
8-10 Apr	Command and Staff	2C-64	Carrier Striking Force
24-30 Apr	Naval Warfare	SWG	Political-Military
6- 8 May	Command and Staff	3C-64	Antisubmarine
13-15 May	Naval Command Course	4F-64	Joint and Combined
1- 4 Jun	Command and Staff	4C-64	Joint and Combined
2- 3 Feb	Naval Command Course	1F-65	Escort of Convoy
31 Mar -2 Apr	Naval Command and Staff	2C-65	Carrier Striking Force
20-23 Apr	Naval Warfare	SWG	Political-Military
29-30 Apr 3- 4 May	Naval Command and Staff	3C-65	Antisubmarine
11-13 May	Naval Command Course	3F-65	Joint and Combined
19-21 May	Naval Warfare	1NW-65	Surveillance and Quarantine
1- 3 Jun	Naval Command and Staff	4C-65	Joint and Combined

* An indoctrination game was conducted for students of the Naval Command Course on 7 February, 1964. Two voluntary participation antisubmarine warfare games were conducted for students of the Naval Warfare Course on 25 May, 1964; and two carrier striking force games on 26 May, 1964.

NAVAL WAR COLLEGE CURRICULUM GAMES CONDUCTED IN THE NEWS
1964-1965

Figure 5-10

When a one-sided game is played, an opposition module is added to the control group organization. The personnel in this module control all opposition forces and, when possible, employ known opposition tactics. The opposition forces, weapons, and sensors are assigned characteristics which conform to the most recent intelligence estimates.

Fleet Games. It is convenient to classify Fleet games into two categories: local play and remote play. Local-play games are similar to curriculum games in that the players occupy the command headquarters and command centers in the NEWS. For remote play, however, the players are stationed in their own real-world command and control spaces, and play the game with the facilities and personnel that are normally available in the situations simulated.

Both local-play and remote-play games are one-sided. The opposition is planned and executed by officers of the War Gaming Department with the assistance and advice of the sponsoring Fleet Command, and often with the aid of other Commands. For example, for an antisubmarine warfare game, submarine commanding officers might be ordered to the College in order to provide the most realistic opposition.

As in the case of curriculum games, local-play Fleet games have been conducted at both the unit and task group levels, with the majority played at the latter level. These games employ techniques similar to those used in curriculum games.

For remote-play games "secure" land-line communications, or combination land-line radio-links are established between the participating Fleet Commands and the NEWS. Additionally, "unsecure" telephone circuits are also used for starting and stopping the game, and for unclassified communications.

The players are furnished game clocks. These are portable clocks which can function at the various NEWS game speeds. They can be connected with the NEWS by leased lines, or operated by local power sources (60 cycle, 115 volt AC). In the latter case the clocks are synchronized with the NEWS game clock, started and stopped, and clock speeds set in accordance with telephoned instructions from the game director in the NEWS.

Remote-play games are conducted at the task-group and higher levels. Except that the players are not in command centers in the NEWS, these games are conducted in the same manner as the curriculum task-group-level games described in the preceding section. The players receive intelligence in the same manner and in the same format as in a real-life emergency or war-time situation; the control group in the NEWS drives the ships and aircraft, and report and respond to their player-superiors in the same manner as real-world ship and aircraft commanders. From the players' viewpoint there is only one difference between the game situation and the real situation: in the latter case, many circuits are used; in the game, the many circuits are simulated by one. However, at the command levels involved, this diminution in communications nets has not, apparently, degraded the quality of remote simulations; for the post-game comments of participating Commanders have invariably emphasized the realism of the play.

As in curriculum and local-play Fleet games, remote-play games are conducted during normal working hours. But, as in the other games, accelerated game speeds keep the game clock up to and usually ahead of the real-world clock. For example, CANUSTREX 1-64 was played at game speeds varying from one to ten times normal clock speeds, and five and one-half days of game play were conducted in four normal days.

Thirty-four Fleet games were conducted in the NEWS during the 1958–1965 period. Figure 5-11 lists the 1964 and 1965 games. This figure shows the sponsoring Fleet command. Most of these games also included participating subordinate commands. Thus, the personnel of ten operation control centers or emergency defense control stations participated in CANUSTREX 1-64; in PHIBNEWS 1-65, commanders and staffs of such commands as Amphibious Group Two, Carrier Division Eighteen, and Cruiser-Destroyer Flotilla Two.

Like a local-play game, a remote-play game provides a Fleet Commander and his staff with an opportunity to execute his war plan with planned wartime forces and against a highly likely wartime opposition. But a remote-play game offers other advantages. It exercises operations control center personnel, and enables a commander to check and evaluate command and control procedures. It minimizes the need for travel funds; keeps the greater part of the staff "down on the farm." For these reasons the remote-play game is becoming increasingly popular. Of the eight Fleet games conducted during 1964 and 1965, five were remote-play games.

Game Design and Rules. NEWS games are usually designed (and programmed) by gaming teams of War Gaming Department officers. A team consists of one or more officers from each of the three branches of the Operation, Evaluation and Research (OER) Division of that Department. As shown in Figure 5-1 the three branches of the OER Division are: Gaming Development, Operations and Programming, and Evaluation and Research.

The Destroyer School Game is a relatively simple game. It is conducted one day each quarter, and three games are played each day in order that the students may rotate positions. Every game played uses the same area of operations, forces, command structure, communications, and so forth. Therefore the same rules and programming forms can be used over and over again. This is seldom true of other NEWS games. War College curriculum games are usually sufficiently different from year to year to require different (or at least updated) rules. Fleet games are in the same category. Each requires new or updated rules, programming forms, and so on.

Whenever a War College operations problem, planning problem or planning exercise culminates in a NEWS war game,* the cognizant War Gaming Department gaming team maintains liaison with the sponsoring school or department during

* The one exception is the School of Naval Warfare's Strategic War Game. This game is conducted by that school. The Engineering and Maintenance Division of the War Gaming Department provides support and communications personnel as requested.

Date	Sponsoring Fleet Command	Game	Type of Operations Simulated by Friendly Side
6 Mar	COMSUBDEVGRU TWO (Commander Submarine Development Group Two)	No name assigned	Antisubmarine
27-29 Jul	COMSECONDFLT (Commander U.S. Second Fleet)	Teamwork	Carrier Striking Force
31 Aug - 3 Sep	COMPHIBLANT (Commander Amphibious Forces, U.S. Atlantic Fleet)	PHIBNEWS I-64*	Amphibious (Movement Phase)
12-15 Oct	COMASWFORLANT (Commander Antisubmarine Forces, U.S. Atlantic Fleet)	NEWSBEX I-64*	Antisubmarine Warfare Barrier
7-11 Dec	COMASWFORLANT and CANCOMARLANT (Commander Antisubmarine Forces, U.S. Atlantic Fleet and Canadian Commander Maritime Forces, Atlantic)	CANUSTREX I-64*	Escort of Convoy and Antisubmarine Warfare
13-17 Sep	COMASWFORPAC (Commander Antisubmarine Forces, U.S. Pacific Fleet)	GOLD TIDINGS 1*	Antisubmarine Warfare
5- 7 Oct	COMASWFORLANT (Commander Antisubmarine Forces, U.S. Atlantic Fleet)	NEWSBEX I-65*	Antisubmarine Warfare Barrier
9-10 Nov	COMPHIBLANT (Commander Amphibious Forces, U.S. Atlantic Fleet)	PHIBNEWS 1-65	Amphibious (Opposed Sortie, Movement Phase, Operations in Objective Area)

* Remote-Play Game

FLEET WAR GAMES IN THE NEWS
1964-1965

Figure 5-11

the planning for and the writing of the directive or syllabus. The directive or syllabus describes the general situation, the special situations, and the planning requirements. The students involved are divided into committees or staffs, as appropriate, and issued the pertinent instructions and information. They determine their missions, list and compare possible courses of action, and prepare plans.

As the students develop their concepts and write their plans, members of the gaming team monitor their progress, select an area of operations for the NEWS master plot, and assist the officers conducting the problem or exercise in the selection of the student plans to be gamed and the assignment of students to player staffs and the control group.

Concurrently with its monitoring and advisory duties, the gaming team develops a concept of play. It devises a control group organization tailored to the concept of play and the player-planned command structure. The team plans the organization of player-supporting and other modules, and assigns personnel to the various control group billets. It designs game control communications nets, status boards, game forms, assigns NEWS forces and command centers, and compiles the characteristics of forces and weapons. It initiates requests for charts, maps, slides, and other graphic materials needed for play. Then the group prepares the rules of the game, the pregame briefings, and the programming forms.

If the game is to be one-sided, the War Gaming Department team, in cooperation with the sponsoring school or department, plans the opposition, assigns forces and weapons in conformance with the general situation, and assigns personnel to man the opposition module during the play of the game.

A Fleet game is initiated by a letter from the sponsoring command to the President of the Naval War College. The War Gaming Department assigns a team to design and program the game, and arranges for one or more pregame conferences between Fleet and department representatives. These discussions raise and resolve such questions as: "What is the purpose of the game? What forces will be simulated? What plans, orders and instructions are pertinent?" Then, maintaining close liaison with the sponsor's representatives, the gaming team proceeds in the same manner as in curriculum gaming to develop and program the game, and to write the rules and prepare the briefings.

Rules. The rules for NEWS games are divided into player rules and control group rules. For a two-sided game, two sets of player rules are required, one for each of the opposing sides; for a one-sided game, one set of player rules. Umpires and certain other control group members receive, or have access to, copies of all the rules.

The player rules describe the communications and other facilities that will be available during a game. They explain how and in what form intelligence will be received. The rules describe the methods to be used by the players to implement their decisions; for example, what buttons to press to turn on the sonar in a destroyer, or, perhaps, what forms to fill out to initiate an air strike (if the umpires are acting as subordinate commanders), and so on. They tell the players to use call signs, or instead, to employ organizational titles, hull numbers, and aircraft flight numbers. They list a phone number to call in case of equipment failure and other details that will assist the players. But the player rules do not explain—or even suggest—how the players should organize their staffs and command centers. It is up to the player-commanders, as it is up to commanders in the real world, to organize their staffs and procedures to utilize best the available command and control facilities.

The control group rules describe the organization of the control group, and the locations and functions of modules and members. They assign personnel to all of the control group positions. The rules describe the available facilities, and explain their use. They describe inter-module and inter-umpire coordinating procedures, the flow, dissemination, and posting of information and intelligence, and the forms and procedures for compiling material for the critique.

The control group rules provide the necessary data or guides and describe the methods to be used for monitoring the employment of forces, evaluating interactions, and injecting constraints due to logistics, weather, sea states, and so on. They contain information and procedures for determining and recording aircraft availability, fuel expenditures, repair times, and the like, and provide umpiring guides for translating per cent losses in effectiveness into the kinds of information and reports that are received by a commander in the real world. And if the umpires are maneuvering forces as subordinates to player-superiors, then the umpire rules may specify the NEWS forces that are available to each of the modules, their programmed characteristics, the procedures for activating and employing the forces, and for varying the characteristics when necessary.

Programming. Programming the NEWS for a game consists, essentially, of two phases. The first phase is the preparation of a set of programming instructions by the gaming team; the second, the programming of the equipment by the Engineering and Maintenance Division.

The programming instructions assign umpire and player spaces and facilities, and the characteristics of forces, weapons and sensor systems in terms of dial and potentiometer settings, and switch positions. The instructions are written on a series of forms and cards. These forms and cards are prepared in accordance with information contained in the *NEWS Programming Guide*.[45] This reference publication for War Gaming Department personnel describes in detail the operational capabilities of the NEWS, and contains all pertinent programming information and data.

Depending upon the type of game, up to five subsets of programming instructions may be required. These contain, respectively, the information and data for programming the following five areas: command headquarters and command centers, umpire area and communications room, control room, equipment room, and damage computer.

The command headquarters and command center programming instructions consist of a set of forms containing the assignment of centers and forces, number of salvos per weapon, rates of fire, and dead reckoning tracer (DRT) and azimuth range indicator (ARI) scale settings. The forms also list all the required labels and readout cards.

Umpire area and communications room information includes a layout of the umpire area showing the equipment required and its location, control group communications nets, side panel displays, status board formats, and passive information display equipment and labels. Also, as needed, the inter-player communications nets and the assignment of channels and facilities are listed.

Control room programming information contains the ocean scale setting, and the shape and color of each of the projected force images. It also includes all of the necessary inputs for the characteristics panels and navigation computers for the active NEWS forces, the setting for the 14 fixed forces, and the settings of the position matching switches.

The equipment room programming sheets contain two different types of information. The first furnishes the dial settings for the rates of ascent and descent of active NEWS forces; the second, potentiometer settings for the "look" and "detectability" values for active NEWS forces, and "detectability" values for fixed forces.

Damage computer programming forms specify the potentiometer setting for the parameters of each weapon-type/target-type combination. They assign a target-type to each NEWS force, and a weapon-type to each weapon. These forms indicate whether or not a player will receive an indication if one or more of his weapons scores a hit, and if so, the length of time each hit indication light will remain illuminated. They specify the initial effectiveness remaining meter settings for each force and whether or not the offensive capability of individual forces will be reduced as a function of damage received.

The personnel of the Engineering and Maintenance Division arrange the equipment and facilities, prepare the status boards, set up labels and readout cards, establish communications nets, and set the dials, potentiometers and switches in accordance with the programming instructions and information provided by the Operations, Evaluation and Research Division team. When these tasks are completed, the master plot screen drawn, and charts, slides and other visual aids prepared and distributed, then the NEWS is programmed and ready for the players and control group.

Participants. As in manual games, the participants in a NEWS game are divided between the players and the control group. The players are War College students, Fleet officers, or Destroyer School students. Occasionally, War Gaming Department officers participate as players. This is usually in games such as the Destroyer School's where players are needed to man the aircraft, or in the few experimental in-house games that have been conducted by the War Gaming Department.

The control group is headed by the Director of the Game. The director is usually the Head of the Operations, Evaluation and Research Division of the War Gaming Department. In the case of a College curriculum game, a senior officer from the sponsoring School or Department serves as an advisor and consultant. For Destroyer School and Fleet games, representatives from the sponsoring activity perform a similar function.

Module directors are provided by the OER Division; umpires, damage assessors, historians and other key control group members by the War Gaming Department and by sponsoring and supporting activities. In games where there is a fairly large number of spectators, a member of the control group serves as a commentator. This officer describes and discusses the events as they occur in the game, and his comments are broadcast into the balcony and umpire areas.

Communications equipment operators, status board keepers, plot console operator, talkers, and messengers are furnished by the War Gaming Department with assistance from supporting and sponsoring activities as required.

Briefings and Rehearsals. The gaming team briefs the Director of the War Gaming Department and other members of the department on the general concept of play, and upon the rules and procedures. If some of the players and supporting control group personnel are not familiar with the NEWS, the gaming team arranges a tour of the system, a tour which emphasizes the facilities and equipment that will be used during the game. Then the team briefs the entire control group; the modules organize, and the director conducts a short control group rehearsal and critique of the game rules and programming. The gaming team initiates programming changes suggested by the critique, and corrects programming errors. Finally, a brief rehearsal is held for both players and control group and, upon its completion, the participants and the system are ready to begin the game.

Critiques and Post Game Reports. At the end of each local-play game, the players are assembled in the umpire area and shown the master plot screen. The director describes briefly the major events that occurred during the game, and the sponsor's representative comments on the highlights of the play. In the case of Fleet and Destroyer School games, a short critique usually follows; in the case of a College game, the critique is generally held at a later date and in one of the College's auditoriums.

For College games, the information compiled by the control group during the game, the comments of module directors and umpires, and slides of the master plot are turned over to the sponsoring school or department for the preparation of the critique. The War Gaming Department assists, as requested, in the preparation of the critique and in its conduct.

At the end of a Fleet game, either local-play or remote-play, the War Gaming Department prepares a report of the game and transmits it to the sponsoring command. This report then becomes the property of that command.

Following every game, the officers and the Operations Research Analyst of the War Gaming Department submit comments on the methods, procedures and data used in the game. These are filed for future reference. The operations orders, rules, programming forms and cards, maps, slides, and all other materials used in programming and conducting the game are filed in a "game package." This material is then available in case another or a similar game is scheduled.

Demonstrations. As mentioned previously, the War Gaming Department designs and conducts dynamic NEWS demonstrations of various types of naval warfare. These demonstrations are presented in the Umpire Area. These are conducted for the Schools and Naval Command Course of the College in support of their curriculums, and for students of the Destroyer School in support of its curriculum. Each serves to integrate and illustrate the overall aspects of a particular type of naval warfare: antisubmarine warfare, antiair warfare, mine warfare, and so on.

The demonstrations are developed and programmed by OER Division teams in somewhat the same manner as games are developed and programmed. Demonstrations use the master plot screen, side panels, navigation computers, projected images, and a variety of supporting visual techniques. They also use supplementary screens for the projection of film clips and slides to support and enhance the master plot display and the narrator's commentary. In some cases the scopes of the azimuth range indicators are tilted to a horizontal position so that the spectators can see the same scope presentation, say, of one of the bombers in the demonstration. The movements and interactions of all force images projected on the master plot and scopes are manipulated by personnel in the control room, and are keyed to the narrator's script.

In addition to the naval warfare demonstration, dynamic demonstrations are also presented to the students of the war gaming courses conducted by the War Gaming Department. These demonstrations illustrate the uses of the equipment in the umpire area, and the various techniques that are employed in NEWS games. Modified versions of these demonstrations are also conducted for distinguished guests and for visiting groups from military and civilian organizations.

Chapter VI
Computers and Computer Games

The computers that are used for computer and computer assisted war games are general purpose stored program digital computers. They were not developed for gaming but were designed and constructed in response to the computational and data processing needs of the mid-twentieth century. However, it was recognized that many of the capabilities of digital computers were applicable to war gaming and, as a result, these modern electronic devices were soon employed to assist in the conduct of war games and, also, to play entire games without benefit of human participation.

In order to understand how such general purpose computers can be used in war gaming, it is beneficial to know what sort of older processes, devices, and games they have replaced, and how the computers can take over their functions. For these reasons, brief descriptions of certain manual processes, the development of computers, and an explanation of binary representation, computers, and their functioning precede the description of computer-assisted and computer games.

Rigid Umpiring. When the rigid method of evaluation is employed in a manual game, the umpires adhere to the prescribed rules and procedures. For instance, at the beginning of a move, a player decides to fire weapons. The damage assessment umpire would then receive weapons employment cards similar to the one shown in Figure 6-1. The data in columns 1 through 15 have been entered, as appropriate, by the players and other umpires, and monitored according to the rules of the game. The damage umpire processes the data on each card by following the procedures shown in Figure 6-2, and places them in an outgoing box. The cards are then used by recorders and other umpires as the rules dictate—updating status boards, furnishing intelligence to the players, degrading the capabilities of forces, etc.

To process the information on each card, the damage assessment umpire needs, in addition to the flow chart or model, a random device and the following data: weapons ranges, hit probabilities, and damage per hit. These data may be changed from play to play without affecting the game procedures.

WEAPONS EMPLOYMENT CARD

	FIRING FORCE								TARGET							OUTCOME			
				LOCATION								LOCATION							
MOVE NO.	NO.	TYPE	E.R.	X	Y	Z	TYPE WEAPON	NO. OF FIRINGS	NO.	TYPE	E.R.	X	Y	Z	RANGE (NAUT. MI.)	IN RANGE	NO. HITS	PERCENT DAMAGE	E.R.
7	25	CLG	.80	1300	0800	0000	SAM	02	06	4AC	.75	1700	0900	0070	40	*YES*	*01*	*25*	*.50*
1	2	3	4	5	6	7	8	9	10	11	12	13	14	15	16	17	18	19	20

COLUMN NUMBERS

NOTE: E.R. INDICATES EFFECTIVENESS REMAINING

WEAPONS EMPLOYMENT CARD

Figure 6-1

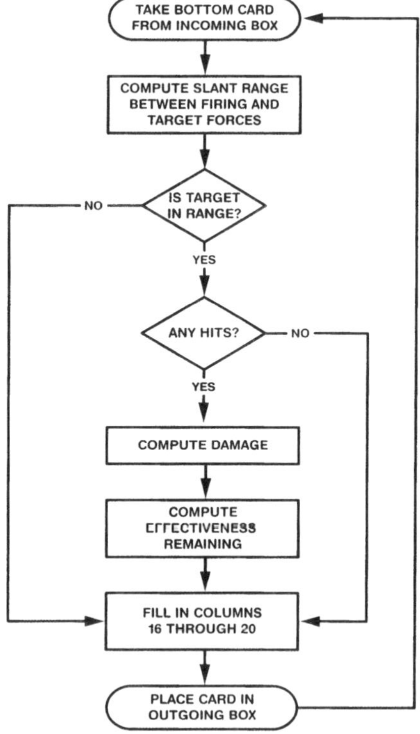

FLOW CHART — DAMAGE ASSESSMENT UMPIRE

Figure 6-2

In the rigid method of evaluation, the umpire makes a few calculations, refers to a table of probabilities, employs a chance device, and makes his decisions on the basis of numerical comparisons. His duties require no particular professional military experience or judgment. These factors are applied when the procedures are developed, the rules written, and the data compiled.

Because rigid umpiring is a routine and time-consuming process, numerous computing and recording aids have been devised. Among these were Livermore's firing-board,* the Naval War College's circular slide rules for damage assessment, and a wide variety of graphs, nomograms, and slide rules. One relatively recent gadget is the RAND Corporation circular slide rule for computing nuclear bomb damage effects. The object of such devices is to simplify and speed-up one or a limited number of the umpiring processes. For instance, a graphical device of some sort could be employed to compute slant range. Or a less specialized aid such as a desk calculator might be used to assist in the process.

Following their development, digital computers have been used to assist umpires in handling lengthy and tedious calculations. However, these computers have other capabilities in addition to those of performing rapid computations. They can store and retrieve data and act as a chance device. They can also make decisions on the basis of numerical comparisons and, as a result, change their sequence of operations. In short, they are capable of performing all such umpiring chores as those envisioned in Figure 6-2. For example, instead of the weapons employment card being placed in an incoming box, they might be punched and fed into an input device of a computer. The computer would then read, process, and turn out the completed card in much the same manner as the human umpire. A more ambitious program might instruct the computer to combine and carry out additional umpiring procedures. For instance, it might monitor the E. R. (effectiveness remaining) of column 4 of the cards to determine if the firing force was capable of firing the weapons in accordance with the rules and if the number of missiles entered in column 9 were available.

Rigid-play Games. Prior to World War II most rigidly evaluated games were conducted for educational purposes. The players were confronted with situations requiring command decisions. Control groups assisted in the process by performing routine and predetermined functions. If control group members gained military experience from the pregame procedures and the plays, it was more or less an added bonus. The relatively few rigidly umpired games which were devised to

* "No clerks are required to make the computations, which involve no more labor than to score at Cribbage; ..."[19]

obtain decision-making information were, for the most part, played to test or to rehearse a plan, or to assist in its development. Only one, or a very limited number of play-throughs were made. Usually, as in educational games, the players made command decisions. The control group furnished supporting services.

The war years and those that followed accelerated the evolutionary growth of conventional military hardware and, in addition, introduced a variety of radical, expensive, and rapidly changing weapons systems. Responsible military officials were faced with a wide and bewildering variety of choices. Which of the many competing weapons systems should be selected to meet best the threat of tomorrow as well as that of today? How should they be employed? How could they be integrated into the overall military structure? The need for decision-making information curved in an exponential fashion.

To meet the requirements for statistically significant data, the mathematical techniques of the war-nurtured applied science of operations research were mobilized and refined. In situations where mathematical methods were impracticable, analysts turned to the traditional military testing tool, the analytical war game. The overall results—from a war gaming point of view—were a renaissance of the ancient art, its introduction into civilian activities, and the development and utilization of a previously somewhat neglected and more scientific approach, an approach which might well be termed the "rigid-play" game.

Rigid games are designed chiefly for the conduct of repeated trials under controlled conditions. Their purpose is to provide data which are statistically sound. The players do not make command decisions; like the umpires in a rigidly evaluated game, they are required to adhere to predetermined doctrines and procedures. A player's judgment may urge him to hold his fire until a better target presents itself; but if the rules say "fire," he fires. If a player learns something in an early play, he cannot, unless the rules permit, use this knowledge in later plays.

In completely rigid games, both the players and the umpires make their decisions according to rules which refer to or include numerical data, and which require some sort of arithmetical and logical manipulations for their implementation. Hence, rigid games are also called "computational games." Since the players are not permitted to use their own experience or judgment, and must base all their decisions on calculations or codified rules, some writers have distinguished this type of endeavor by the name "simulation," and have reserved the title of "game" for simulations in which either the players or both the players and umpires are allowed to make decisions.[46] Using this terminology, a manual rigid game is called a "manual simulation," but a manual play in which the players exercise choice and the umpires follow the rigid method of evaluation is known as a "manual game."*

The formulation and conduct of rigid games has a greater appeal for analysts and researchers than for many professional military officers. However, the latter are definitely concerned with the doctrines and data which are used, and with the results that are obtained, e.g., what is the range of possible outcome, what are the sensitive parameters and which of them can be controlled, etc.

The rigid games that were devised and conducted in the early 1950's were manual games. And as in other manual games, various devices and computing aids were developed and used to speed parts of the simulation process. But despite these aids, the procedures were rather slow, and there was seldom sufficient time or people to play the number of games or examine all of the variations that were deemed desirable.

With the advent of electronic digital computers with fairly large storage capacities and with the ability to perform both arithmetic and logical operations, it became possible to instruct them not only to play the umpiring roles, but also to act as the players in a completely rigid type of play. Thus, computer gaming—fast, and as completely objective as only a machine can be—was born.

Computer games are sometimes referred to as "computer simulations,"[46,6] or as computational games for the same reasons that these terms are used in conjunction with or in reference to rigid manual games. Like their hand-played counterparts, computer games are conducted to obtain decision-making information. They are analytical rather than educational in nature.

Development of Computing Devices and Systems. There are four general classes of computing devices and systems. In order of their development they are: the manual, the mechanical, the electromechanical, and the electronic.**

The earliest manual devices evolved from the use of the fingers as counting and computational aids and are, therefore, known as "digital" devices. Of these, the familiar abacus has survived. In this device, discrete quantities are represented by beads.

A later and entirely different kind of manual computing aid uses a continuous scale to represent numbers and quantities. One common example of this type of computing device is the slide rule; others, graphs and nomograms. Because, in

---

* See footnote, page 19.

** *An Introduction to Automatic Computers*, by Ned Chapin, (D. Van Nostrand Company, Inc. 1957) contains a chronology of computing developments and automatic computers from earliest times to 1956.

these tools, there is an analogy between the measurements and the quantities represented, they are known as "analog" computational devices.

The abacus and, in general, the slide rule are used for the solution of a variety of problems. Hence, they may be termed "general" or "multi-purpose" computers or computing aids. Graphs and nomograms, on the other hand, are usually constructed for the solution of a particular type or class of problems. They are "special-purpose" computers. Most of the manual computational aids that have been or are used in war gaming are special-purpose devices.

The first mechanical computer appears to have been an adding machine built in France in 1642 by Pascal. A somewhat similar device was constructed later in the century by Leibnitz of Germany. These two machines might be considered as the ancestors of today's desk calculators.

In France about 1746, Jacques devised a method of using punched cards to control the operations of a loom. Some forty years later Müller of Germany conceived the idea of an automatic computer, a machine that could by itself carry out a sequence of operations. Babbage, in England, extended the work of Jacques and Müller and around 1830 constructed a model of a card-controlled digital computer. The British government financed the building of a full-scale version, but its completion was beyond the technology of the times. However, a different type of computer was constructed in 1876 by Lord Kelvin. This was a special-purpose analog device for calculating the motion of the tides. Its purpose, as stated by the inventor, was "... to substitute brass for brain in the great mechanical labour of calculating ..."*

Toward the end of the nineteenth century, Hollerith and Powers of the U.S. Bureau of the Census combined the earlier idea of punched cards with electromagnetic techniques, and developed methods and equipment for recording, sorting, and tabulating the data collected during the census of 1890. Modern punched-card systems and equipment are highly improved versions of their data processing machines.

In the 1930's, Dr. Bush of M.I.T. designed and built a mechanical analog computer for the solution of various types of differential equations. This machine was called a "differential analyzer," and is considered by some to be the first of the modern computers.[47] Improved types were used during the second world war to solve problems in ballistics. Later on, analog computers were built with electromechanical and electronic components.

---

* *Encyclopedia Britannica*, Vol. 4, page 549, 1960.

The first automatic digital computer was completed in 1944. Built at Harvard University by H. Aiken and a group of engineers and graduate students, it used electromagnetic components as computing elements, and was known as the Mark I Relay Computer, or the Automatic Sequence-Controlled Calculator. It performed about three additions per second.[48]

Realizing that many complicated mathematical problems could be solved by reducing them to the basic arithmetic processes,* Dr. J. W. Mauchley of the U.S. Bureau of Standards suggested that a high-speed digital computer would make this approach practicable.[47] To obtain the necessary computational speeds, he proposed that vacuum tubes be used as computing elements. Under Mauchley's and J. P. Eckert's direction, the design and construction of an electronic computer was begun in 1942 at the University of Pennsylvania. The result was ENIAC (Electronic Numerical Integrator and Automatic Calculator). Completed in 1946, it was the original high-speed digital computer, the first to take advantage of the swift motions of electrons. ENIAC handled up to 5,000 additions per second.[48]

Since the construction of ENIAC, a large number of general purpose digital computers of various sizes and capacities have been built, and continuing improvements made in their design, versatility, and speed. These are the sort of computers that are used as adjuncts to manual games and for the conduct of computer games.

Binary Representation. The counter wheels and other components of a mechanical digital computer are constructed with ten positions or states, each corresponding to one of the ten decimal digits. A group of components represents a decimal number. The components of an electronic digital computer, however, are two-state or binary devices. Transistors and vacuum tubes are either conducting or not conducting, magnetic materials are magnetized in one direction or in the opposite direction, and so on. If data are to be represented by these components, either a series of pulses in time must be used to indicate decimal digits, or a system of data representation compatible with the bi-state nature of the electronic components and circuits must be selected. The latter course has proven the better. Today, digital computers are designed to function in their natural or binary mode. The decimal system employs ten digits, 0 through 9. Their place values are based on a progression of powers of ten. For example, the decimal number 36 has a 3 in the 10^1 or tens position, and a 6 in the 10^0 or units position, i.e.,

* Transforming a mathematical problem into a series of arithmetic steps is called "numerical analysis."

$$36 = 3(10)^1+6(10)^0.$$

The number system employing two digits, 0 and 1, is called the binary system. Place values correspond to powers of two (see Table 6-1). Thus, in the binary number 100100 the most significant 1 is in the 2^5 or thirty-twos position, the left 0 in the 2^4 or sixteens place, the next 0 in the 2^3 or eights position, and so forth, or:

$$100100 = 1(2)^5+0(2)^4+0(2)^3+1(2)^2+0(2)^1+0(2)^0$$

Its equivalent decimal number is found by computing the powers of two and adding:

$$1(32)+0(16)+0(8)+1(4)+0(2)+0(1) = 36$$

Using the bases or radices as subscripts to indicate the respective number systems:

$$100100_2 = 36_{10}$$

Table 6-1

POWERS OF TWO

2^0	1		2^{17}	131,072
2^1	2		2^{18}	262,144
2^2	4		2^{19}	524,288
2^3	8		2^{20}	1,048,576
2^4	16		2^{21}	2,097,152
2^5	32		2^{22}	4,194,304
2^6	64		2^{23}	8,388,608
2^7	128		2^{24}	16,777,216
2^8	256		2^{25}	33,554,432
2^9	512		2^{26}	67,108,864
2^{10}	1,024		2^{27}	134,217,728
2^{11}	2,048		2^{28}	268,435,456
2^{12}	4,096		2^{29}	536,870,912
2^{13}	8,192		2^{30}	1,073,741,824
2^{14}	16,384		2^{31}	2,147,483,648
2^{15}	32,768		2^{32}	4,294,967,296
2^{16}	65,536		2^{33}	9,589,934,592

Table 6-2

DECIMAL AND BINARY EQUIVALENTS

Decimal	Binary Place Values							Decimal	Binary Place Values						
	64	32	16	8	4	2	1		64	32	16	8	4	2	1
0							0	17			1	0	0	0	1
1							1	18			1	0	0	1	0
2						1	0	19			1	0	0	1	1
3						1	1	20			1	0	1	0	0
4					1	0	0	21			1	0	1	0	1
5					1	0	1	22			1	0	1	1	0
6					1	1	0	23			1	0	1	1	1
7					1	1	1	24			1	1	0	0	0
8				1	0	0	0	25			1	1	0	0	1
9				1	0	0	1	30			1	1	1	1	0
10				1	0	1	0	40		1	0	1	0	0	0
11				1	0	1	1	50		1	1	0	0	1	0
12				1	1	0	0	60		1	1	1	1	0	0
13				1	1	0	1	70	1	0	0	0	1	1	0
14				1	1	1	0	80	1	0	1	0	0	0	0
15				1	1	1	1	90	1	0	1	1	0	1	0
16			1	0	0	0	0	100	1	1	0	0	1	0	0

As shown in Figure 6-3, the binary number 100100 can be represented at one instant in time by a group of common binary indicators, light bulbs. The decimal number 36 requires fewer bulbs, but each must be flashed an appropriate number of times.

In the upper part of Figure 6-3, a light represents the 1 of binary notation; no light, the 0. Similarly, within a computer, one of the two states of a component represents one of the binary symbols, and the second signals the presence of the other.

The binary symbol 1 or its electronic indicator is called a "bit," a shortened form of binary digit. The 0 is sometimes referred to as a "no-bit"; more often its presence is simply inferred. The binary number 110 can be described as having a no bit in the 1 position, and a bit in the 2 and 4 positions; or merely by noting that it has a bit in the 2 and 4 positions.

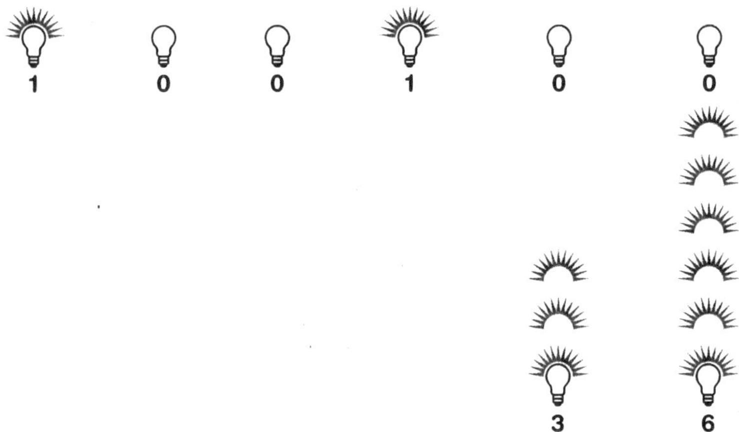

BINARY AND DECIMAL REPRESENTATION OF DATA

Figure 6-3

While some computers employ the binary system of notation, others use various codes based on that system. One such scheme is known as the "binary coded decimal," or "BCD." As illustrated in Table 6-3, this system uses four bit positions to represent in binary form any of the decimal digits or "characters," and combinations of the four-bit binary representations to form decimal numbers.

Table 6-3

FOUR PLACE BINARY REPRESENTATION OF DECIMAL DIGITS 0–9

Decimal	9	8	7	6	5	4	3	2	1	0
Binary	1001	1000	0111	0110	0101	0100	0011	0010	0001	0000

BINARY CODED DECIMAL REPRESENTATION OF DECIMAL 36

Decimal	3	6
BCD	0011	0110

A computer may store and process data character by character. In such a case, if data were represented internally as shown in Table 6-3, the computer would handle four bit positions (one character) at a time. In a second method a computer manipulates a larger number of bit positions called a "word." A word might consist of, say, 32 bit positions. This number is referred to as the "word length." The left bit position of a word is frequently reserved for a sign bit. Then a bit in that position is a signal to the computer that the number is negative; the absence of a bit, that it is positive. If the left bit of a 32-bit word is used as a sign bit, the word is capable of representing a decimal number of up to 2^{32}-1, or 4,294,967,295 (see Table 6-1).

Generally speaking, input data for a computer are expressed in the normal decimal fashion, and the computer performs the chore of translating the decimal numbers into the proper form for internal storage and processing. After processing, the computer translates the binary representations back to decimal form for the end results or output. An understanding of how data are represented within the computer is, however, necessary for preparing the program, and to interpret data that are visually displayed at the console.

Digital Computers. A digital computer consists of five functional components: input device, storage or memory, control unit, arithmetic-logical unit, and output device. It is controlled externally from a console which contains the keys and switches for starting, stopping, and resetting. The console also contains keys for the manual insertion of data, and lights so that data within the system may be displayed visually.

Input devices read instructions and data from punched cards, punched tape, or magnetic tape into the main or primary memory component.

The main memory accepts and stores information and furnishes it to other computer elements. In addition, some computers possess an auxiliary or secondary memory. Data stored in auxiliary memory are transferred through main memory and, when needed, routed back into main memory before processing. Since this takes longer than getting data directly from primary memory, the secondary memory is also called the "slow access" memory; the primary memory, the "rapid access."

In order that information may be stored and located as needed, each location or position of storage has an address. When data are inserted at an assigned memory address, it replaces any information already there. However, data taken from storage for processing or transfer are in effect copied rather than removed, and remain in the memory location unless erased by a specific instruction or replaced by other information.

The control unit coordinates the activities of the computer components and directs their operations according to a program stored in memory. The arithmetic-logical unit performs the basic arithmetic processes of addition, subtraction, multiplication, and division. This unit can also compare two numbers in somewhat the same way as an umpire in a war game compares the numbers appearing on the faces of a pair of dice with a hit probability. The unit, like the umpire, decides whether to take the next step in the program, or branch to another instruction. Results of processing are placed in storage either for further processing or for transfer to an output device.

Output devices take information from the main memory and record it on punched cards, punched tape, magnetic tape, or prepare printed copy. Additionally, by means of cathode ray tube display units, some computers can present graphical displays of the output data.

Input and output devices may be located at some distance from the other components, thus enabling several activities to use the same computer (processing and storage units) on a time-sharing or on a priority basis.

Stored Programs. Each computer has a built-in capability for performing a certain number of specific operations such as: read data into memory, add the contents of one memory location to another, move data from one location to another, make comparisons, print out information, and so on. It carries out each operation in response to a coded instruction. The instruction tells the computer the operation to perform and provides the addresses of the necessary data. The series of instructions required to carry out a procedure is called a "program."

A program for a digital computer is usually recorded on punched cards or tape. When it is desired to use the program, the cards or tape are read into the main memory. After that job is completed, another program may be stored and another procedure carried out. Because it is able to store its own program of instructions, a digital computer can be used for many problems simply by "loading" the proper program and the necessary data into its memory.

Developing a Program. The development of a digital computer program is usually a long and rather involved process. It requires an understanding of the problem, a knowledge of the instructions which the computer is capable of performing, the code by which it operates, the capacity of the memory, and the method of data representation.

The first step in the preparation of a computer program is the construction of a generalized model. For instance, a program for damage assessment might originate with a flow chart such as the one depicted in Figure 6-4. This model differs from that for the human damage assessment umpire (Figure 6-2) in only the input and output steps. It indicates that for this particular case punched cards will be used as input and output mediums.

The flow chart shows what is to be done, not how to do it, and a computer must be told "how." The next step is to prepare more detailed charts. Thus, the

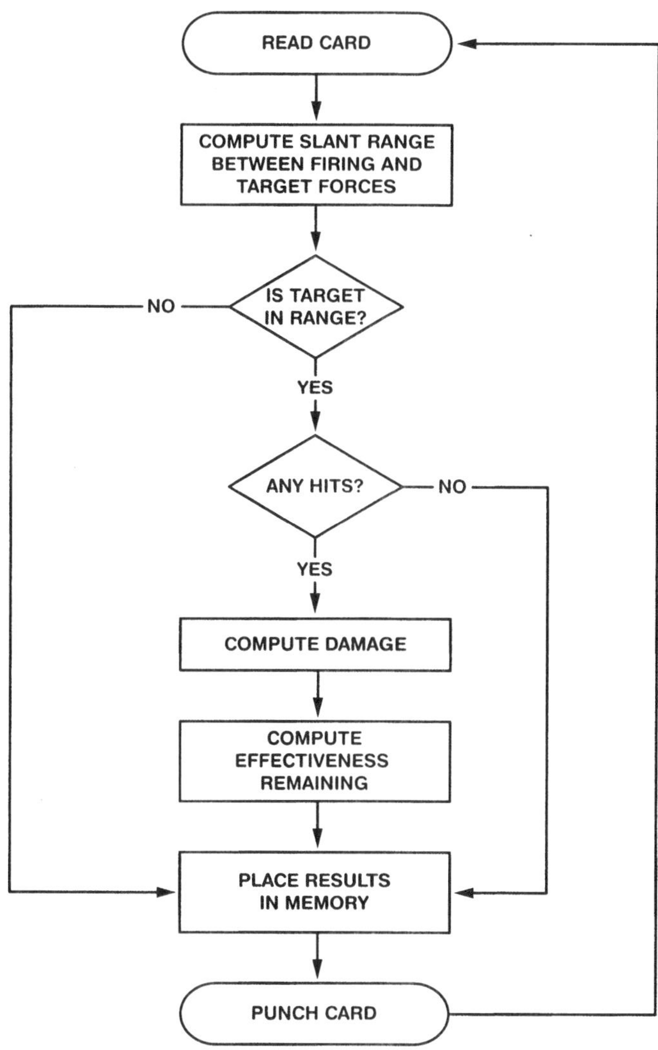

FLOW CHART — DAMAGE ASSESSMENT MODEL

Figure 6-4

second box of Figure 6-4 might be expanded as shown in Figure 6-5. In this chart X_w represents the X-coordinate of the force firing the weapon; X_t, the X-coordinate of the target. ΔX represents their difference. The symbols for the other coordinates follow a similar pattern.

Charts such as Figure 6-5, which are concerned chiefly with how data are to be processed within a computer, are sometimes called "block diagrams" rather than flow charts.

When the entire sequence of logic and arithmetic operations has been graphically delineated, the charts are used as guides for writing each step or instruction in the language of the computer. As noted earlier, the series of coded instructions for an entire process is called a program. The program is recorded on a deck of punched cards, a punched tape, or a magnetic tape.

The last step of Figure 6-5 calls for the calculation of a square root. Because digital computers can only add, subtract, multiply, and divide, this step needs to be expanded into a sequence of operations which the computer is capable of performing. However, programs for the solution of such common problems as the computation of square roots are usually available. They can be stored in memory and tied into the main program as needed, and are usually referred to as "subroutines."

Programming Languages. Preparing a program in the form of a series of coded computer instructions is a long and exacting process, and one that requires a detailed knowledge of the computer and its coded language. To provide faster and more efficient means of writing computer programs, programming languages such as FORTRAN (FORmula TRANslation Language) and COBOL (COmmon Business Oriented Language) have been developed. These languages require less detailed knowledge of the computer. They more closely approximate the everyday language of the programmer and hence are relatively easy to learn. A program written in such a language is called a "source program."

A source program is fed into a computer along with a "processor." A processor is a computer program that translates the source program into a series of coded computer instructions, and produces as an output a program in computer language. This program is called the "object program." The object program can then be used by the computer to carry out the desired procedures.

Computer Processing. Prior to the use of a computer, the deck of punched cards (or tapes) on which the program is recorded is loaded into memory. Then the subroutines and necessary data, which are also recorded on cards or tapes, are read

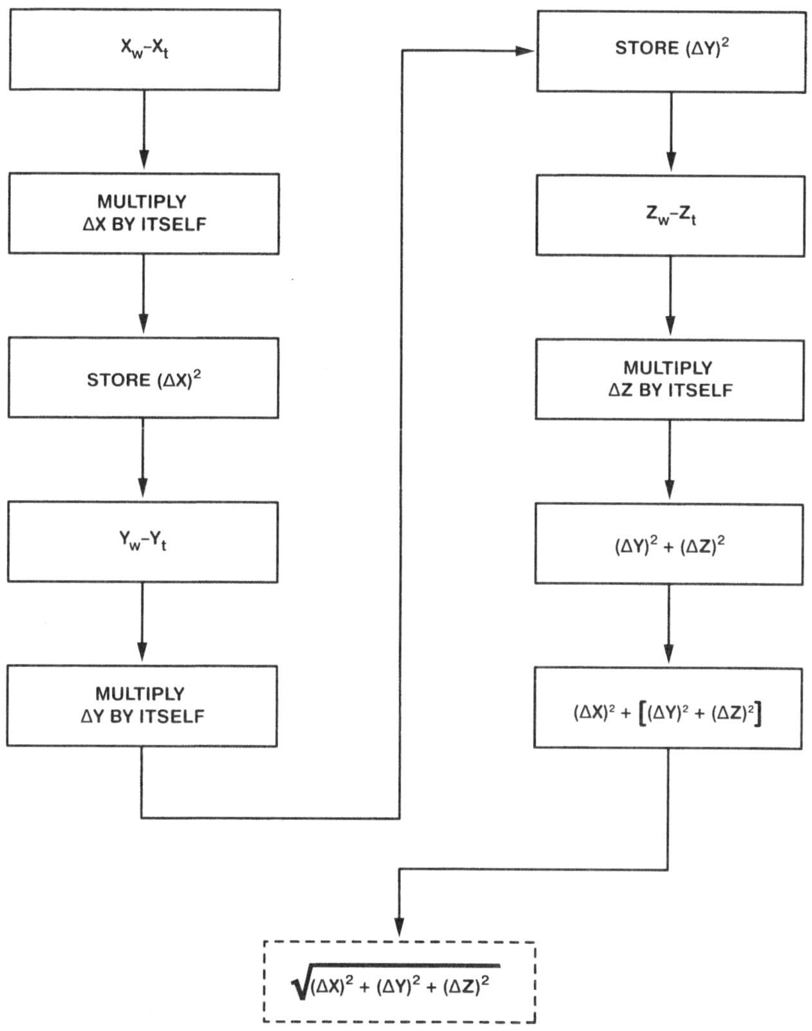

BLOCK DIAGRAM — SLANT RANGE COMPUTATION

Figure 6-5

and stored. These would include, in the case of the damage assessment routine, a square root subroutine, a random number generating subroutine (which replaces the dice roll or random number table of the human umpire), weapon ranges, hit probabilities, and damage per hit.

A sample problem is placed in the computer and the results of each step are checked against those obtained by hand or desk calculator processing. In this way, errors or so-called "bugs" in the program are located and corrected, a procedure known as "debugging." The debugging of complicated programs usually requires a great deal of time and skill.

When the program is debugged, the computer is started. The control unit locates the first instruction stored in memory. It interprets the instruction and commands the operation called for to be performed. It then takes, analyzes, and executes the next instruction, and so on, step by step until it processes all the data, completes the program, or reaches a halt instruction. For example, let's suppose that the weapons employment cards for a move are stacked in the card hopper. The computer takes the first card and reads the information on it into memory. It processes the information according to the stored program and punches out the results on the card. It then reads, processes, and punches out the next card, and so on until the last card is stacked at the outgoing end.

The weapon ranges, hit probabilities and incremental damage which were stored in memory for use with the damage assessment program may be changed from play to play without requiring any changes in the computer routine. However, if the procedures are changed or new ones added, the computer program must be modified or rewritten. To facilitate the introduction of modifications, some routines are designed so as to consist of a sort of master program and a number of subroutines. Subroutines may be replaced by improved versions without affecting the overall pattern. Modular programs usually require a larger amount of memory, and take longer to run.

Computer-Assisted Games. The damage assessment program previously discussed serves to illustrate in a very general way how a digital computer might be used to assist in the control of a manual game. In the particular case cited, it would handle the duties of a damage assessment umpire, and perform them faster and without arithmetical errors. And in practice, additional programs would be developed to handle other control group functions. General Rogers had this to say about the use of computers in a 1960 United States Continental Army Command war game. "To reduce the effort involved in making needed evaluation, a small electronic digital computer is available. It is used for such things as evaluating casualties due to conventional or atomic artillery, infantry engagements, and tank or tank-antitank firefights. As time goes on, more and more such tasks which are primarily arithmetical in nature will be assigned to the computer … Additionally, work is underway to simplify the bookkeeping effort associated with data storage. Eventually the files on units which show strengths, casualties, logistics situation, position, and similar data, may be put on tape or punched cards. Already the computer is used for keeping an intelligence file up-to-date and deciding, on the basis of the probabilities involved, which units are detected and at what time in the course of play."[49]

Computers are also employed to assist in post game evaluations of manual games. For example, detailed records of many aspects of the plays of the game known as INDIGO (Intelligence Division Gaming Operation) were "… put on punched cards for computer associated analysis of several phases …"[6]

TACSPIEL, described briefly in Chapter IV, is a computer-assisted game dealing with land warfare at the division and lower levels. Assessment data, unit identification and position information, etc., are punched on cards. These cards are used as inputs to the computer which processes the information and performs bookkeeping operations. Another and related manual game (also mentioned in Chapter IV) which employs computer assistance is THEATERSPIEL. This is played on a higher level (theater) than TACSPIEL. Players receive intelligence from the control group and from the outputs of the intelligence model. The players evaluate the information in view of their overall objectives and prepare mission type orders. The orders are sent to the appropriate sections of the control group. The members of the control group evaluate the orders and "… make appropriate computer inputs to the field or model they control. These computer inputs are then punched on IBM punch cards, put into the computer and a day's operation is generated within the computer. The number of computer input cards have been averaging about 1200 per day for a typical cycle of play assessing division units in the theater level setting. This cycle of play is a 24 hour game cycle and is generally assessed in a period of some three working days."[42]

THEATERSPIEL contains five computer models: air operations, ground combat operations, combat support, logistics, and combat recovery. Guerrilla activity, small unit actions, and political-military affairs are hand-assessed. The intelligence model was played by hand, but is now computerized.

Computer outputs include a casualty assessment report and a master status report. The casualty assessment report results from the interaction of three models: air, ground, and support. The status report provides the updated position, strength, and supply level of all units. It also provides the combat potential of ground combat units, and the weapons potential of artillery units. The control group combines the information contained in these reports with its hand-assessed results and the outputs of the intelligence model. It prepares and issues evaluated intelligence reports to the players. Upon receipt of this information, the players are ready to begin the next cycle of play.

The use of computers in conjunction with manual gaming techniques has several advantages. The computer frees the control group from tedious and time-consuming computations and bookkeeping, and allows the game to progress at a more acceptable rate. It makes possible rigid and rapid damage assessment in games in which the decisions are made by the players as well as in those in which the players and the umpires follow predetermined doctrines and decision rules. And in either case, this type of gaming permits the players and umpires to utilize map displays and to follow the course of events as they would in a similar but purely manual game.

A computer-assisted game is an amalgam of computer models, hand-played models and value judgments. It allows for a gradual development and substitution of computer models for hand-played models and hand-played models for control group judgment when and as experience indicates that each such substitution is both practicable and desirable. Computer-assisted games can use smaller and less costly equipment than those needed for computer simulations, and usually require less of an investment in programming time. They appear to be suited to gaming activities which do not have direct access to a computer, but which may, through the use of remote input-output devices, share one with a number of other activities. As pointed out by Morgenthaler,[46] computer-assisted gaming may be more efficient than computer simulations for large-scale games which are to be run once or a limited number of times.

Computer-assisted games require careful planning so that computer inputs and outputs form a logical part of the overall flow of information. They are adaptable to a time-step type of play in which players make decisions, the control group, with the aid of the computer, monitors and assesses the resulting movements and interactions, and then informs the players of the results. Computer-assisted games are less rapid than computer games, and are not suited to situations which require a large number of replications.

Computer Gaming. Computer games are conducted entirely on a digital computer. Once the program and data are loaded, and the start button pressed, the computer itself simulates the conflict in accordance with the instructions stored in its memory. Computer games are analytical, and completely rigid. As noted earlier, they are sometimes called computer simulations or computational games.

Although the programming of a computer for a game may be a lengthy and involved process, it follows the same basic procedures that are required for programming an umpire routine, or any other sort of problem. First, a general model or flow chart is constructed. Detailed block diagrams are prepared, and a program written. The program is recorded on punched cards or on tapes. The program, subroutines, data, and parameters are read into memory, and the program is debugged. Then the game is ready to be played. As in the umpiring program, parameters such as hit probabilities, weapon ranges, etc., may be changed to suit the purpose of the game. Additionally, since the model for a computer game includes the decisions and actions of the players, provisions are made to reflect a number of player decisions or doctrines by a selection of suitable input parameter.

During and at the end of a game, the computer can print out the desired results according to instructions. For instance, in an antiair warfare game, "The 'print-outs' can show numbers of aircraft shot down by missiles and by interceptors. It can show numbers and types of ships sunk, and it can show each event in chronological order together with the time it occurs. If the machine has the necessary accessories, a graphic presentation showing attacking bombers and defending ship tracks can be printed out during or at the end of the game."[31]

The pregame procedures for a computer game are similar to those for other types, but require more careful and detailed planning. The model, for example, must be constructed so that all desired aspects are considered and described precisely. If some contingency is not programmed, an umpire cannot step in and make a decision, or stop the play until a rule is formulated. As observed previously, changes in program logic require a rewriting of the routine.

Because the preparation of a computer model requires that every step be thought out in advance, it is sometimes constructed with the aid of manual gaming techniques. The hand-plays provide the model designers with an opportunity to see and examine all possible events and interactions, to gain an appreciation of their interrelationships and relative worth, to determine feasible aggregations, and to experiment with various procedures.

Computer models, like other game models, may be either deterministic or stochastic in their treatment of chance events. "A deterministic model has the property that the result of a modeled event is completely determined by the data which describe the situation. In such a model the results of probabilistic events are determined by expected values for the events; e.g., if the probability of a bomber's survival over a given route is 0.20, then of ten bombers flown along this route the deterministic model shows exactly eight killed and two alive at the end of the route. A stochastic or Monte Carlo model has the property that the result of a modeled event is determined by the interaction of the model rules with a random process (or processes). For instance, the stochastic model might determine how many of the ten bombers survive by comparing ten random numbers with the survival probability 0.20; for each number less than 0.20 a bomber survives.

"Repeated runs of a stochastic model reveal the distribution of possible outcomes, not just an expected outcome."[6] Stochastic models are also called probabilistic models. Outcomes are subject to chance or probability. Some models use both expected value (deterministic) and stochastic (probabilistic) techniques.

Time-Step and Event-Store Games. Usually, computer games are conducted according to either a time-step or event-store method. In the former case, as mentioned in Chapter III, the procedures are similar to those used in a manual game in which all moves are made for a fixed time interval. The computer calculates the positions of all forces at regular time steps. At the end of each step, it examines each interaction that might have occurred, decides if it did occur, and if it did, determines the outcomes.

"For any particular play of a game the time interval is a constant, but may be changed from play to play if so desired. ... In a time step game, when two things occur within the same interval, either extra calculations must be made to determine which occurred first, or the programmer must have arbitrarily decided which item takes precedence. A small time step can be employed to eliminate most occurrences of this nature but (this increases the running time of a game)."[50]

In the event-store or critical event method, the computer, instead of advancing the game by constant time increments, jumps ahead to the next event that has a probability of occurring and that is vital to the outcome of the game. "No positions, distances, or times are determined until they can be used."[50]

As each new event is generated an "event word" is formed. This word tells when the event will occur, what type of action is to be taken, and what offensive and defensive units are involved. The word is then stored according to its time of occurrence in a chronological list of future events.

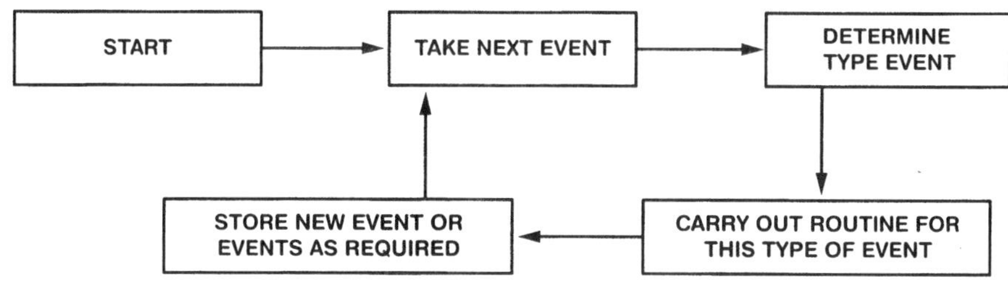

EVENT STORE ROUTINE

Figure 6-6

"The sequence of the game is as follows: input data and program are read into the computer and the machine then calculates and stores, in proper order, all events that can be predicated at the start of the game. The program then takes the first event in store, calculates the outcome, stores this, forms words for any required new events, and removes any units that will no longer affect the game results. With further events in store, they are considered in order, until the last event is treated. Then the game is completed. As an alternative procedure the game can be terminated at some fixed time, or when some specific event occurs."[50]

One advantage of the event-store method is that events—detections, weapon releases, weapon kills, etc.—occur in proper time sequence; another, the ease and flexibility of programming. "All of the various sections of the event store game are loosely coupled through the control routine which selects the next event in store and determines its type. If it is found that new events are desirable, or if revisions to existing events are indicated, these can be inserted without affecting the entire game. This is particularly true when an effort is made in the original coding to (1) allow space in the computer store for expansion, and (2) to make each event a self-contained routine. Since experience shows that all games need some modifications when used to study varied military problems, this feature is well appreciated."[50]

One disadvantage of the event-store technique is that "Initially, the programmer encounters difficulty with the logic because the normal chronological sequence is not obvious. ... This difficulty is overcome by experience and many persons then find the event concept the simpler."[50] A second limitation is the amount of memory that must be set aside for storing future events. This difficulty may be minimized by combining the time-step and event-store methods into a so-called "Periodically Supplemented Event Store" technique. In this method "A time step is added to the control program by storing at a stated interval a type of event that will look forward and determine which of the participants can have interactions in the coming time interval. Events occurring farther ahead than one time interval will not be stored unless the necessary data could only now be available."[50]

Some Advantages and Disadvantages of Computer Gaming. Computer games are strictly analytical games. They are another tool for the analysis and evaluation of military operations.

The chief advantage of computer gaming is replication. Within a reasonable amount of time, a game can be replicated sufficiently often to obtain a range of results which gives an indication of "... how bad the situation could be, how good it might be, and what the average results are."[31] Then one or more parameters can be varied, another series played, and a new distribution of results obtained. A comparison of the distributions reveals the effects of the parameter variation or variations.

A computer can perform a tremendous volume of routine calculations and bookkeeping, and examine and consider more factors than human players. Additionally, it can play the same game over and over again without becoming bored, making mistakes in arithmetic, forgetting to follow some of the rules, neglecting to consider all pertinent aspects, or injecting into the game information acquired in a preceding run.

On the debit side, the development of a computer model, its programming, and debugging may require a great deal of effort and time, far more than usually needed for other types of games. For instance, Morgenthaler[46] noted that one medium-sized computer simulation took one man-year to formulate, program, and check. He pointed out, however, that as analysts acquire that priceless commodity, experience, the time required for model building and programming will be reduced.

Dr. A. W. Pennington of the Planning Analysis Group of the Applied Physics Laboratory of the Johns Hopkins University noted a second difficulty: "I feel that the real limitation of the (computer) war game is the difficulty of translating the intention of the model to the computer."[51] Clayton J. Thomas, in Chapter 10 of *Progress in Operations Research* voiced a similar opinion.[52]

Although some computer games dealing with ground operations include the physical and military characteristics of terrain, their insertion in some games have presented programming and storage problems. In an article published in 1960, Colonel E. S. Maloney, USMC, stated that this difficulty is a fundamental limitation to the application of computer gaming to ground operations, and he wrote: "The mathematical expression of such factors as cover and concealment, visibility, and trafficability for each distinct terrain section has been attempted but requires such a tremendous amount of detail as to absorb, or exceed, the entire capacity of the computer. There is at this time no proven and fully accepted method of inserting terrain factors in a computer-played war game."[53]

Because computer games are analytical games, readers are always cautioned that the outputs of a game are no better than the inputs, or that the method is no better than the inputs. "This, of course, is true but I would point out also that this is true of any study and if valid inputs are available for other types of studies they must also be available for war games. In addition, I would point out that in every operations research study mathematical approximations are made just so the mathematics are tractable and often these assumptions are not immediately apparent to any but the most sophisticated mathematician. This never need be the case in a war game. … When the problem can be reduced to a logical flow, but the interactions are too complicated for direct calculation in a reasonable time, use the digital computer"[51] (game).

Since the late 1950's, computer gaming has probably become the most popular form of war gaming, and a surprisingly large number and variety of models and routines have been developed by both military activities and civilian contract organizations. In early 1966 about seventy-five computer models and routines were being used to assist in studies and analyses of cold, limited, and general war. These models ranged from tactical games such as CARMONETTE III to strategic simulations such as STAGE.

CARMONETTE III was developed by the Research Analysis Corporation for the Army. This game plays the actions and interactions of opposing ground units. It includes individual soldiers, mortars and artillery pieces as well as supporting tanks, helicopters, and aircraft. STAGE, at the opposite end of the spectrum, was developed by Technical Operations, Inc. for the Air Force. This game simulates a two-sided nuclear exchange, and plays such details as aircraft sorties, fuel states, missile flights, and ground zeros of individual weapons.

In addition to the computer games that have been developed to simulate ground and air warfare, a number have been devised to simulate the various aspects of naval warfare. A few of these games are discussed in the remaining part of this chapter.

Navy War Games Program Computer Games.[54,55] As part of the Navy War Games Program, a number of computer games and game analyses have been developed and conducted by technical support groups operating under the direction of the Assistant to the Chief of Naval Operations for War Gaming Matters (Op-06C).*

* The other part of the Navy War Games Program consists of "The examination of current fleet and force exercises and plans using the Naval Electronic Warfare Simulator (NEWS) at the Naval War College."[31]

The major customers for these games and analyses are the Joint War Games Agency of the Joint Chiefs of Staff, the operating forces of the Navy, and study groups sponsored by the Chief of Naval Operations.*

The Planning Analysis Group (PAG) of the Applied Physics Laboratory, Johns Hopkins University, is the technical support group that develops and conducts simulations and analyses of naval warfare. Among the games produced by this group are the Strike Warfare Model Mark II, the Anti-Air Warfare Systems Interaction Model, the Sea Warfare Intermediate Model, and the SSBM Detection Model.

Strike Warfare Model Mark II

This game is an improved and expanded version of an earlier strike warfare model. It provides a means for rapidly examining the interplay of opposing plans and forces in a two-sided, global, nuclear war, thus permitting numerous runs of the same situation. The model is an event-store type. Running time is approximately two hours. Outputs include a battle history which contains an account of each event that occurred.

The area of operations for the game is divided into blocks measuring five degrees of latitude by five degrees of longitude. Each base is located within its appropriate block. A base is a target in the game. Bases may be airfields, carriers, missile sites, and so on. The characteristics of the bases are inputs to the game.

Characteristics of the opposing forces and the details of the opposing plans are also inputs to the game. These inputs may be real or hypothetical, and include such details as take-off bases, take-off times, and flight profiles.

Play begins with one of the opposing sides initiating a nuclear attack. After a time delay, the side under attack takes retaliatory action. Aborts, in-flight and warhead reliabilities are stochastically examined. The impact points of ballistic missiles are determined and damage to bases assessed.

The game also includes in-flight interactions between the penetrators (bombers, air-to-surface missiles and decoys) and the defenses (interceptors and surface-to-air missiles), and the refueling and rearming of aircraft that return to base.

* Thomas Bush. "War Gaming in the Navy." A lecture delivered at the School of Naval Command and Staff, Naval War College, Newport, R.I.: September 29, 1965.

Anti-Air Warfare Systems Interaction Model

The Systems Interaction Model (SIM) provides a means for evaluating the antiair warfare capabilities of a naval task force against an air threat. By a choice of inputs, the user can describe the desired tactical situation, the doctrines of the opposing sides, and the characteristics of opposing forces and weapons. The game can simulate all aspects of a naval force versus air attack, selected portions of the defensive system or, by means of suitable inputs, air attacks against land bases.

The model is capable of conducting a search-for-the-fleet game in an area of up to 16,000,000 square miles, but usually uses smaller areas and situations in which the approximate location of the fleet is known.

The concept of sector defense is employed. A vital area contains the ships that perform the task force's basic mission; other sectors outside the vital area contain radar pickets, early warning aircraft, and combat air patrols. However, by using suitable inputs to describe the sectors, almost any disposition including dispersed dispositions can be represented.

The task force can include any desired naval vessels, and employ any desired tactics, weapons, and sensor systems. Weapons include shipborne missiles and guns and airborne air-to-air missiles. Both defensive and offensive electronic countermeasures can be played.

"The attack is composed of one or more raids, each having one or more aircraft, which fly a mission profile controlled by take-off time, course, speed, altitude and maneuvering inputs. The raids may conduct search and attack with airborne radar, passive ECM equipment, and offensive weapons which include air-to-surface missiles, rockets, and bombs in various combinations. Raids may also use active ECM equipment capable of jamming search and track radars and communications. Fighter cover and decoys may also be provided for the attack."[54]

Damage to ships is computed from delivery accuracy, warhead size, and target characteristics.

Sea Warfare Intermediate Model (SWIM)

The Sea Warfare game is designed to simulate the play of a Blue carrier striking force and supporting antisubmarine warfare units against a coordinated attack by Red submarines armed with torpedoes and cruise missiles.

The area of operations is a rectangle which may represent any desired size and location. The striking forces consist of a carrier, cruisers, and destroyers, and it may be supported by a hunter-killer group. Ship, weapon and sensor characteristics are inputs, as are the positions of ships in the force and group dispositions. Ship positions in the formations remain constant throughout the game; however, destroyers may leave the formations to prosecute a submarine contact, returning afterwards to their original positions. The carrier of the hunter-killer group provides fixed-wing aircraft and helicopters for patrols and the prosecution of submarine contacts.

Red forces consist of nuclear and conventional submarines. Prior to play, a number of the submarines may be assigned cruise missiles for use against the surface forces. The missiles are equipped with terminal active-radar homing.

"Communications between the units in the Blue force is assumed throughout the game so that the current status of all 'datums' is known to the main task force and so that units on the same datum carry out coordinated tactics ... There is no communication between the individual Red submarines during the game; however, it is assumed that all have access to periodic broadcasts from a Red Intelligence Center (RIC)."[55]

The game usually begins with both sides in a high state of readiness. The carrier striking force is deployed in a general operating area; Red submarines are on patrol stations and have general knowledge of Blue's operating area. Depending upon input times, the Blue force proceeds to a launch area, launches its strikes, and moves to the recovery area; the Red submarines leave their stations and attempt to close, and then attack. The hunter-killer group conducts searches and conducts hold-down tactics until the strikes are launched or until an overt attack by Red submarines. A concentration of submarine contacts during the game, or a submarine attack can cause changes in Blue's timetable.

While this game does not contain provisions for Red air attacks on the Blue forces, it is planned to include this feature in future versions.

SSBM Detection Model

This model simulates ballistic-missile submarines approaching missile launching sites off a coast line, and their interactions with submarine surveillance systems and associated aircraft.

Detections obtained by the surveillance system are relayed to antisubmarine warfare patrol aircraft. Depending upon the information received, the aircraft proceed along a bearing line or to a designated area and attempt to detect, localize, and kill. Aircraft have the capability of detecting

> submarines by radar, visually, or by means of sonobuoys. Freighters proceeding through the area allow for contacts which may be misclassified by the surveillance system.
>
> Submarines may detect aircraft, and attempt to remain undetected by the aircraft. They can also detect the freighters. Conventional submarines may recharge their batteries on the surface or by snorkeling. Nuclear submarines remain submerged, and transit the area either above or below the layer.

In addition to the four games described above, the Planning Analysis Group has developed a number of other games and computer routines. These include air strike models, antiair warfare models, antisubmarine barrier models, a submarine versus submarine approach and attack model, and a torpedo salvo assessment routine. This latter model is designed to provide the data needed to assess the effects of non-homing torpedo firings for both hand-played and computer games.

All current Planning Analysis Group models are run on IBM 7090 and 7094 computers. In most cases reprogramming would be necessary if different computers were used.

Unclassified descriptions of the Planning Analysis Group's games are contained in *The Navy War Games Manual*[54] and the Planning Analysis Group's publication, *Simulation Digest I*.[55] Reports published by PAG are distributed by the Assistant for War Gaming Matters, Office of the Chief of Naval Operations (Op-06C).

The Computation and Analysis Laboratory of the U. S. Naval Weapons Laboratory is the group that provides technical support to Op-06C in the major areas of amphibious warfare and damage assessment. This activity has developed three amphibious warfare models: Embarkation Planning Support, Supporting Arms, and Ship-to-Shore.

> **Embarkation Planning Support Model**
>
> "This model can simulate the embarkation of an entire Marine Expeditionary Corps with associated shipping. Minimum amphibious and MSTS (Military Sea Transportation Service) shipping requirements are determined, assigned to ports of embarkation and scheduled in a manner which will accomplish embarkation and movement to the pre-rehearsal or Amphibious Operation Area (AOA) in the shortest possible time.... By varying input parameters, various alternatives of any given plan can be investigated."[54]

Supporting Arms Model

The Supporting Arms Computer Model simulates the naval gunfire and air support portions of an amphibious operation during the pre-assault phases (pre-D-day and D-day (pre-H-hour) time period).

The naval gunfire portion of the model simulates target acquisition, firings, and damage; the air support portion simulates planned and alert status air strikes and consequent damage. Damage to aircraft by opposition groundfire can also be played.

Weapons data can be supplied by the Naval Weapons Laboratory. Operational data, however, is supplied by the user for his particular operation plan.

Game outputs list the status of each element (targets, aircraft, etc.) at desired times. Summaries provide such information as types and amount of ordnance expended, targets destroyed, and number of sorties flown.

Ship-to-Shore Model

The Ship-to-Shore model provides a means for playing in detail "the movement of troops, vehicles, equipment and supplies from ships to a beach or landing zone by means of surface craft, LST's, and helicopters.

"This model can be used to determine the craft and shipping requirements to effectively achieve a certain build-up rate ashore, as well as the time required to land a certain force level or the time required to complete the operation. A wide variety of present or proposed characteristics of ships, landing craft, helicopters, force composition, and beach handling rates can be investigated."[54]

Sealift I.[56] The Sealift I game simulates the convoy-submarine battle. It was developed by the Naval Warfare Analysis Group, Center for Naval Analyses, to assist in the study of convoy protection, primarily against submarines, and to examine its effects on the sealift supply rates in a limited war.

During the game, and at times determined by inputs, convoys are formed in a home port. Each convoy is composed of three types of ships: cargo, antisubmarine, and forward screen ships. The forward screen may also include aircraft, sonobuoys, and submarines. The ships in a convoy are drawn from a port "pool." "This pool is stocked by ships from returning convoys and by the ship building rate. If the required ships are available, the convoy sails toward its delivery port; if not, the game is stopped, and a 'printout' is made of the game results to date including the event that caused the stoppage."

As the convoy and its escorts proceed toward the delivery port, the ships encounter various types and degrees of opposition: mine fields, air attacks, surface attacks, and submarine attacks. Each of the various types of opposition may be included, or not, as desired. The emphasis, however, is on the submarine opposition. Ships lost during the transit are recorded by ship types, method and time of loss. Losses of escorts decrease the antisubmarine capability of the force.

"After reaching the delivery port, the convoy unloads and stays in port a prescribed number of days. During this period the cargo ships are again liable to air attack. Of those ships sunk in an air attack, one-half are assumed to be sunk before unloading and one-half after unloading."

On the homeward trip, the convoy reverses its route, and is subject to the same kinds of opposition that it encountered on the outbound trip. When it reaches port the ships are placed by types in various "ship pools." The ship pools are then used to make up future convoys.

There can be up to three types of submarines in the game. At the start of play, a selected percentage of the opposition submarines are in port and the remainder are on station. The time remaining on station for those on patrol is determined by a uniform random distribution.

As the game gets under way, submarines in port depart for their patrol areas at times determined by inputs. Those in port are subject to damage by strikes. Additionally, new construction adds to the submarine force as the war progresses.

Submarines in transit to and from station encounter good and bad sonar conditions, and are subject to various types of opposition and interactions including antisubmarine barriers and possible attacks by a hunter-killer group.

If a submarine detects the convoy, it tries to penetrate the convoy's defense and sink cargo ships. Escorts then form surface attack units and attempt to locate and destroy the submarine. If the user so desires, the submarines may attack escorts rather than cargo vessels, i.e., conduct an anti-escort campaign.

When a submarine has either completed its time on station or fired its maximum permissible number of torpedoes, it begins the return trip. If and when a submarine reaches its home port, it will stay there for a predetermined period of time for overhaul and resupply, and then sail again for a patrol area.

Barrier Submarine Computer Game.[57] This game was designed and programmed by Commander William A. Van Train, USN, in partial fulfillment of the requirements for a degree at the United States Naval Postgraduate School, Monterey,

California. It was evolved to illustrate the advantages of using computer gaming to assist in the design of submarine barriers, and was programmed for play on the 1604 Computer manufactured by the Control Data Corporation.

Essentially, the game provides a means for conducting parametric analyses of submarine barriers to determine:

(1) The best design of a submarine barrier, and

(2) The optimal sample size required for a computer output in order to achieve a reasonable degree of sensitivity in the analysis.

In the program a game play begins with the attempt of a single transiting submarine to penetrate a submarine barrier, and ends when the penetrator succeeds or is destroyed. A game unit constitutes 100 plays, and a single data run is as many game units as the analyst desires.

For the play of a data run, a one, two, or three line barrier is selected. Barrier submarines are positioned probabilistically in the vicinity of their assigned stations, and the transitor is assigned a track angle in a similar fashion. The transitor then attempts to penetrate the barrier. Following its success or failure, the barrier submarines are redistributed, the transitor repositioned, and another play started. After 100 plays the data are stored, and another unit of plays started. Upon completion of the predetermined number of game units, a statistical analysis subroutine computes the sample mean and variance of detections, interceptions, and kills for each 100 plays, and additional data for the specified number of 100-transit runs. The general procedures are shown in the simplified flow chart of Figure 6-7.

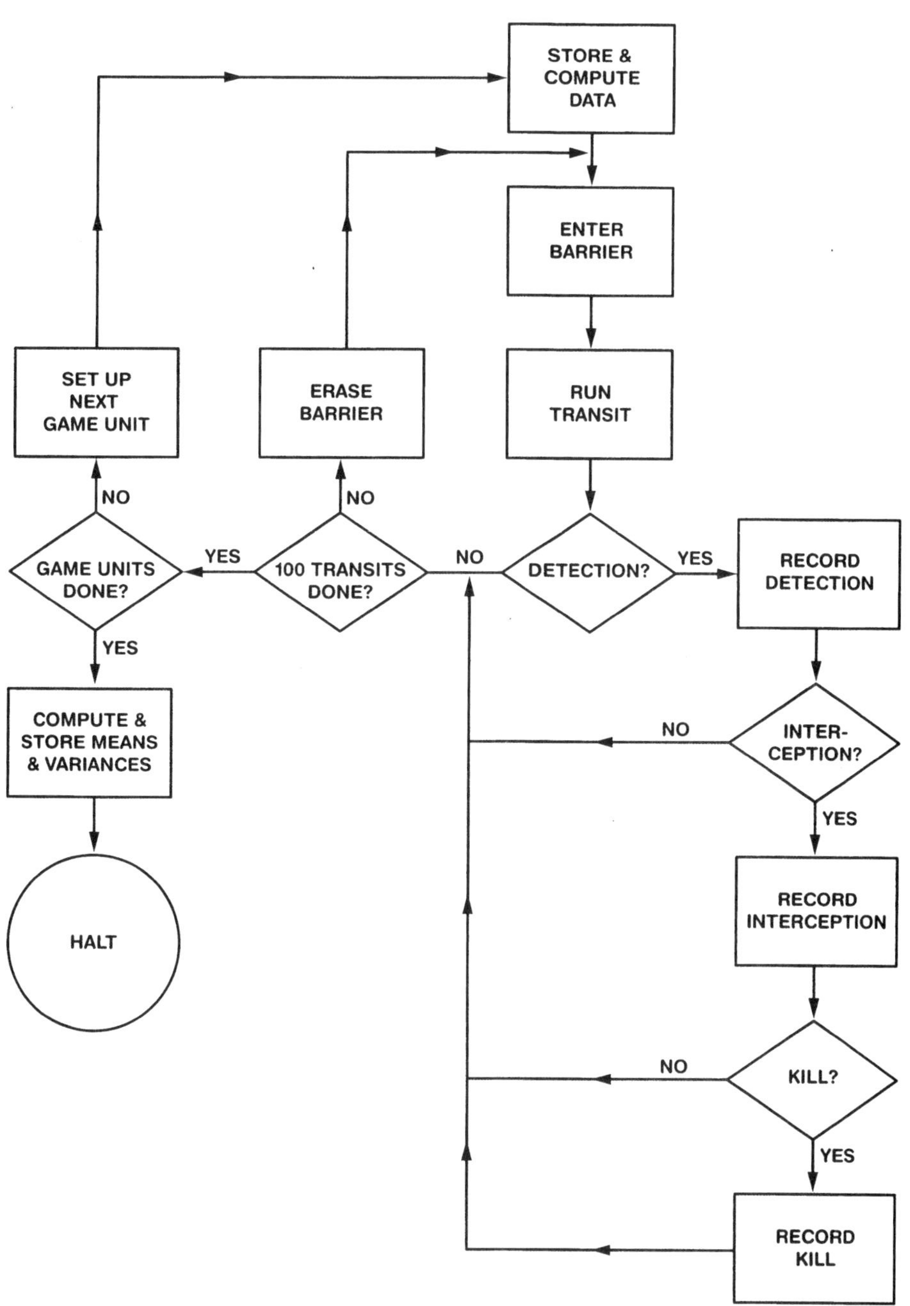

FLOW CHART—BARRIER SUBMARINE MODEL

Figure 6-7

Appendix A
Chance Devices

Chance Devices. A coin may be used to simulate an event with a 0.5 probability of success; an ordinary die to determine the success or failure of an event in a war game having a 1/6, 1/3, 1/2, 2/3 or 5/6 probability of occurrence. Both are chance devices of somewhat limited usefulness. A more versatile device is nothing more than a box or bag containing, say, 10 cards, each bearing a different digit. If a card is drawn with any number from 1 to 8, an event with a probability of happening of 0.8 occurs; if a 9 or a 0, it does not happen. The card is replaced, the box shaken, and it is ready for the next drawing. Or in the proportions indicated by past records, the cards might be labelled according to different weather conditions. Then if a card is drawn with the word "fog," a heavy blanket settles over the area of operations. Various types of roulette wheels and spinning devices such as those used in the Coast Artillery Game[24] are sometimes useful, and even roller skate wheels with subdivided rims have been employed as random devices. But despite the usefulness of some of these methods, the traditional—and until recently the most popular—war gaming chance device is a pair of ordinary 6-sided dice.

Table A-1 illustrates how a pair of 6-sided dice may be employed to produce various probabilities. Thus, if an event has a 50 percent probability of happening, and a roll of the dice results in a 2, 4, 5, 6, or 8, it happens; if any other value turns up, it doesn't. Again, if the probability is 0.80, and the upturned faces of the two dice add up to any of the following: 2, 4, 5, 6, 7, 8, 9, or 12, the event occurs.*

* With the exceptions of 0.25, 0.50, and 0.75, the probabilities listed in Table A-1 are approximate values. For example, the probability of rolling a 3 with a pair of unbiased dice is $\frac{2}{36}$, or 0.056; of rolling a 2, 4, 5, 6, 7, or 10, is $\frac{22}{36}$ or 0.611. (See Table B-2, Appendix B.)

Table A-1

PROBABILITIES RESULTING FROM A SINGLE ROLL OF TWO 6-SIDED DICE

Probability	Value of the Throw
.05	3
.10	5
.15	3 or 4
.20	2 or 7
.25	2, 3, or 7
.30	6 or 7
.35	3, 6, or 7
.40	2, 4, 5, 6, or 12
.45	2, 3, 4, 5, 6, or 12
.50	2, 4, 5, 6, or 8
.55	2, 3, 4, 5, 6, or 8
.60	2, 4, 5, 6, 7, or 10
.65	2, 3, 4, 5, 6, 7, or 11
.70	2, 4, 5, 6, 7, 8, or 12
.75	2, 3, 4, 5, 6, 7, 8, or 12
.80	2, 4, 5, 6, 7, 8, 9, or 12
.85	2, 3, 4, 5, 6, 7, 8, 9, or 12
.90	2, 4, 5, 6, 7, 8, 9, 10, or 12
.95	2, 3, 4, 5, 6, 7, 8, 9, 10, or 12
1.00	2, 3, 4, 5, 6, 7, 8, 9, 10, 11, or 12

Somewhat reminiscent of an early World War II put-it-together-yourself approximation of the globe is a relatively new and simple chance device, the 20-sided or random number generating die. It is in the form of an icosahedron, one of the five regular polyhedra. Each of the 20 bounding surfaces is an equilateral triangle, and each of the 10 digits, 0 to 9, appears twice on its faces. The probability of any particular digit appearing on a single roll of a die is 2/(2+18) or 0.10, and all have an equal probability of showing. Dice in the form of icosahedra are packaged in sets of three, each one of a different color, so that one, two, or three random digits may be produced by a throw of one, two or three dice respectively.*

For an 80 per cent probability, a throw of an unbiased 20-sided die must turn up any one of 8 digits. Which 8, of course, are determined in advance of the roll. The usual choices are 1 to 8 with 9 and 0 spelling failure; or 0 to 7 inclusive, yes; 8 and 9, no.

Two different colored dice are useful for simulating an event with a probability of success of say, 0.41. A red die might be selected for the first digit of the

* Sets of 3—one each of red, yellow, and blue—are manufactured and sold by the Japanese Standards Association, Kobikikan-Bekkan Building, 6-1, Ginza-higashi, Chuo-ku, Tokyo, Japan. The price is $2.50 per set, plus $0.70 postage (up to 9 sets).

number; a yellow, for the second. Since with two dice there are 100 equally likely ways of turning up a two digit number, 00, 01, 02, to 99, then 41 of the numbers, usually 01 to 41, or 00 to 40, are selected to indicate success.

Three 20-sided dice are used in the same manner as two to derive probabilities such as 0.504 that are expressed in thousandths. However, three-place accuracy is seldom possible or even desirable in war gaming and, for that reason, three dice are not used very often for evaluating interactions.

Twenty-sided dice are also used for randomly rounding-off fractional values. For example, suppose that the application of the damage rules in a war game resulted in 1.75 hits, then a pair of dice may be rolled to determine whether one or two hits are assessed. A roll of 01 to 75 rules two hits; a roll of 76 to 00, one hit.

Currently, the most widely used war gaming chance device is a table of random numbers. A portion of such a table is shown below:

09	10	25	27	91
40	46	59	89	64
87	41	30	06	53
68	95	56	09	47
81	33	80	83	28
14	96	15	09	50
95	05	31	61	84
91	88	24	32	97
48	46	80	68	53
10	29	76	42	90

The numbers in a random number table are grouped for convenience in reading. The columns in some tables consist of rows of two digits, as above; in others, of rows of three, four or five digits. Usually, there is an extra space between every five or ten rows.

Random number tables are often compiled by electronic devices or computers. A number of tables is available in pamphlet or book form; for example, the *Table of 105,000 Random Decimal Digits* prepared by the Interstate Commerce Commission's Bureau of Transport Economics and Statistics, and the RAND Corporation's *A Million Random Digits* published by the Free Press, Glenco, Illinois. Smaller tables are found in the back of such books as *The Compleat*

Strategyst by J. D. Williams (McGraw-Hill, 1954), and in the control group's section of the rules of some manual war games.

Random number tables can also be constructed by any manual process which selects one of the ten digits in such a way that each is equally likely to be chosen, and that each selection is in no way affected by previous selections. For instance, a random number table can be prepared, three digits at a time, by rolling three unbiased 20-sided dice, and writing down the digits as they appear on the upper faces of, let's say, the red, yellow and blue dice. Or a random number table might be constructed, one digit at a time, by drawing at random one of ten cards numbered from 0 to 9 from a box, then replacing the card, shaking the box and drawing again.

A third method uses an ordinary die and a table such as shown below. If the first roll results in a 3, and the second in a 6, then the first digit in the random number table is an 8. If the next trial results in a roll of a 2 and a 4, respectively, the second digit in the table is a 0, and so on. If, on any trial, a 6 is turned up on the first roll, the die is rolled again.

		SECOND ROLL					
		1	2	3	4	5	6
FIRST ROLL	1	1	2	3	4	5	6
	2	7	8	9	0	1	2
	3	3	4	5	6	7	8
	4	9	0	1	2	3	4
	5	5	6	7	8	9	0
	6	—	—	—	—	—	—

In order to use a random number table, a starting number is chosen at random, and a direction of movement selected. Thus, prior to the play of a game, for example, the number 89 in the second row from the top in the random number table shown on page 209 is selected as the first number, and the decision made to proceed downward. (Tables usually cover several pages and the direction of movement can be up, down, right or left.) It is also decided that numbers beginning with 01 and ending with the given probability times 100 will be used to represent successes, i.e. 01 to 20 will indicate success when a weapon with a 0.20 single shot hit probability is fired, 21 to 00 failure, and so on.

As the game progresses a weapon is fired five times, each firing having a hit probability of 0.20. The starting number, 89, rules a miss on the first firing. The results of the next four firings are: 06, a hit; 09, a hit; 83, a miss; and 09, a hit. Thus, in this particular case, chance has determined that the weapon scores three hits out of five firings, even though its single shot hit probability is only 0.20.

As each number in the random number table is used it is crossed out. Assuming that the same weapon is again fired five times, and its hit probability remains unchanged, the next five numbers in the table (61, 32, 68, 42, and 91) rules five misses.

Random number tables are also used in a manner similar to 20-sided dice to round-off fractional values. Thus, if during a game it is determined that 3.28 aircraft are destroyed, and it is desired to round-off this amount by a random round-off process, then the next unused number in the table is used to determine whether three or four aircraft are destroyed. A number from 01 to 28 rules that four aircraft are destroyed; one from 29 to 00, three aircraft. The next unused number in the random number table on page 209 is 64; therefore, in this instance, three aircraft are destroyed.

Where a sequence of possible events is concerned, one of two alternative chance evaluation procedures may be used. For example, suppose that the situation involves a fighter attacking a bomber and that the events are:

1. The fighter acquires the target on its air-intercept radar (detection);
2. The fighter attains a firing position (conversion);
3. The fighter's weapons destroy the bomber (kill); and the respective probabilities of success of each event are known.

Then one procedure is to use a chance device to determine if a detection occurs (assuming that there is an opportunity for a detection), and if a detection does occur, to use the chance device to determine whether or not the fighter attains a firing position, and so forth. A second procedure is to compute the overall probability of success by multiplying the probabilities of success of each of the component events, and to use this value in conjunction with a chance device to determine whether or not the fighter destroys the bomber.

Another example of the use of chance devices is illustrated by Table A-2. The values in the right column are taken from Figure 3-6, Chapter III. The first column relates the probabilities (as taken from Figure 3-6) associated with the hours in the right column to the roll of a pair of 20-sided dice; the second, with the numbers found in a table of random numbers; and the third, with the throw of a pair of ordinary 6-sided dice. If, for example, a roll of the 20-sided dice, or a table of random numbers turns up any number from 46 to 75 inclusive, or the regular dice show a 6 or a 7, then the equipment will function 700 hours without maintenance.

Table A-2

HOURS SINCE LAST MAINTENANCE PERIOD TO BREAKDOWN

Decision Numbers			
20-sided dice	Random Number Table	6-sided dice	Hours
01 - 05	01 - 05	3	400
06 - 20	06 - 20	3 or 4	500
21 - 45	21 - 45	2, 3, or 7	600
46 - 75	46 - 75	6 or 7	700
76 - 95	76 - 95	2 or 7	800
96 - 00	96 - 00	3	900

It is interesting to note the heading of the first three columns of Table A-2: "Decision Numbers." This term is used because the decisions made by the umpire or by the computer are determined by the numbers turned up by the dice or a random number table. It is a relatively new war gaming term and has been applied chiefly to decisions made in accordance with numbers obtained from random number tables, although it is equally applicable to numbers produced by dice as illustrated in Table A-2. Usually, a table such as Table A-2 contains only the column of decision numbers that is associated with the type of chance device provided for the game.

In computer games the computer generates or stores random numbers, and these numbers are used to determine the outcomes of chance events in stochastic models. The NEWS damage computer behaves in somewhat the same way. It measures the range at the time of firing, looks at the stored probability of the weapon versus the target at that particular range and, by means of a randomizing device, comes up with a hit, or a miss.

Appendix B
Probability Distributions

When a coin is tossed the results may be tabulated as follows:

Table B-1

Number of Heads	Probability
1	0.5
0	0.5

or shown graphically as in Figure B-1.

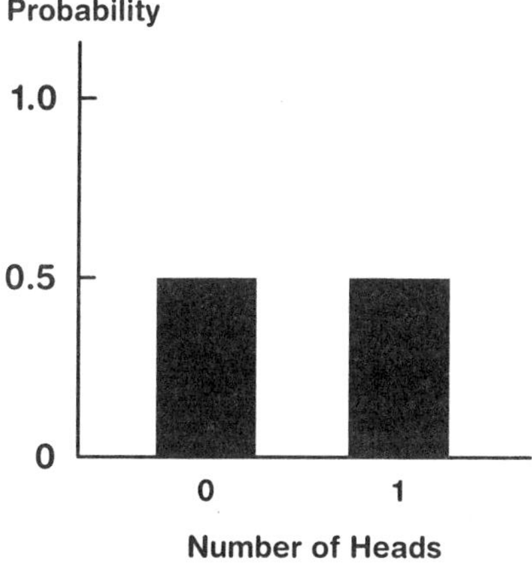

Figure B-1

These are two examples of a simple probability distribution, a tabular and a graphical. In the graph, the values of the random variable—in this case the number of heads—appear along the abscissa or horizontal axis; the probability along the ordinate or vertical axis.

Since a coin cannot show both a head and a tail, these events are mutually exclusive. Since it must fall in one of these ways, the sum of the probabilities equals 1, or certainty.

If two bombers in an aggregated force of four carry nuclear bombs, two conventional bombs, and two are destroyed en route to the target, how does the umpire determine which two are destroyed? Let A and B represent the two aircraft carrying nuclear weapons, and C and D those with the less lethal punch. As shown below, there are 6 possible combinations* of two aircraft:

A and B	B and C
A and C	B and D
A and D	C and D

The first includes both bombers packing a nuclear wallop; the next four, one nuclear bombing plane; and the last, no nuclear carrying aircraft. The graphical probability distribution is shown in Figure B-2. The number of nuclear bomb carrying aircraft destroyed may be determined by the roll of a single regular die: 1, no nuclear carrying aircraft destroyed; 2, 3, 4, or 5, one such bomber killed; and 6, both aircraft with nuclear weapons destroyed. Or 20-sided dice or a random number table might make the decision: 01 to 17, 18 to 83, and 84 to 00; 0, 1, and 2 nuclear carrying bombers respectively. Again, a 20-sided die or a table of random numbers could be used as follows: 1, 0 nuclear bomb lugging planes; 2, 3, 4, and 5, 1 such airplane; 6, 2 of the bombers with the big payload; 7, 8, 9, and 0, no go; and another roll is made, or the next number in the table selected.

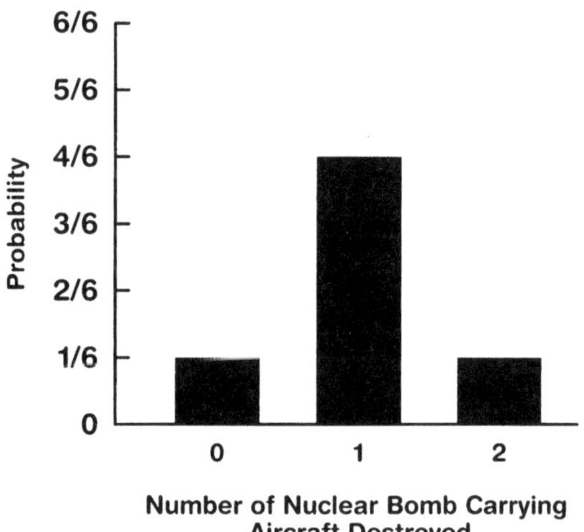

Figure B-2

* A combination is a group of things without regard to order. Thus, A and B, or B and A, are one combination.

When something can happen in m ways, and something else in n ways, together they can happen in m times n ways. For instance, 1 regular die can fall in 6 ways; two dice, in 36 ways. Extending this idea, three dice can fall in 6 x 6 x 6, or 216 ways. If a missile can either hit or miss its target, then in two independent trials there are 2 x 2 or 2^2, or 4 possible results: 2 hits; 1 hit, 1 miss; 1 miss, 1 hit; or two misses. When three missiles are launched there are 2^3, or 8 possible results, and so on.

In the case of two regular dice, there are 36 equally likely ways in which they can fall; 11 different values from 2 to 12 that then can show. The probability of any particular value appearing on a single throw of two dice is, therefore, the number of ways that the value can appear divided by 36. Thus, as shown in Table B-2, a 10 can turn up in three ways: 4, 6; 5, 5; or 6, 4, and the probability of rolling a 10 is 3/36. The probability distribution is delineated in Figure B-3. The random variable, the value of the throw, is shown along the abscissa; the probability along the ordinate. A table such as Table A-1 in Appendix A is compiled by changing the desired probability into 36ths and finding a number of throws with a total probability equal to the desired probability. For example: 0.60 equals (0.60 x 36)/36 or 21.6/36. This value is approximately equal to 22/36. 22/36 is equal to the sum of the probabilities of rolling a 2, 4, 5, 6, 7, or 10. (Other throws with probabilities adding up to 22/36 could just as well be used: 2, 3, 4, 5, 6, 7, and 12, for instance.)

Table B-2

2 REGULAR DICE

						6,1					
					5,1	5,2	6,2				
Numbers on upper faces of two dice				4,1	4,2	4,3	5,3	6,3			
			3,1	3,2	3,3	3,4	4,4	5,4	6,4		
		2,1	2,2	2,3	2,4	2,5	3,5	4,5	5,5	6,5	
	1,1	1,2	1,3	1,4	1,5	1,6	2,6	3,6	4,6	5,6	6,6
Value of the throw	2	3	4	5	6	7	8	9	10	11	12
Number of equally likely ways	1	2	3	4	5	6	5	4	3	2	1
Probability of the throw	1/36	2/36	3/36	4/36	5/36	6/36	5/36	4/36	3/36	2/36	1/36

Counting hits and misses, there are 2 x 2 x 2 or 8 ways in which three firings of a gun can affect the target. These are listed in the left column of Table B-3. If the single shot hit probability is 0.4, the probability of a miss is 1-0.4, or 0.6. A method

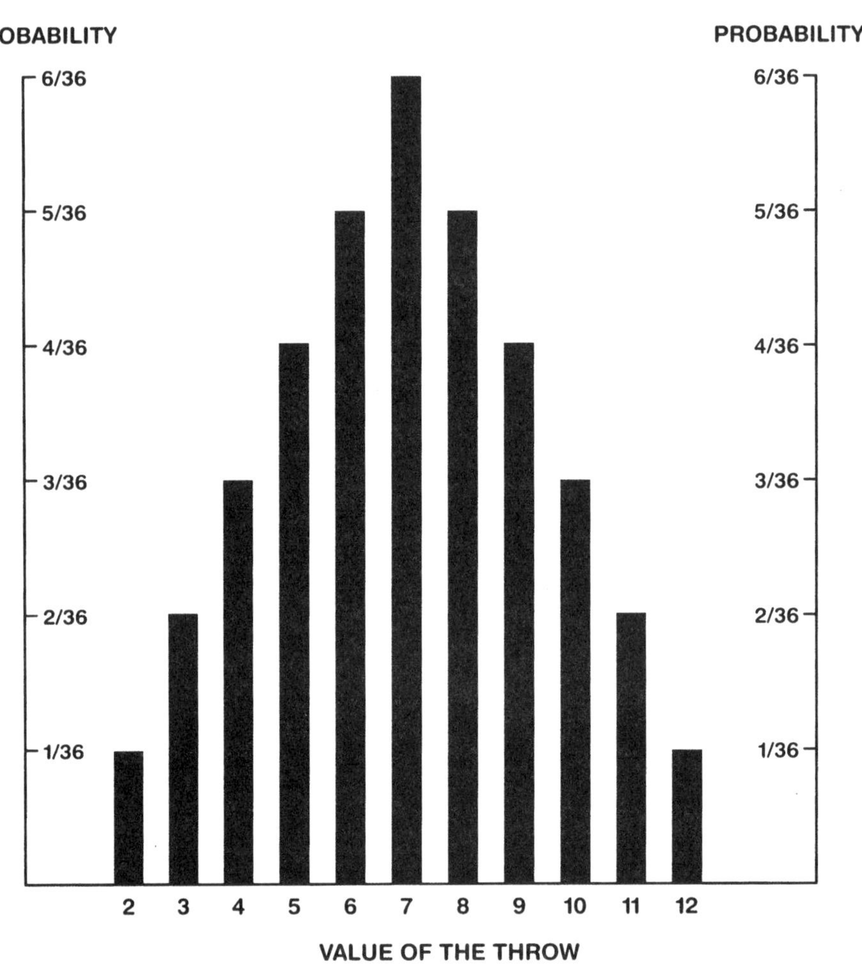

PROBABILITY DISTRIBUTION FOR TWO DICE

Figure B-3

for computing the hit probability of each combination is illustrated in the second column of the table. The probabilities of getting two hits and a miss, or one hit and two misses are summed, and the third column gives the probabilities of getting 3, 2, 1, and 0 hits; 0.064, 0.288, 0.432, and 0.216, respectively. These are sometimes referred to as the probabilities of "exactly" 3 hits, exactly 2 hits, etc. This is to distinguish them from other probabilities, for example, the probability of "at least" 2 hits, which in this case is the sum of the probabilities of getting 3 and 2 hits, or 0.064 plus 0.288, or 0.352. The probability of getting at least one hit is the sum of the probabilities of exactly 3, 2, and 1 hits, 0.064+0.288+0.432, or 0.784.* The chances of getting "at most" 1 hit, that is the probability of getting 1 or 0 hits, is 0.432+0.216, or 0.648.

Table B-3

THREE ROUNDS — SSHP = 0.4
(H indicates a hit; M, a miss)

Ways		Probabilities	Number of Hits
HHH	0.4 x 0.4 x 0.4 = .064	0.064	3
HHM HMH MHH	0.4 x 0.4 x 0.6 = .096 0.4 x 0.6 x 0.4 = .096 0.6 x 0.4 x 0.4 = .096	0.288	2
HMM MHM MMH	0.4 x 0.6 x 0.6 = .144 0.6 x 0.4 x 0.6 = .144 0.6 x 0.6 x 0.4 = .144	0.432	1
MMM	0.6 x 0.6 x 0.6 = .216	0.216	0
		1.000	

If the symbol ${}_nP_h$ represents the probability of exactly h events occurring in n independent trials, and p is the probability of occurrence in a single trial, the following formula can be used in place of the method indicated in Table B-3:

---

* The probability of at least one success in n independent trials can also be found by the following formula:

$$P_1 = 1 - (1-p)^n$$

For example: Let p = 0.4, and n = 3

$$P_1 = 1-(1-0.4)^3 = 1-0.216 = 0.784$$

This checks with the results obtained above.

The number of firings, n, necessary to obtain a probability of P_1 of at least one hit with a SSHP of p is:

$$n = \frac{\log (1-P_1)}{\log (1-p)}$$

Thus the number of firings needed to obtain a probability of 0.784 of at least one hit when the SSHP or p equals 0.4 is:

$$n = \frac{\log (1 - 0.784)}{\log (1 - 0.4)} = \frac{\log 0.216}{\log 0.6} = 3$$

$$_nP_h = \frac{n!}{h!\,(n-h)!}\; p^h\,(1-p)^{n-h} \qquad \text{(see footnote 1)}^{*}$$

Thus, the probability of exactly 3 hits in 3 trials when the SSHP or p equals 0.4 is:

$$_3P_3 = \frac{3!}{3!\,(3-3)!}\; 0.4^3\,(1-0.4)^{3-3} \qquad \text{(see footnote 2)}^{**}$$

$$= \frac{6}{6}\;(0.064)\,(1), \text{ or } 0.064$$

The probability of exactly 2 hits in 3 trials is:

$$_3P_2 = \frac{3!}{2!\,(3-2)!}\; 0.4^2\,(1-0.4)^{3-2}$$

$$= \frac{6}{2}\;(0.16)\,(0.6), \text{ or } 0.288$$

The probability of exactly 1 hit equals:

$$_3P_1 = \frac{3!}{1!\,(3-1)!}\; 0.4^1\,(1-0.4)^{3-1} = 0.432,$$

and the probability of 0 hits:

$$_3P_0 = \frac{3!}{0!\,(3-0)!}\; 0.4^0\,(1-0.4)^{3-0} = 0.216$$

Since the events are mutually exclusive, and 3, 2, 1, and 0 hits exhaust all possibilities, the sum of the probabilities equals 1. For gaming purposes the probabilities would most likely be rounded to 2 places, i.e., to 0.06, 0.29, 0.43 and 0.22 respectively.

The number of hits resulting from 3 firings of a weapon with a SSHP of 0.04 can be determined by use of Table B-4 and 20-sided dice, or by employing that table and a table of random numbers. If these chance devices are not available, 100 slips of paper numbered from 00 to 99 can be placed in a box and a slip drawn to

---

* 1) This is called the "binomial law." The values of $_nP_h$ versus h is known as the "binomial distribution." This distribution is a discrete distribution, i.e., a missile can score a hit, or 2 hits, etc., but not 1.17 or 2.39 hits, and so on. The binomial law is useful in many aspects of war gaming.

Two other well known distributions are the "Poisson distribution" and the "normal (or Gaussian) distribution." The former is a discrete function that approximates the binomial distribution when there are a large number of trials and the probability of success of a single trial is small. The normal distribution is a continuous function.

** 2) n! is read, "n factorial"; 3!, 3 factorial, etc. 3! equals 3x2x1; 2! equals 2x1, etc. 0! equals 1 by definition, i.e., (3-3)! = 1.

A number raised to a zero power equals 1. Thus, $(1-0.4)^{3-3} = 1$.

obtain the decision number. Another method employs a pair of regular dice and a compatible decision number table.

Table B-4

Decision Number	Number of Hits
01 - 06	3
07 - 35	2
36 - 78	1
79 - 00	0

Figure B-4 illustrates a mathematically determined probability distribution for five firings of a missile with an overall hit probability of 0.60. A distribution such as this may be computed according to the method indicated in Table B-3, or by use of the formula for ${}_nP_h$.

When a probability distribution is difficult or impossible to compute it may be approximated by simulating a number of trials, that is, by use of the Monte Carlo technique. Any of the chance devices may be employed—tables of random numbers, 20-sided dice, etc. For instance, the NEWS damage computer was used to simulate a number of trials of five firings of a missile with an overall hit probability of 0.60. After each trial of five firings the number of hits was recorded. At the end of 100 trials a probability distribution was prepared. It is shown in Figure B-5.

A comparison of the distributions of Figures B-4 and B-5 illustrates one instance of how a distribution obtained by simulation tends to approach its theoretical counterpart. If the distribution of Figure B-4 were not available, then the probability distribution obtained by the Monte Carlo method could be employed.

The relative frequency of hits, that is, the ratio of hits to firings obtained from the experiment conducted with the NEWS damage computer is shown in Figure B-6. Fifty firings with an overall hit probability of 0.6 resulted in 31 hits, or a relative frequency of 31/50 or 0.62. One hundred attempts scored 60 hits; 150 tries, 85 hits for a ratio of hits to firings of 0.57. After about 180 trials the relative frequency of hits remained very close to 60 percent.

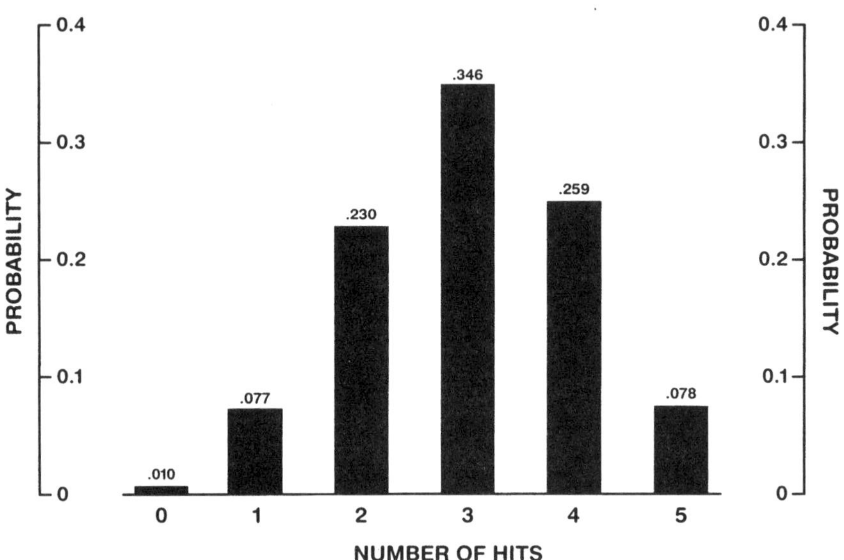

PROBABILITY DISTRIBUTION FOR 5 ROUNDS—OHP=0.6

Figure B-4

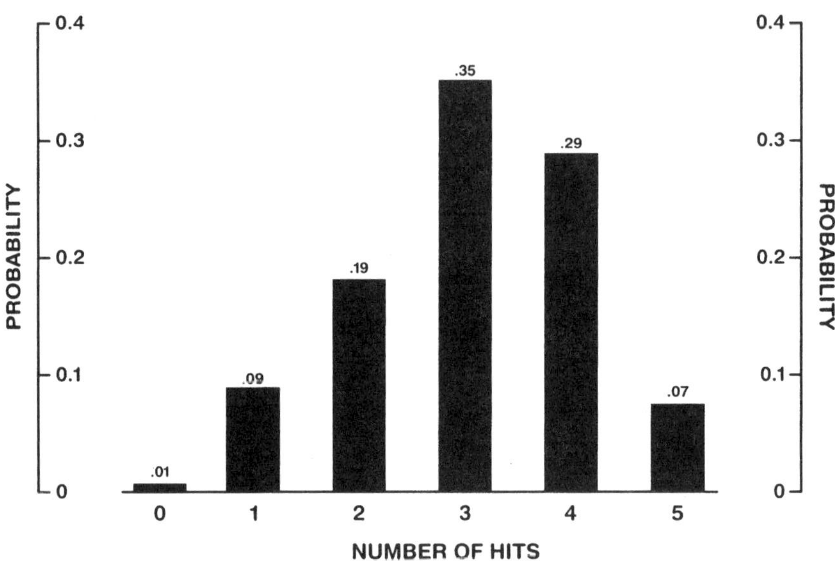

PROBABILITY DISTRIBUTION FOR 100 TRIALS OF 5 ROUNDS EACH—OHP=0.6

Figure B-5

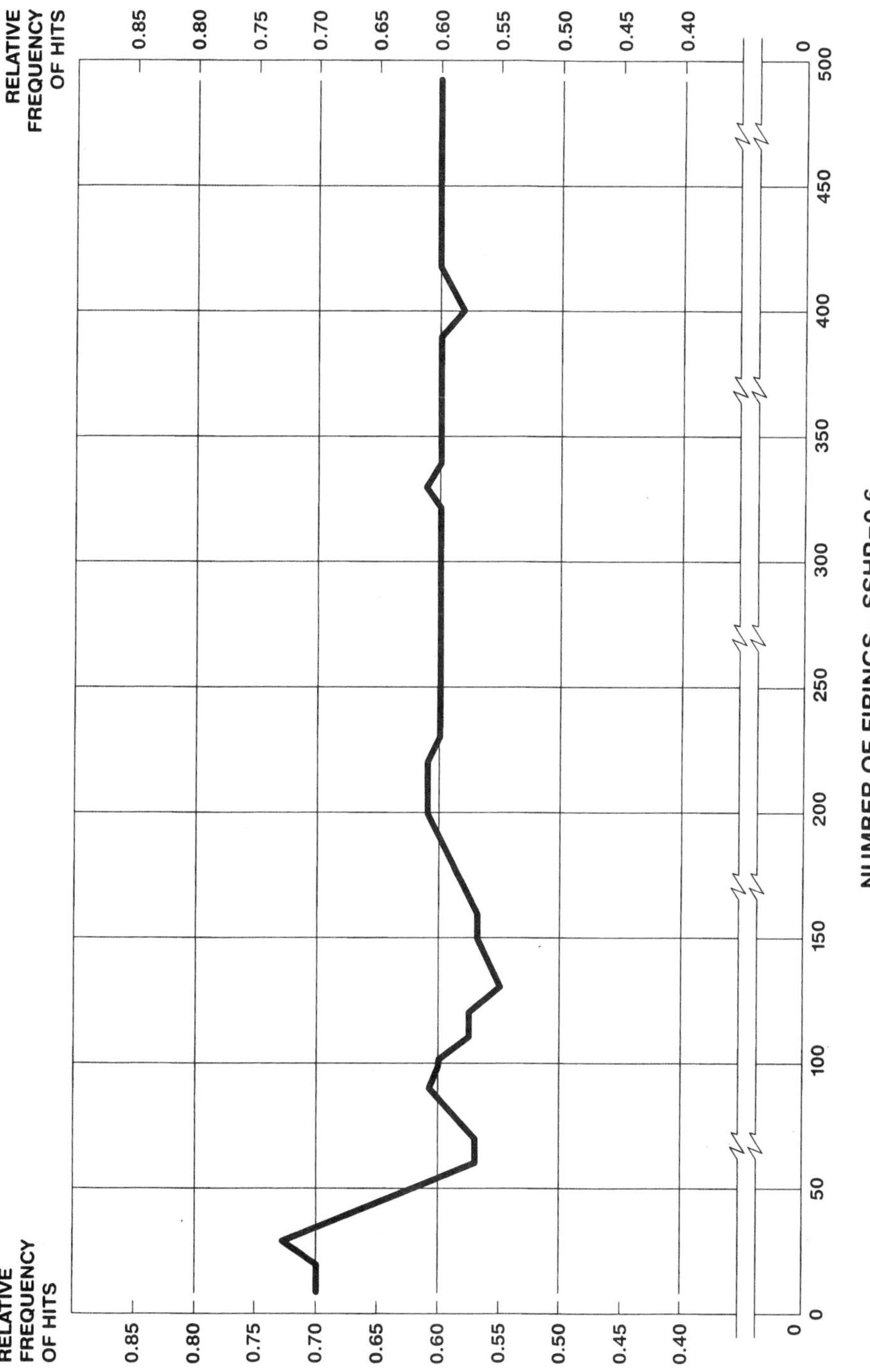
RELATIVE FREQUENCY OF HITS
0.85
0.80
0.75
0.70
0.65
0.60
0.55
0.50
0.45
0.40
0
0
50
100
150
200
250
300
350
400
450
500
NUMBER OF FIRINGS—SSHP=0.6

Figure B-6

Appendix C

A Glossary of War Gaming Terms

Aggregated Force
A single symbol, model, or NEWS force which represents a real-world force composed of two or more units.

Analytical Game
A game conducted for the purpose of deriving information which may be used to assist military commanders and executives in reaching decisions.

Board Game or Board Maneuver
A manual naval war game employing a game board to represent the area of operations. Formerly, another name for a tactical naval war game.

Chance Device
A device used to simulate an event which may or may not happen, but which has a known probability of happening. Common chance devices are regular dice, 20-sided (icosahedron) dice, and tables of random numbers.

Chart Game or Chart Maneuver
A manual naval war game employing a chart (or map) to represent the area of operations. Formerly, another name for a strategic naval war game.

Closed Game
A game in which players receive the amounts and kinds of information and intelligence of friendly and enemy forces that they would normally receive in a similar real-world situation. Most war games are closed games.

Computer Game
A game conducted on a digital computer. No human participants are involved in its play. Also called a computer simulation; and sometimes a machine game or a machine simulation.

Computer-Assisted Game
A manual game utilizing digital computer assistance for bookkeeping and damage assessment. Also called a manual-computer game.

Conflict Situation
One in which two or more individuals, organizations, nations, or allies are competing for the same goal, or have opposing objectives.

Constructive Force
A force represented by manual methods, and employed in a game conducted on the NEWS and in conjunction with NEWS forces.

Control Group
The director's staff. Its members advise and assist him in the planning, conduct, and critique of the war game.

Deterministic Model or Game
An expected-value model.

Director
The individual responsible for a war game and its critique. Also known as the controller and, in early Naval War College games, as the arbitrator.

Educational Game
A game conducted to provide military commanders or executives with decision-making experience, and to familiarize them with the operations and problems involved.

Electronic Maneuver Board System (EMBS)
A former name of the Navy Electronic Warfare Simulator (NEWS).

Event-Store or Critical Event Method
A technique used in computer games wherein the computer determines the times of possible future events, and stores them in a chronological list. The game advances from event to event rather than by fixed intervals of time.

Expected-Value Model or Game
One wherein the outcomes of chance events are determined by average or expected values. Also known as a deterministic model or game.

Game Board

A deck (floor) divided into squares and used to represent an area of operations in a manual naval war game. The squares facilitate the plotting and recording of the movements of naval units. The game board is also known as a maneuver board.

An array of squares or hexagons used to represent an area of operations, or employed as an overlay to a map or chart which depicts the area of operations.

Game Theory

A mathematical theory which, under certain conditions, can be employed to determine the optimum strategy or course of action to pursue in a conflict situation.

General Situation

A general description of the conflict situation that exists or is assumed to exist at the start of player-planning for the play of a war game. The general situation is issued to all players, and is usually supplemented by special situations. Also called the scenario.

Kriegsspiel (Kriegspiel)

War play or war game.

Level

The range of the echelons of military command which are represented by the players in a war game. Also, the lowest echelon of command which is represented by players.

Machine Game

A game conducted by means of equipment specifically designed to simulate military operations. At the Naval War College, the term is applied to a game played on the Navy Electronic Warfare Simulator (NEWS).

Maneuver Board

A game board.

Manual or Hand-Played Game

A game in which the forces are represented by models, pins, pieces, or symbols, and the participants move them about by hand on a chart, map, board, or terrain model which represents the area of operations.

Manual-Computer Game

A computer-assisted game.

Manual-Machine Game
A game employing a mixture of manual and machine (NEWS) simulation techniques.

Map Game or Map Maneuver
A manual war game employing a map (or chart) to represent the area of operations.

Model
A representation of an object or structure, or an explanation or description of a system, a process, or a series of related events.

Model, War Game
The procedures and rules required for the control and conduct of a war game.

Monte Carlo Technique
The use of a chance device to determine the outcomes of chance events, or to approximate a probability distribution that is difficult or impossible to compute.

Multi-Sided or N-Sided Game
A game in which there are more than two players or player teams involved in a conflict situation.

Naval War Game
A war game representing a conflict between naval forces, or a war game in which naval forces predominate.

Navy Electronic Warfare Simulator (NEWS)
A large and complex simulation system which is installed in Sims Hall of the Naval War College. It is designed specifically for the simulation of naval warfare.

NEWS Area of Operations
The geographical area represented on the master plot screen of the Navy Electronic Warfare Simulator for a specific war game.

NEWS Force
A means of representing a military force within the Navy Electronic Warfare Simulator. A NEWS force can be programmed to approximate the mobility, firepower, and intelligence and communications facilities of a single or aggregated real-world force. It can be detected by other NEWS forces, and can sustain damage from the weapons of opposing NEWS forces.

A NEWS force can be controlled by players, or if desired, by the control group.

NEWS Game
A game played on the Navy Electronic Warfare Simulator. Also called a machine game.

One-Sided Game
A game in which the opposition is furnished by the control group, or by Nature.

Open Game
A game in which all players receive or have access to all information and intelligence of the actions of all friendly and enemy forces. Usually played in one room and on a single map or chart.

Operational Gaming
The application of gaming techniques to non-military situations. Also used to describe the simulation of both military and non-military operations.

Parameter
A value such as a hit probability, a detection range, an ammunition allowance, etc., that remains constant for the play of a game, but that may be varied from play to play as desired.

Player
A participant in a war game who is not a member of the control group, and who plays the role of a real-world commander or a staff officer of a military unit or units.

Probabilistic Model or Game
A stochastic model.

Probability
The probability of the occurrence of an event is the ratio of the number of equally likely ways in which the event can happen to the total number of equally likely ways in which the event can and cannot happen.

Program
Noun: A series of instructions required to complete a given procedure.

Verb: To prepare a program.

Programming
Preparing a program.

Purpose
The general and specific reason or reasons for which a war game is planned and played.

Scenario
A chronological listing of pre-planned situations, events, messages, etc., to be generated by the control group in order to confront the players with situations requiring decisions during the play of a one-sided game.

A description of the conflict situation. Also known as the general situation.

Scope
The scope of a war game is expressed by the range of command levels represented, the military services involved, the contemplated types of operations, and the size of the area of operations.

Simulation
An operating representation of events and processes.

Special Situation
A description of the elements of a conflict situation that can only be known with certainty by one of the contesting sides, e.g., order of battle, weapons characteristics, etc.; plus intelligence estimates of similar information concerning the enemy. A special situation is prepared for and issued to each of the opposing sides. The special situations supplement the general situation.

If there is a time lag in the game world between the completion of the players' plans and the start of game play, a description of the events that occur during this period is also called a special situation. One such special situation is usually prepared for each side. Sometimes referred to as an intelligence pass or a situation summary.

Stochastic Model or Game
One wherein the results of chance events are determined by the use of a chance device. Also known as a probabilistic or Monte Carlo model or game.

Repeated trials of a stochastic game provide a distribution of possible outcomes.

Subroutine
A program which can be stored in the main or auxiliary program of a digital computer and used as part of other programs to perform a specific operation; e.g., a square root subroutine.

Time-Step Method
A technique employed in computer games wherein the game advances by regular time steps. At the end of each time step the computer decides if the interactions occurred, and if they did, it determines the outcomes. For any particular play of a game the time interval is constant, but in some cases it may be changed from play to play if so desired.

Two-Sided Game
A game in which there are two opposing players or teams of players.

Umpire
A member of the control group who performs one or more of the following duties: monitors player actions, evaluates interactions, provides intelligence to players.

Umpiring, Free
The results of interactions are determined by the umpires in accordance with their professional judgment and experience.

Umpiring, Semirigid
Interactions are evaluated by the rigid method, but the outcomes can be modified or overruled by the umpires. The term is also used when certain specified interactions are evaluated by rigid umpiring; other interactions, by free umpiring. Also called free-rigid.

Umpiring, Rigid
The results of interactions are determined by umpires, simulation equipment, or computers in accordance with predetermining rules, data, and procedures.

War Game
A simulation, in accordance with predetermined rules, data, and procedures, of selected aspects of a conflict situation.

Appendix D
References

References Cited

1. U.S. Naval War College. *Rules for the Conduct of the War Games, 1900–1905.* Washington: U.S. Govt. Print. Off., 1900–1905.

2. Young, John P. *A Survey of Historical Developments in War Games.* Bethesda, Md.: Johns Hopkins University, Operations Research Office, 1959.

3. Little, W. McCarty. "The Strategic Naval War Game or Chart Maneuver." *U.S. Naval Institute Proceedings*, December 1912, p. 1213–1233.

4. Sayre, Farrand. *Map Maneuvers and Tactical Rides.* 3d ed. Fort Leavenworth, Kan.: Army Service Schools Press, 1910.

5. McDonald, John D. and Ricciardi, Franc M. "The Business Decision Game." *Fortune*, March 1958, p. 140–142.

6. *Joint War Gaming Feasibility.* Washington: Technical Operations, 1961.

7. "The War Game and How It Is Played." *Scientific American*, 5 December 1914, p. 470–471.

8. Hofmann, Rudolf. *War Games.* Washington: U.S. Dept. of the Army. Office of the Chief of Military History, 1952.

9. Zimmerman, Richard E. "A Monte Carlo Model for Military Analysis." McClosky, Joseph E. and Coppinger, John M., eds. *Operations Research for Management.* Baltimore: Johns Hopkins Press, 1956. v. II.

10. Clerk, John. *An Essay on Naval Tactics.* Edinburgh: Constable, 1790.

11. Deems, Paul S. "War Gaming and Exercises." *Air University Quarterly Review*, Winter 1956–1957, p. 98–126.

12. Fuchida, Mitsuo and Okumiya, Masatake. *Midway: the Battle That Doomed Japan.* Annapolis: U.S. Naval Institute, 1955.

13. Thomas, Clayton J. and Deemer, Walter L. "The Role of Operational Gaming in Operations Research." *Operations Research*, February 1957, p. 1–27.

14. Haywood, O.G., Jr. "Military Decision and the Mathematical Theory of Games." *Air University Quarterly Review*, Summer 1950, p. 17–30.

15. _______. "Military Decision and Game Theory." *Operations Research*, November 1954, p. 365–385.

16. Beebe, Robert P. *Military Decision from the Viewpoint of Game Theory.* Newport, R.I.: U.S. Naval War College, 1957.

17. Cushen, Walter E. "Operational Gaming in Industry." McCloskey, Joseph F. and Coppinger, John M., eds. *Operations Research for Management.* Baltimore: Johns Hopkins Press, 1956. v. II.

18. Totten, Charles A.L. "Strategos: the American Game of War." *Journal of the Military Service Institution*, 1880. v. I, p. 185–202.

19. Livermore, William R. *The American Kriegsspiel.* rev. ed. Boston: Clarke, 1898.

20. Middleton, Lt. Col. *Explanation and Application of the English Rules for Playing the War Game.* London: Mitchell, 1873.

21. Verdy du Vernois, Julius A.F.W. von. *Simplified War Game.* Kansas City, Mo.: Hudson-Kimberly, 1897.

22. Totten, Charles A.L. *Strategos: a Series of American Games of War.* New York: Appleton, 1880. v. II.

23. Knight, Austin M. and Puleston, William D. *History of the United States Naval War College.* Newport, R.I.: U.S. Naval War College, 1916.

24. Chamberlaine, William. *Coast Artillery War Game.* 3d ed. Fort Monroe, Va.: Coast Artillery School Press, 1914.

25. *The Solution of Map Problems.* Fort Leavenworth, Kan.: General Service Schools, 1925.

26. "War Games for Battalion, Regiment and Division." *Military Review*, March 1941, p. 48–51.

27. U.S. Army Strategy and Tactics Analysis Group. *Directory of Organizations and Activities Engaged or Interested in War Gaming.* Bethesda, Md.: 1962.

28. Adams, R.H. and Jenkins, J.L. "Simulation of Air Operations with the Air Battle Model." *Operations Research*, September–October 1960, p. 600–615.

29. Bloomfield, Lincoln P. "Political Gaming." *U.S. Naval Institute Proceedings*, September, 1960. p. 57–64.

30. Van Arsdall, Clyde. "Joint War Games." War Gaming Symposium, Second, 1964. *Proceedings*. Washington: Washington Operations Research Council, 1964. p. 117–128.

31. Davis, John B., Jr. and Tiedeman, John A. "The Navy War Games Program." *U.S. Naval Institute Proceedings*, June 1960, p. 61–67.

32. Bellman, Richard, et al. "On the Construction of a Multi-State, Multi-Person Business Game." *Operations Research*, August 1957, p. 469–503.

33. Musgrove, Edgar F. "No Game." *Marine Corps Gazette*, August 1965, p. 53–56.

34. Brooks, F.C. and Merriam, L.W. "CORG Plans Tomorrow's Army Today." *Army*, February 1956, p. 28–31.

35. Newton, J.M., et al. "Submarine Tactical Games." *Naval Research Reviews*, June 1959, p. 14–17.

36. Andrus, Alvin F. "Bringing War Game Simulations into the Classroom." War Gaming Symposium, Fourth, 1965. *Proceedings*. McLean, Va.: East Coast War Games Council, Research Analysis Corporation, 1965. p. 195–203.

37. "Why Navy Will Be Ready for Tomorrow's War." *Armed Forces Management*, December 1958, p. 24–26.

38. General Dynamics Corporation. Electric Boat Division. *Gaming: a Method of Studying Submarine Tactics*. Groton, Conn.: 1958.

39. Bloomfield, Lincoln P. and Whaley, Barton. "The Political-Military Exercise: a Progress Report." *Orbis*, Winter 1965, p. 854–870.

40. McDonald, Thomas J. "JCS Politico-Military Desk Games." War Gaming Symposium, Second, 1964. *Proceedings*. Washington: Washington Operations Research Council, 1964. p. 63–74.

41. Dondero, Lawrence J. "TACSPIEL Orientation." War Gaming Symposium, Fourth, 1965. *Proceedings*. McLean, Va.: East Coast War Games Council, Research Analysis Corporation, 1965. p. 253–263.

42. Kerlin, Edward P. "A Description of THEATERSPIEL: a Theater Level War Game." War Gaming Symposium, Fourth, 1965. *Proceedings*. McLean, Va.: East Coast War Games Council, Research Analysis Corporation, 1965. p. 171–183.

43. Renshaw, J.R. and Heuston, A. *The Game Monopologs*. Santa Monica, Calif.: Rand, 1960.

44. Brooks, Richard S. "How It Works—the Navy Electronic Warfare Simulator." *U.S. Naval Institute Proceedings*, September 1959, p. 147–148.

45. McHugh, Francis J. and Ames, Chauncey, P., eds. *NEWS Programming Guide*. Newport, R.I.: U.S. Naval War College, War Gaming Dept., 1964.

46. Morgenthaler, George W. "The Theory and Application of Simulation in Operations Research." Ackoff, Russell L., ed. *Progress in Operations Research*. New York: Wiley, 1961. v. I.

47. Woodbury, David O. *Let ERMA Do It*. New York: Harcourt, Brace, 1956.

48. Berkeley, Edmund C. *Giant Brains or Machines That Think*. New York: Wiley, 1949.

49. Rogers, Gordon B. "Battle without Bloodshed." *Army Information Digest*, December 1960, p. 32–39.

50. Pennington, A.W. *War Game Techniques*. Silver Springs, Md.: Johns Hopkins University, Planning Analysis Group, 1960.

51. _______. "Computers and Computer War Gaming." Lecture. U.S. Naval War College, Newport, R.I.: 1 November 1961.

52. Thomas, Clayton J. "Military Gaming." Ackoff, Russell L., ed. *Progress in Operations Research*. New York: Wiley, 1961. v. I.

53. Maloney, E.S. "Modern War Gaming: State of the Art." *Marine Corps Gazette*, November 1960, p. MCA10–MCA12.

54. U.S. Office of Naval Operations. *The Navy War Games Manual*. Washington: 1965.

55. Johns Hopkins University. Applied Physics Laboratory. Planning Analysis Group. *Simulation Digest I*. Pam-80. Silver Springs, Md.: 1964.

56. Center for Naval Analyses. Naval Warfare Analysis Group. *An Event-Store Computer Program for Determining Sea Lift Capabilities and Attrition in an ASW Environment*. Washington: 1964.

57. Van Train, W.A., Jr. *Submarine Barrier Analysis by a Computer War Game Method*. Monterey, Calif.: U.S. Naval Postgraduate School, 1961.

General Bibliography

Abhau, Conrad. "Operations Research, Aid to Military Decision." *U.S. Naval Institute Proceedings*, August 1959, p. 137–138.

Abt, Clark C. "War Gaming." *International Science and Technology*, August 1964, p. 29–37.

Archer, W.L. "The Technique of Modern War Gaming." *Canadian Army Journal*, Fall 1961, p. 15–25.

"The Armored Cavalry Trainer (ACT)." *Armor*, July-August 1965, p. 57–58.

Ashby, Raymond C., Jr. "Realistic Umpiring—Map Maneuver Mainspring." *Military Review*, November 1952, p. 37–42.

Bloomfield, Lincoln P. and Whaley, Barton. "POLEX, the Political-Military Exercise." *Military Review*, November 1965, p. 65–71.

Bond, Brian. "Some Attractions and Pitfalls of Military History." *Military Review*, February 1965, p. 87–96.

Brackney, Howard. "The Dynamics of Military Combat." *Operations Research*, January–February 1959, p. 30–44.

Brodie, Bernard. *The American Scientific Strategists*. Santa Monica, Calif.: Rand, 1964.

Chastain, John A. "The Role of Computers in Combat Control." *US. Naval Institute Proceedings*, September 1961, p. 59–70.

Cockrill, James T. "The Validity of War Game Analysis." *U.S. Naval Institute Proceedings*, January 1966, p. 44–53.

"CONARC Engineer Notes." *The Military Engineer*, September–October 1960, p. 417.

Conolly, Robert C. *Selected Probabilistic Concepts Used in War Gaming*. Newport, R.I.: U.S. Naval War College, 1962.

Cushen, Walter E. *Generalized Battle Games on a Digital Computer*. Tech. Memo. ORO-T-263: Chevy Chase, Md.: Johns Hopkins University, Operations Research Office, 1954.

Dalkey, Norman C. *Games and Simulators*. Santa Monica, Calif.: Rand, April 1964.

Davis, Lee J. "Map Maneuvers—Their Preparation and Conduct." *Military Review*, November 1951, p. 16–24.

De Quoy, Alfred W. "Operational War Gaming." *Armor*, September–October 1963, p. 34–40.

"Fabulous 'War Game' Ready." *Naval Aviation News*, January 1959, p. 16–17.

Featherstone, Donald F. *Naval War Games; Fighting Sea Battles with Model Ships*. London: S. Paul, 1965, p. 21–26, 145–174.

Flagle, Charles D. "Simulation Techniques." Flagle, Charles D., et al., eds. *Operations Research and Systems Engineering*. Baltimore: Johns Hopkins Press, 1960. p. 425–447.

Fredericks, Pierce G. "And Now Wide-Screen Warfare." The *New York Times Magazine*, 7 December 1958, p. 96–97.

The Game of War. Burlington, Mass.: Technical Operations, 1960.

Geisler, Murray A. "A First Experiment in Logistics System Simulation." *Naval Research Logistics Quarterly*, March 1960, p. 21–44.

Haak, Frank S. "Formula for the Future—Operations Research." *U.S. Naval Institute Proceedings*, April 1961, p. 50–55.

Hammon, Colin P. *The Design and Construction of a Computer Simulation.* Monterey, Calif.: U.S. Naval Postgraduate School, 1964.

Helmer, Olaf. *Strategic Gaming.* Santa Monica, Calif.: Rand, 1960.

Jane, Fred T. *How to Play the Naval War Game.* London: Samson Law, Marston, 1912.

_______. "The Naval War Game." *U.S. Naval Institute Proceedings,* September 1903, p. 595–660.

Jepson, Hans G. "Are We Ready?" *Ordnance,* November–December 1955, p. 431–434.

Johns Hopkins University. Operations Research Office. *Bibliography on War Gaming.* Chevy Chase, Md.: 1957.

_______. _______. *The Stratspiel Pilot Model.* Bethesda, Md.: 1960.

Kahn, Hermann and Mann, Irwin. *War Gaming.* Santa Monica, Calif.: Rand, 1957.

Kelley, Laurence B. "Fighting a Logistics War in the Laboratory." *U.S. Naval Institute Proceedings.* September 1959, p. 126, 129.

Malcolm, Donald G. *A Bibliography on the Use of Simulation in Management Analysis.* Santa Monica, Calif.: System Development Corporation, 1959.

_______. "Bibliography on the Use of Simulation in Management Analysis." *Operations Research,* March–April 1960, p. 169–177.

McHugh, Francis J. "Gaming at the Naval War College." *U.S. Naval Institute Proceedings,* March 1964, p. 48–55.

_______. "The Oldest Training Device." *Naval Training Bulletin,* Fall 1964, p. 8–12.

Nagle, Frederick W. "Weather and Command Decision." *U.S. Naval Institute Proceedings,* January 1964, p. 44–48.

"Navy Unveils Electronic War 'Game'." *U.S. Naval Institute Proceedings*, January 1959, p. 136–137.

Niblack, A.P. "The Jane Naval War Game in the Scientific American." *U.S. Naval Institute Proceedings*, September 1903, p. 581–594.

Nolan, John E., Jr. "Tactics and the Theory of Games; the Theory of Games Applied to the Battle of Guadalcanal." *Army*, August 1960, p. 77–81.

Paxson, E.W. *War Gaming*. Santa Monica, Calif.: Rand, February 1963.

Pratt, Fletcher. "A Naval War Game and a Formula." *U.S. Naval Institute Proceedings*, December 1932, p. 1758–1762.

Specht, Robert D. *War Games*. Santa Monica, Calif.: Rand, 1957.

Thrall, Robert M. "An Air War Game." *Research Review*, December 1953, p. 9–14.

"War Games." *Military Review*, June 1961, p. 68–77.

"War Games: Key to Doctrine?" *Marine Corps Gazette*, November 1960, p. MCA9-MCA10.

Willard, D. *Lanchester as a Force in History: an Analysis of Land Battles of the Years 1618–1905*. Bethesda, Md.: Research Analysis Corporation, 1962.

Zimmerman, Richard E. "Simulation of Tactical War Games." Flagle, Charles D., et al., eds. *Operations Research and Systems Engineering*. Baltimore: Johns Hopkins Press, 1960. p. 711–762.